School of American Research
Advanced Seminar Series

DOUGLAS W. SCHWARTZ, GENERAL EDITOR

SCHOOL OF AMERICAN RESEARCH
ADVANCED SEMINAR SERIES

Reconstructing Prehistoric Pueblo Societies
New Perspectives on the Pueblos
Structure and Process in Latin America
The Classic Maya Collapse
Methods and Theories of Anthropological Genetics
Sixteenth-Century Mexico
Ancient Civilization and Trade
Photography in Archaeological Research
Meaning in Anthropology
The Valley of Mexico
Demographic Anthropology
The Origins of Maya Civilization
Explanation of Prehistoric Change
Explorations in Ethnoarchaeology
Entrepreneurs in Cultural Context
The Dying Community
Southwestern Indian Ritual Drama
Lowland Maya Settlement Patterns
Simulations in Archaeology
Chan Chan: Andean Desert City
Shipwreck Anthropology

Shipwreck Anthropology

This Advanced Seminar
was made possible by the
generous support of
E. E. FOGELSON

SHIPWRECK ANTHROPOLOGY

EDITED BY
RICHARD A. GOULD

A SCHOOL OF AMERICAN RESEARCH BOOK
UNIVERSITY OF NEW MEXICO PRESS • Albuquerque

School for Advanced Research Press
Post Office Box 2188
Santa Fe, New Mexico 87504-2188
sarpress.sarweb.org

Library of Congress Cataloging in Publication Data

Main entry under title:
Shipwreck anthropology.
  (School of American Research advanced seminar series ; 45)
  "A School of American Research book."
  Papers from a conference held at the School of American Research,
May, 1981.
Bibliography: p.
Includes index.
  1. Underwater archaeology—Congresses. 2. Shipwrecks—Congresses.
I. Gould, Richard A. II. School of American Research (Santa Fe, N.M.)
III. Series.

CC77.U5S53 1983   930.1'028'04   83-1363
ISBN 0-8263-0687-X

Dedicated to the memory
of our esteemed colleague
KEITH MUCKELROY

Contents

Acknowledgments

Feeling something like an "old grad" now, I continue to marvel at how well these School of American Research Advanced Seminars do what they do. There probably is no better opportunity today for a small number of colleagues to debate and discuss archaeological and anthropological topics of mutual interest in such congenial surroundings as those in Santa Fe at the School. On behalf of the participants in the seminar on shipwrecks as anthropological phenomena, I wish to thank all the staff members of the School of American Research for their consideration and attention to details that made this such an enjoyable and worthwhile gathering.

Special thanks go to Dr. Douglas Schwartz for his efforts in making this seminar a success. Above all, it was his willingness to explore the relatively new and untried idea that shipwrecks offer the possibility of anthropologically significant discoveries that led to this conference in May, 1981. While in no sense downplaying the value of earlier work done in the field of shipwreck archaeology, this seminar points the way to new and perhaps wider applications within this field. It was within this atmosphere of friendly yet critical debate that we were able to try out this new approach, and this atmosphere owes much to Dr. Schwartz's efforts over the years to maintain the seminars and the high standard of the publications arising from them. We are all proud to be associated with the seminars and publications of the School of American Research.

Finally, I wish to thank each of the contributors for their enthusiasm during discussions and their thoughtful and scholarly papers. Thanks to such efforts, the archaeological study of shipwrecks will continue to represent some of the finest work in the field of archaeology as a whole. I appreciated, too, the concern shown for the dangers of looting and treasure hunting of wrecks. We are now more aware than ever of the urgency of this problem and the need to speak out whenever these abuses occur.

RICHARD A. GOULD

Statement by
Seminar Participants

on the Present Looting of
Shipwrecks in Florida and Texas

Shipwrecks and wreck sites in Florida and the Gulf Coast are currently being looted on an unprecedented scale by professional treasure hunters and amateur divers. These wrecks, many of them dating back to the sixteenth and seventeenth centuries, are an irreplaceable resource for archaeology and anthropology. They offer unique opportunities for studying human behavior in relation to a wide range of maritime-related problems. Looting by treasure hunters and amateur divers destroys these sites. Recent court decisions in Florida and Texas can be expected to produce even more looting in the near future.

We want the anthropological profession to be aware of this, and we ask our colleagues to take every opportunity to oppose this activity. Our position is that the same scientific, legal, and ethical standards that apply to archaeology on land should also apply to archaeology under water. Archaeology for gain, by selling gold and other materials taken from wrecks for personal or corporate profit, is not acceptable. Nor is any indirect involvement by archaeologists in activities that foster a market in such antiquities. We urge that our colleagues refrain from working or consulting for treasure hunters and avoid trafficking in gold or other loot taken from wrecks. Professional archaeologists will need to consider carefully any action they may take that could support treasure hunters, and they should consider the implications of anything they might do that affects these wrecks and the materials taken from them.

The position taken here is entirely consistent with that of the Society for American Archaeology ("Four Statements for Archaeology," *American Antiquity* 1961 (27): 137–38) and with the views expressed recently by Karen D. Vitelli ("The ABCs of the Antiquities Market," *Early Man*, Spring 1982, pp. 29–32).

GEORGE F. BASS
CHERYL CLAASSEN
WILBURN A. COCKRELL
RICHARD A. GOULD
DANIEL J. LENIHAN

MARK P. LEONE
LARRY MURPHY
PETER R. SCHMIDT
E. GARY STICKEL
PATTY JO WATSON

Shipwreck Anthropology

1
Looking Below the Surface:

Shipwreck Archaeology as Anthropology

RICHARD A. GOULD

Consider the predicament of an underwater archaeologist about to confront a series of wrecks in a setting like Truk Lagoon or the Great Lakes, where the materials consist of ships wrecked fairly recently and on a massive scale. The accepted image of shipwreck archaeology is based on work done on wrecks of great classical or historical antiquity and finite or limited scale—for example, amphora wrecks of the Mediterranean or Spanish wrecks from the Armada of 1588. Descending into Truk Lagoon or Lake Superior, our hypothetical underwater archaeologist soon perceives that the inherited wisdom of wreck archaeology may not help him as much as he would like. For one thing, the sizes and numbers of ships involved preclude any realistic attempt at total excavation. And their relative recency, in some cases as little as thirty-five or forty years, confounds the conventional view of archaeology as dealing only with the ancient past. What is our hypothetical underwater archaeologist doing here anyway?

In fact, as the readers of this book probably know already, there is nothing hypothetical about this situation. Underwater archaeologists, especially those working for various public agencies such as the National Park Service, are often called upon to deal with these kinds of shipwrecks, along with those of a more conventional nature. As this

3

kind of work proceeds, the question of an appropriate scholarly rationale inevitably arises. Most underwater archaeologists agree that mere relic collecting will not suffice, even though this is the aspect of their work that is likely to have the most appeal to the lay public (along with the adventuring and treasure-hunting aspects that often accompany relic collecting). The dangers of what Ivor Noël-Hume (1969: 10–11) aptly refers to as the "shrine complex" are well known to most archaeologists. That is, an undue emphasis upon the excavation and restoration of relics associated with national heroes and historically famous accomplishments can lead to the neglect of less spectacular, but possibly more informative, sites and materials.

Historical particularism—and I do not use this term here in any negative sense—justifies much of the current work in shipwreck archaeology, since shipwrecks are undeniably part of the total body of material studied by historians and historical archaeologists. Again, most professional archaeologists and enlightened amateurs agree that historical sources should be mastered and used in a detailed and competent way whenever they are available. Noël-Hume's negative views notwithstanding (1969: 12–13), most of the anthropologically trained archaeologists I know who have become involved in historic archaeology, including the study of shipwrecks, acknowledge the need to know the documented history of the materials they study, including mastery of relevant languages and detailed knowledge of the technologies and historic sources they use. The shipwreck archaeologist, like any historical archaeologist, must first examine the documentary information that is available. This historical expertise can be delegated, to a degree, since no one scholar can reasonably be expected to master all the various special skills needed for competent archaeological research. Indeed, this kind of division of labor has long been a standard practice of both anthropological and historical archaeologists. In other words, historical skills having to do with such things as documentation of pottery, metalworking, and other industries that produce archaeological remains are essentially similar to specialized expertise in such fields as faunal analysis, lithics, palynology, and other fields that have supported archaeology for a long time. The argument I am offering here, by way of an overview of this School of American Research seminar volume, is that we will achieve more by viewing archaeology as a unified approach to the study of human behavior than by arguing over alleged differences between "historical" and "anthropological"

4

archaeology. Shipwrecks are part of the legitimate domain of archaeology and can produce results that are as significant for our ability to explain variability in human behavior as any other kind of archaeology, whether it deals with stone tools in a European Paleolithic rockshelter or ceramics contained in a sixteenth-century Spanish shipwreck.

If one provisionally accepts this argument, then the next question is: What is it that unifies the field of archaeology in spite of differences in the materials being studied and the skills required to study them? My suggestion is that the unity of archaeology rests not with the materials being studied or the particular methods that are applied but in the reasoning used to draw conclusions about behavior from the physical remains of past human activities. Discussions and debates that occurred during this seminar and the papers presented by the seminar participants offer ideas and evidence that provide us with a preliminary indication of how the study of shipwrecks can inform and enlarge our general view of man's relationship to his maritime environment, especially with respect to voyaging and matters of commerce, warfare, and other relevant factors.

In planning this seminar, variety was sought and achieved. Participants included both "land" and underwater archaeologists. Historical, classical, and anthropological traditions in archaeology were all represented, as were more specialized approaches like ethnoarchaeology, experimental archaeology, and public archaeology. So, in searching for unifying principles, one should not assume beforehand either that the views of all of the participants in this seminar were identical or that the ideas and conclusions arrived at represent a complete or final statement about the essential nature of shipwreck archaeology. Indeed, the liveliness of the debate at times indicated that differences between land and underwater archaeologists extend considerably beyond the fact that one species wears cowboy boots while the other wears flippers. In this summary chapter I shall try to indicate what I think are the approaches and reasoning that link shipwreck archaeology to the larger domains of social history and science. But I shall also attempt to do justice to the differences that exist under the intellectual umbrella of archaeology, leaving it up to the individual reader to decide how much variety his or her particular brand of archaeology can accommodate.

On a more personal note, let me also explain why this book is dedicated to the memory of Keith Muckelroy. I first met Keith in Cambridge in 1977 while he was seeing his book, *Maritime Archae-*

ology, through the editing process for publication. We had several opportunities to discuss his work and what he saw as the future for shipwreck and underwater archaeology, and I was much impressed by his enthusiasm, his considerable knowledge of the field, and his intellect. So it was only natural, when the idea of this seminar was first suggested to me by Douglas Schwartz, Dan Lenihan, and Larry Murphy, that Keith's name appear at the head of the list of possible participants. In due course, I invited Keith to participate, and he accepted the invitation. It was a profound shock to learn that Keith drowned in a diving accident in Loch Tay on September 8, 1980. This feeling of loss was shared by all of the other seminar participants, and it is therefore our wish to mark his memory by dedicating this volume to him.

In attempting an overview of the seminar, I shall first examine the goals and reasoning that seem to be emerging in shipwreck studies and then look at the implications these goals and arguments have for the ways in which shipwreck archaeology can, or perhaps should, be done.

SHIPWRECKS AS "DEEP STRUCTURES"

This pun is not intended to suggest that French Structuralism or any other particular school of anthropological thought should be brought to bear on shipwreck archaeology. But it does imply that generalizations about various ways the human species has adapted to the conditions of voyaging and its use of the maritime habitat may be possible on the basis of evidence provided by shipwrecks. Anthropology has been a useful source for generalizations about human behavior, but, as Lenihan cautioned during the discussion of his paper, there is nothing inevitable about the relationship between shipwreck archaeology, or any other kind of archaeology, and anthropology. This relationship, which has seen its greatest development among American-trained scholars, is not a necessary one, and its value must be demonstrated by those who advocate it. It is with this point in mind that we must view the questions raised by Bass as to whether or not an anthropological approach really adds anything to our understanding of human behavior connected with shipwrecks. In other words, the burden is on anthropologically oriented archaeologists of all kinds, including shipwreck specialists, to demonstrate the explanatory value of their approach. Also, there is what Watson referred to in discussions as the "present inchoate nature of anthropology," by which she means that anthropology today is too varied to offer a consistent basis for attempting scientific generalizations about human behavior. Thus, she cautions, archaeologists should be careful about jumping onto some sort of anthropological bandwagon when the anthropologists themselves are uncertain about what kind of social science, if any, they are involved with.

With these cautionary points in mind we can begin to consider what kinds of theoretical "glue" might lead shipwreck archaeology to adhere to the rest of archaeology and provide a basis for larger generalizations about human behavior. All of archaeology is based upon the study of various material residues of human activities. The links between these residues and the behavior that produced them are at the center of all archaeological reasoning. Most flaws in archaeological reasoning turn out to be failures of one sort or another to account for all of the links involved in this relationship in any given case. For example, it was common for archaeologists studying Paleolithic and Paleo-Indian sites to identify concentrations of flaked stone artifacts and debris in habitation sites as stone-chipping workshops—in other words, to equate the material by-products of a particular activity with the physical locus of that activity. Increased awareness by archaeologists of the complexities of behavior relating to how different materials come to rest in a given physical context in actual habitation sites has led to a reexamination of that assumption. Indeed, archaeological associations of all kinds are now being reexamined in this manner, with respect to both natural and cultural factors that affect their occurrence, and the results of this kind of examination are proving beneficial to archaeological interpretation.

Wrecks in general, and shipwrecks in particular, are subject to this same kind of examination. Recent work in shipwreck archaeology reveals systematic and skillful efforts to control for a wide array of natural variables such as currents, sea bottom conditions, salinity, and other factors in explaining the particular characteristics of different kinds of wrecks (Muckelroy 1978: 157–213). But comparable controls in explaining how behavioral variables operate to produce different kinds of physical associations are still uncertain and untried. Ambiguities abound in this domain, and this seminar, above all, has addressed the issue of identifying consistent and reliable relationships between particular kinds of human behavior and certain shipwreck remains.

DIG WE MUST—MUST WE DIG?

If one reads George Bass's (1975) autobiographical account of the development of shipwreck archaeology in America or other, similar books that describe the beginnings of shipwreck studies by English and European scholars (Throckmorton 1969), it becomes clear that this field is now in a period of transition. The pioneers have established momentum for shipwreck archaeology by gaining popular support on the one hand, mainly through books and films, and scholarly results on the other hand in the form of reports on wrecks like the Bronze Age ship at Cape Gelidonya, Turkey (Bass 1961; Bass and Throckmorton 1961, 1967) and systematic publication of research results in special journals like the *International Journal of Nautical Archaeology and Underwater Exploration*. Despite early resistance (Bass 1975: 127–30), classical archaeologists and historians have come increasingly to appreciate shipwreck studies as a valid scholarly approach. The stigma of underwater archaeology as somehow little more than sport diving or treasure hunting has been effectively dispelled.

There have also been dramatic advances in the technology of underwater archaeology, from the invention of scuba apparatus during the 1940s in France by Jacques-Yves Cousteau and Emile Gagnan to recent developments such as side-scanning sonar and minisubmarines. Although many problems remain, it seems fair to say that technological advances and increasing ingenuity in their application mean that the controls available to shipwreck and underwater archaeologists are at least as good as those used by excavators on land.

For land archaeologists in every part of the world there has or will come a time when even greater scholarly and intellectual gains can be made through careful analysis than simply through continued excavation. During the pioneer phase of archaeology in any region, the well-known Consolidated Edison Company's motto "Dig We Must" applies, since the first priority is always to establish secure chronologies and time-space relationships for material assemblages derived from controlled stratigraphic archaeology. But as these assemblages begin

8

to repeat themselves within a given area, and as the number of ex-cavated collections and site reports grows, this motto is increasingly replaced by the question, Must We Dig?

This is not a call to archaeologists to drop tools and cease excavating. Digging and its underwater counterpart will always continue to play a key role in mature regional archaeology. Rather, it is a call for more selective digging, and now is the time for shipwreck archaeologists to consider the principles that will guide the process of selection. In looking back over the discussions during this seminar, one can identify several of these guiding principles.

Survey Instead of Search

During an orientation session intended to acquaint the land ar-chaeologists with some of the problems and approaches of underwater archaeology, Larry Murphy emphasized the importance of surveying rather than searching for wrecks. This idea was later reinforced in his paper by this discussion of wrecks found in the vicinity of Isle Royale in Lake Superior. In both instances, Murphy advocated a regional approach to the study of wrecks, emphasizing the need for systematic methods of sampling. He approached this issue from the viewpoint of a public archaeologist whose primary concern is to identify zones for the protection of different sorts of cultural resources. Later discussions, however, emphasized the wider implications of this argument. Perhaps the easiest way to summarize these discussions would be for me to suggest that there may be at least two kinds of survey strategies involved in studying shipwrecks. First, there are *surveys of elimination*, by which I mean surveys that systematically eliminate ambiguities about what wreck materials may or may not be present within a given area. In surveys of elimination, the aim is to cover an area completely by means of a reliable sampling technique in order to determine unambiguously both the presence and absence of wreck materials within the area. And, second, there are *surveys by design*, in which the particular wreck materials being surveyed are selected on the basis of a hypothesis. Those wreck materials are, in fact, whatever is required to test the particular hypothesis. So, for example, when Murphy offered the "one more voyage" hypothesis in his paper, he also specified what materials an underwater archaeologist would need to look at during a survey in an area like the Great Lakes in order to test this hypothesis effectively.

In this case, the argument is that iron or steel ships have longer use-lives in the Great Lakes, which are freshwater bodies, than in their saltwater counterparts because there is less damage to hulls from corrosion. Or, in freshwater contexts, hulls last longer than machinery such as engines and steering equipment. Many shipowners today tend to extend the life of their ships beyond safe limits, as is amply demonstrated by recent hazards posed by aging supertankers (Mostert 1974) and the widespread use of flags of convenience by owners to avoid regulations that might bring about their ships' retirement. Murphy's hypothesis is that shipowners may always have been tempted to use their vessels beyond their normal, safe use-lives. To test such an idea, one would have to examine the wrecks in the Great Lakes to see if it was failure of the hulls or failure of the machinery that was the primary factor leading to the loss of these ships. By asking this kind of question, Murphy is presenting a hypothesis that is capable of being disproved. Certainly, an underwater survey in the Great Lakes that consistently determines hull failure as the primary cause of these losses could effectively disprove this hypothesis, especially if compared with wrecks in saltwater. In this case, the research design demands a test of this kind, and the survey would, of necessity, focus on those elements of ship construction (i.e., hulls, engines, steering machinery, etc.) that provide this test.

Ideally, both strategies are combined in an effective survey to ensure complete regional coverage as well as attention to relevant details of ship construction, marine architecture, or whatever the hypothesis demands. Anything less than a complete survey, in both senses proposed here, will leave important questions unanswered. For example, during a search an archaeologist may find several exciting wrecks without knowing for sure whether other wrecks of equal or greater importance exist in the same area. Any decision to allocate funds and resources for excavation of these wrecks will need to take this kind of question into consideration. Of course, as in land archaeology, certain regions have been so little explored that searches are still the only feasible first step in opening up the area to archaeology. But as work proceeds further, as it did in places like the American Southwest and Great Basin (Thomas and Bettinger 1976), so, too, grows the importance of systematic regional surveys based upon hypotheses that can be tested.

10

It is in these "mature" areas of archaeological research, as opposed to the "pioneer" areas, that shipwreck studies, like land archaeology, need to place greater emphasis on surveys rather than searches.

Partial Instead of Total Excavation

Total excavation of wrecks would be ideal if one were planning to attempt detailed reconstructions of ancient ships and trying to understand such essentials as their cargo capacity and overall dimensions. Yet all kinds of practical limitations impose themselves in the real world of underwater wrecks. Incomplete preservation, damage from looting or teredo worms, and other factors constantly impinge upon the totality of underwater archaeology, just as they do on land. So, understandably, shipwreck specialists can increasingly be heard to argue for more effective use of limited remains:

Nearly complete old and ancient hulls do not solve all the mysteries. They only provide us with enough intelligence to notice new ones. . . . There are . . . discoveries to be made on many poorly preserved hulls, if only we take the trouble to carefully scrutinize them (Steffy 1978: 53).

To the limiting factors mentioned above, we can also add problems of funding and support for excavation that are well known to all archaeologists. In short, there is no perfect world in which total excavation can consistently take place, and we must, as Steffy (1978) exhorts, try to obtain "maximum results from minimum remains."

But practical problems are not the only ones that may limit the totality of shipwreck excavation. Even if one had unlimited funds and time for research, it would not always be a good idea to attempt total excavation. The kind of careful scrutiny Steffy is advocating can be applied to any wreck, including one in a good state of preservation, if that scrutiny is directed toward solving a problem or testing a hypothesis. Not only is it impossible to attempt total excavation of extremely large wrecks like Great Lakes ore carriers or Japanese transports from World War II, but it may even be undesirable. As Bass pointed out during discussions, the new willingness by archaeologists to examine everything from early, prehistoric wrecks to recent historical or even contemporary wrecks means that we do not have to depend upon well-known historic wrecks in places like the Mediterranean, the Car-

11

ibbean, or the British Isles, even though we tended to limit our studies to these in the past. These are all fair game for archaeology. This is also what Sonny Cockrell referred to as the "unexamined assumption" of shipwreck archaeology, namely the traditional emphasis on wrecks from historically prominent places like the Mediterranean. Instead of limiting our research to such obvious cases, Cockrell argued, we can now turn our attention to everything from canoes to modern ships. But our success in dealing with this widened range of shipwreck evidence will ultimately depend more upon the questions we ask about them than upon the degree to which we excavate them.

Taking up the theme of sampling along with questions about totality of excavation, Mark Leone raised the possibility, both in his paper and in discussion, of regional approaches to shipwreck archaeology. He disagreed with the argument by Basch (1972: 50–52) that shipwreck archaeology is weakened by its inability to identify with certainty the port of origin of a ship from its remains, or where it was originally built. While many aspects of ships and life aboard ship are undoubtedly independent of particular regions, Leone emphasized that regional studies can be extremely informative about the variability of maritime adaptations in relation to different local or regional conditions. For example, look at the specialized steamboats designed for use on the Tombigbee River and other parts of the "western rivers" system of Alabama and Mississippi. Three of the seminar papers deal explicitly with the explanatory possibilities of using a regional approach and comparing the results—Leone's study of Chesapeake Bay, Schmidt and Mrozowski's on Narragansett Bay, and Murphy's references to Great Lakes archaeology. Each region created special conditions that affected maritime behavior and the wrecks that resulted in different ways. But, as Leone noted, regional approaches to shipwrecks will be effective only if archaeologists are willing to be selective in their excavation and survey practices, by asking important questions and seeking evidence relative to those questions. Thus, when Schmidt and Mrozowski ask general questions about the nature of contraband behavior as inferred from archaeological materials, the Narragansett Bay area takes on special importance for the anthropologist. Similarly, Leone's ideas about capitalistic political and economic relations can be effectively applied to shipwrecks in the vicinity of Chesapeake Bay. Leone's assertion that anthropologically useful questions about vari-

12

ability in human behavior in relation to shipwrecks and remains connected with seafaring can be approached effectively on a regional basis is strongly supported by these papers.

Explicit Instead of Implicit Research Planning

Possibly one of the most jargon-ridden and misunderstood aspects of contemporary archaeology is the idea of research design. In some quarters this phrase has become almost a catechism, ritually chanted by grant applicants and review committees alike. Like all such formulae, the concept of research design needs to be examined from time to time, especially when it may be applied to a domain of archaeology where it is not usually discussed. Nothing could be more fatuous than declarations by land archaeologists to the effect that shipwreck and underwater specialists do not understand or employ research designs, where the implication is that shipwreck archaeology is a sort of underwater Easter egg hunt. With respect to this particular notion, perhaps, the old stereotypes of the shipwreck archaeologist as a sport diver or treasure hunter linger on most noticeably.

Suffice it to say that shipwreck archaeologists today do ask questions and design their archaeological research to answer those questions. These questions range from matters of nautical detail, such as the differences between "shell first" as opposed to "frame first" types of hull construction (Muckelroy 1978: 59–69), to larger questions involving explanations of major historical developments, like the early influence of Middle Eastern bronze working on the technological and artistic traditions of Mycenean Greece (Bass 1975: 58–59). These are different sorts of questions from those ordinarily asked by anthropologically oriented archaeologists, in that they emphasize particular details of nautical history and particular historical traditions and issues, but they are no less valid. Land archaeologists, too, must deal effectively with such particularistic questions in their research, whether or not they attempt to extend their findings to encompass larger generalizations about variability in human behavior.

Perhaps it is in the realm of explicitness that shipwreck and land archaeologists today differ most. Gary Stickel's paper develops this idea most fully, although it is discussed in other papers as well. The question here is whether certain large, perforated stones lying in the waters

13

offshore from Redondo Beach, California, are a by-product of Asian seafaring or can be accounted for by some other, alternative hypothesis. This paper is not so much about the artifacts themselves as it is about the kind of research design needed to resolve problems of this sort. What might at first seem to be theoretical "overkill" with respect to the formal steps involved in such a project can be rationalized as a way of making explicit steps that have generally been assumed or glossed over in underwater archaeology. Opinions may differ about the utility of such an exercise, since the paper is not about shipwrecks per se, and because some archaeologists may regard these steps in archaeological reasoning as obvious and unnecessary. Yet, in defense of this approach, it should be noted that remains of this nature, whether underwater or on land, lend themselves to science-fictional treatment, in the manner of Mu, Atlantis, and "chariots of the gods," unless they are dealt with in an unusually rigorous and convincing way by archaeologists. The case of the Bimini pavement (Valentine 1976)—rows of rectangular stone blocks under water in the Bahamas—might well profit from a similarly rigorous archaeological treatment in order to dispel any ambiguities that might linger concerning these remains.

Cheryl Claassen also addresses the problem of explicitness in research design in her paper on experimental approaches in the field of nautical archaeology. She distinguishes between the goals of replication and the controlled handling of variables in experimental archaeology related to ships and shipwrecks, and she identifies the latter as being more consistent with both the procedures and goals of experimental science. When she states that "there is no problem in archaeology that cannot be better understood through the use of a well-designed and well-executed experiment," she is emphasizing the idea that the effective control and manipulation of variables with the aim of testing alternative hypotheses is the essence of good research design.

A look at the seminar papers reveals many areas where controlled experiments of the kind Claassen is advocating could be usefully applied to problems in shipwreck archaeology. The "cannonball controversy" and Wignall's (1973) claim that the brittleness of sixteenth-century Spanish shot accounts for the relative ineffectiveness of Spanish gunnery against English ships during the Armada battles of 1588 is a case in point. What is needed now is a controlled test of both quenched and unquenched cast iron to determine the differential properties and behavior of these metals in response to various compressive forces and

14

shock. Wignall's hypothesis is fine as far as it goes, but as Claassen pointed out during discussions, it fairly cries out for further by-product testing of the materials involved in order to resolve the question. Further debate of this issue in the literature by historians is unlikely to settle the matter until such test results are available. Then, too, there is the problem of shipwrecks in the Great Lakes, where experiments comparing the relative fatigue rates of metals due to corrosion vs. mechanical stress could be usefully applied to test Murphy's hypothesis. Indeed, the literature on seafaring and nautical history abounds with such possibilities for experimental applications. Take, for example, Drake's raids on Spanish shipping in the vicinity of Sagres in 1587. Historians like Mattingly (1959: 121) have argued that, while the raids' military achievements were not great, they did have a profound effect upon the Armada of 1588 by reducing the Spaniards' ready supply of seasoned barrel staves. Although it may have seemed trivial in 1587, one of the Armada's most acute problems later on concerned spoilage of water and provisions in casks made of unseasoned wood. Controlled experiments to compare spoilage of water and various kinds of food in barrels of seasoned and unseasoned wood could not only test this assertion but also provide information on relative rates of spoilage under these different conditions.

Ethnoarchaeology, too, calls for explicit research design, and there are many opportunities for ethnoarchaeological applications in maritime archaeology. Seminar discussions about the use of ethnoarchaeology in shipwreck studies hinged upon the relevance of uniformitarianist assumptions in connecting events of the past with the present. Ethnoarchaeology goes considerably beyond what Muckelroy (1978: 234) refers to as parallelisms in maritime behavior and technology observed in contemporary ethnology and surviving cultural traditions as applied to the past. He correctly noted that "consideration of other ethnological material can serve a very useful purpose in freeing the researcher from the restricted concepts of his own technical tradition" (Hasslöf, O., 1963, quoted by Muckelroy 1978: 234–35). He further points out that ethnographic studies can provide a greater range of alternative possibilities for explaining particular details of ship or boat handling and construction than might be possible without such studies. While true, such a limited view of ethnoarchaeology can present difficulties, too, because as Leone and Gould both pointed out during the discussions, such ethnographic parallels or analogues can

15

be self-limiting in that they omit alternative possibilities that may have no existing or known ethnographic counterpart. This problem is well known to ethnoarchaeologists who work on land (Freeman 1968; Gould 1978: 29–36), and it can be expected to apply to maritime archaeology as well, especially in non-Western contexts. For example, what ethnographic analogues are there today for the kind of voyaging out of sight of land that we know, on archaeological grounds, occurred across Wallace's Line from Southeast Asia to Australia–New Guinea at least 35,000 years ago (Mulvaney 1975: 130)? As the scope of shipwreck archaeology expands beyond the domain of European traditions of boatbuilding and seamanship, so, too, increase the dangers of applying ethnographic and historic parallels directly to our explanations of past human maritime behavior.

Leone and Gould both asked: What can shipwreck archaeologists do to discover general principles that hold true for both past and present-day human nautical behavior? Such an indirect approach offers a way of escaping the limitations imposed by self-limiting ethnographic parallels, provided, of course, that one has first established a reliable uniformitarian basis for such principles and can also specify the test implications of those general principles in relation to wreck remains. Gould's paper is, in fact, a trial effort to do just that, by specifying the archaeological "signatures" that characterize the behavior of combatants who are adapting to the stresses of extreme defensive isolation during war. This, too, was the intent of Murphy's "one more voyage" hypothesis, which may or may not emerge as a general principle of commercial seafaring, depending upon its testing in the course of further archaeological research. Whether or not such general principles of human behavior hold true for all times and places is less important than the way these principles can direct our efforts at archaeological research in specific directions that extend beyond any ethnocentric or otherwise self-limiting explanations.

In short, it is important to be explicit about our use of ethnographic and historical observations when attempting to explain past maritime behavior. A further case was discussed in the seminar which reveals how true this is. In his analysis of the metal items recovered from the Cape Gelidonya wreck of 1200 B.C., Bass noted several observations of modern and traditional metalworking technology that furnished important clues to his explanation of the particular characteristics of these items and their further implications for understanding the historic relations between Mycenean Greece and other parts of the classical world. This was especially true of the "ox-hide" ingots of copper, so called because of their four-legged shape and one rough or "hairy" side. In a published account of this analysis, Bass (1975: 51) pointed out that it was widely believed that such ingots were cast intentionally to look like dried ox skins, perhaps in order to equal the price of a cow before the invention and use of coinage. Bass's observations of contemporary smelting technology in a Philadelphia foundry led him to support an alternative explanation for the particular characteristics of these ingots:

Five minutes at the Kramer Ingot Company in Philadelphia showed me that, surprisingly, none of the scholars who had written about the ingots had ever watched molten metal being poured. The "hairy" side was the naturally bubbly upper surface of the copper cooling in the open air, not a lower surface formed in a purposely uneven mold; modern founders take care to prevent this rough surface by floating powdered charcoal on the liquid metal. Since the random weights of our ingots varying between thirty-five and fifty-seven pounds were based on no standard at all—another surprise—it was impossible that they had served as currency. There now seemed no reason to believe that the ingots were anything other than simple slabs of copper, their "legs" serving as handles for ease of porterage, to be melted down and mixed with tin to form bronze (Bass 1975: 51).

This is a convincing argument, even without the further evidence Bass found for residues of tin among the ingots on the sea bottom and the sixteen Egyptian tomb paihtings and reliefs he also found showing such "ox-hide"-shaped ingots being carried by men in exactly the manner proposed above.

The questions were, Why is this explanation convincing? What is it that holds true for both the modern and ancient behavior being described? In this case, the bridging element in the argument has to do with the uniformitarian relationship between the metal and the forces applied to it. Copper always reacts in the same way when subjected to heat in the manner described above. Because that is true, we can regard Bass's technological hypothesis rather than the alternative economic hypothesis of these ingots as standardized currency as the most parsimonious explanation for the observed evidence that characterizes these archaeological items. Moreover, certain test implications were borne out in the research, namely in evidence from Egyptian tomb paintings and in the relationship between copper ingots

17

and the wider context of metalworking and trade in the ancient Mediterranean. Uniformity of weights for these ingots would go far toward disproving Bass's technological hypothesis, but, so far, such uniformity has not been shown.

So what we have here is an example of scientific reasoning that can serve as a model for explaining past human behavior using contemporary observations as evidence. As in the case of experimental archaeology, ethnoarchaeology explicitly establishes bridging arguments connecting past and present human behavior based upon acceptable uniformities in the relationships between human behavior and the material by-products of that behavior. Upon hearing his evidence subjected to this kind of analysis during the seminar, George Bass several times uttered the comment: "But we [meaning shipwreck archaeologists in the historic/Classical tradition] have been doing this kind of thing all along!" He meant, of course, that all of the various steps in the archaeological reasoning outlined above were implicit in their research, at least in this case of the so-called ox-hide ingots. In considering this issue, some of the seminar participants were anxious to make these steps explicit in order to make it easier for other scholars to explain shipwreck materials effectively, especially in relation to experimental and ethnographic observations.

Most members of the seminar felt that there was value in being explicit about how one applies the rules of science to explanations of past human behavior, especially when training newcomers to the field or in ensuring that even experienced researchers "touch all the bases" when designing their research. For example, we were never told why Bass went to the Kramer Ingot Company in the first place. Was this by accident or by design? Considering the decisive impact this visit had on his explanation of the characteristics of this particular kind of shipwreck material, it would be reassuring to know that he intended to do this all along as part of his efforts to test the alternative hypotheses bearing on this question. If it was accidental, then the archaeological profession is lucky he was alert to the possibilities presented by these observations. But while serendipity undoubtedly does occur in the process of scientific discovery and should not be underestimated, science in general cannot trust to luck alone. An organized and theoretically self-conscious approach to this question of the "ox-hide" copper ingots from the Cape Gelidonya wreck, with an explicit statement of the questions to be asked, the alternative hypotheses, and the test

18

implications of these hypotheses (and, in this case, also specifying the bridging arguments that allow one to link present-day observations with behavior in the past) would offer greater assurance of convincing results than reliance on intuition and serendipity. Both Lenihan and Watson argue in their papers that wreck archaeology has reached a stage in its historical development where explicit research designs are needed, not so much to replace the insights of established shipwreck scholars, but to provide a basis for both maintaining and improving upon the standards set during the course of this earlier work.

OLD GOLD AND NEW CONCERNS

The United States may well be the only country left in the world where individuals and private companies can legally go out and loot shipwrecks. So no discussion of new directions in shipwreck archaeology is complete without some consideration of this problem. Sonny Cockrell's paper represents an effort to classify various kinds of shipwrecks in relation to what they might offer in the way of anthropologically useful ideas and information, and it provided the basis for our understanding of the magnitude of what might be lost if shipwrecks are destroyed by looters. During our discussions, Cockrell made it clear that this is not simply an academic concern, since large-scale efforts are in progress, mainly along the Florida and Texas coasts, by private companies like Treasure Salvors, to remove gold and other valuables from Spanish wrecks (see also Wade 1981). Adding to this discussion, Barbara Purdy emphasized the peculiar role that avarice connected with gold has played in leading to this large-scale destruction of historic wrecks in Florida. Cockrell's paper, together with his discussions and Purdy's, revealed the extent of destruction of wrecks and wreck sites from looting activities and the damaging implications these activities have for the future of shipwreck archaeology. Bass, Lenihan, and Murphy strongly echoed this view and offered examples from their own experiences.

For the land archaeologists in this seminar this was a new concern, though not entirely an unfamiliar one. Archaeology in general has been and continues to be plagued by looting of all kinds, which persists in the face of legal constraints as long as there are markets for such goods. However, the land archaeologists learned several surprising things from their underwater counterparts during this seminar about the nature and extent of wreck looting.

Underwater looting is unusually destructive, since it involves the use of techniques that irrevocably and totally obliterate site associations and fragile materials. Boat-mounted "blasters" (powerful jets of water reated by funneling a boat's propellor wash through a cylindrical cowling, euphemistically called a "mailbox" in recent treasure hunters' promotional literature [Lyon 1981: 5, 16; 1982: 235]), heavy-duty airlifts, and even explosives are sometimes used. Even when less destructive methods are applied, the results in no way resemble the sort of standards set by the archaeological profession.

Underwater looting may be legal. At least, it will be if the present trend set by the U.S. Federal Appeals Court in Miami, which recently found in favor of Treasure Salvors and against the state of Florida in a major case involving two important Spanish wrecks, continues (Wade 1981).

There is a spurious romance about treasure hunting that garners far more public support than this activity is entitled to. Some of the worst offenders have been recently portrayed in a heroic fashion by the media, without the opportunity for "equal time" by professional archaeologists and shipwreck historians.

The result of all these factors, in addition to the usual ones associated with pot hunting and other forms of looting in land archaeology, has been the rapid destruction of an irreplaceable part of our historic and cultural heritage as well as an important source of anthropological knowledge in general. In comparison with other countries, where both law and public sentiment support preservation and scientifically controlled research on wrecks, the United States appears curiously "underdeveloped" and backward in its treatment of this important cultural resource. Considering the urgency of this matter, the participants in this seminar unanimously agreed to prepare a statement (see p. xiii), which was then sent to archaeological and scientific journals for further dissemination. This statement should be read particularly with reference to the recent legal case over the wrecks of the *Atocha* and *Santa Margarita* between Treasure Salvors and the state of Florida. It would certainly help if we could enlist the general support of the archaeological profession to discourage the looting of wrecks and any involvement or aid by archaeologists in this activity.

20

THINK OR SWIM? NEW DIRECTIONS IN
SHIPWRECK ARCHAEOLOGY

While important differences remain, both among the seminar participants and in the field at large, at least some of the important trends in shipwrecks as anthropological phenomena became clear during the discussions and can be posited as prime considerations for further work in this field. These include:

1. An expansion of the domain of shipwreck archaeology to include wrecks of all kinds—ancient and modern, prehistoric and historic, and non-Western as well as European-derived. Although impressive results have been achieved on historic shipwrecks of European origin, especially in the Mediterranean, the Caribbean, and the waters of northern Europe, there is no necessary reason why shipwreck archaeologists should limit their scope to major historic events within these much-studied areas.

2. Greater explicitness in planning and carrying out research on wrecks. This should not be viewed as a criticism of earlier work, but simply reflects an increased need for self-conscious rationalization of each step in a program of research. For some this may appear pedantic. But experience in land archaeology has shown that there are important benefits to be gained from such explicitness in research design. It is easier to train students and newcomers to the field, and they are trained better. It can eliminate or reduce wasted effort such as the excessive multiplication of descriptive site reports or the preoccupation with material objects for their own sake. And, if used effectively, research designs can lead to our asking more interesting questions about wrecks on the one hand and to achieving more convincing results on the other hand.

3. An interest in applying approaches that emphasize systematic sampling and survey methods, selective or problem-oriented excavation, and experimental and ethnoarchaeological approaches. None of these approaches is new to shipwreck studies, but there are many new ideas entering the field about how to make these approaches more effective.

4. Urgent concern for the conservation and selective study of shipwreck remains as a resource capable of providing unique information and ideas about human behavior.

21

5. A new willingness to posit generalizations about past and present-day human behavior based upon shipwreck remains. For some of us, shipwreck archaeology is viewed as a part of social science. What makes it a science is not the use of scientific techniques and apparatus, but an organized process of reasoning based on the application of certain rules of science, such as the testing of alternative hypotheses, the principle of parsimony, the need for repeatability of results, and the ability to extend the results from a particular case to the realm of general propositions about the nature of variability in the behavior of the human species in a convincing manner.

When V. Gordon Childe attempted to generalize about the course of human history through his concept of the Neolithic Revolution, he changed the direction of archaeology in a way that affected nearly all of the research done since. One does not have to accept his theories about human behavior today in order to appreciate the influence of his scholarship on land archaeology. Seafaring, with its historic effects upon commerce, technology, war, and other key aspects of human behavior, is no less important a topic for potential generalization by archaeologists than agriculture. This seminar demonstrated that the possibility for such generalization exists in the field of shipwreck archaeology. It would be unfair to paraphrase the old Willey and Phillips dictum by claiming that "Shipwreck archaeology is anthropology or it is all wet!" because this is not really true. Classical and historical archaeologists have demonstrated the scholarly importance of their approach to this kind of material, and no doubt their efforts will continue. But there clearly is an anthropological dimension to shipwrecks and wreck sites, and the time has come for anthropologically oriented archaeologists to recognize and explore it in an intelligent and convincing manner.

2
Method and Theory in Shipwreck Archaeology[1]

PATTY JO WATSON

Washington University, St. Louis

SHIPWRECKS AS ARCHAEOLOGICAL PHENOMENA

Human beings have been working underwater at least since the third millennium B.C. when the Mesopotamian culture-hero, Gilgamesh, used the *petra*-diver's technique (attach one or two large rocks to one's ankles and jump into deep water, then release the rocks to return to the surface) to obtain the plant of immortality from the sea bottom (Speiser 1955: 108). However, it was not until A.D. 1828 that the first diving dress was invented, to be used shortly thereafter in salvaging portions of a well-known and important historical wreck, the *Royal George*, during the 1830s (McKee 1968: Chapter 1). Sponge divers using this same type of dress recovered classical Greek sculpture and other material from ancient Roman wrecks during the early part of this century (McKee 1968; Throckmorton 1969; Bass 1980). The post–World War II invention of a very different form of diving apparatus

1. The final version of this paper was prepared at the Center for Advanced Study in the Behavioral Sciences, Stanford, California. I am grateful for financial support provided the center by National Science Foundation Grant no. BNS76-22943.

(SCUBA) placed the undersea world within reach of anyone who could afford the moderate expense of air tanks, fins, mask, and wet suit, with predictable impact on the submerged archaeological record in the hospitable Mediterranean sea:

The forest of pines that borders the coast in the harbor provided shelter for the multicolored tents of a vast international camping ground, from which hordes of pink, chubby little divers from Germany, Belgium, and Switzerland set out in feverish pursuit of nautical souvenirs. They were especially fond of archaeological items, and the wrecks in the vicinity were the victims of regularly scheduled clandestine explorations.

Every day toward evening we would see them coming in little groups, swimming along behind the inflatable mattresses that carried their diving gear. They would land on the Ile d'Or and sit all in a row by the edge of the water, waiting patiently for the *Espadon* to leave so that they could exploit the site for their own purposes (Dumas 1972: 72–73).

The Titan wreck was the last surviving known ancient wreck in reasonably shallow water in the south of France. In the short space of ten years the others had been destroyed without a trace, except for a few amphoras and other objects which found their way to the Musée Borely and were duly studied and published by Benoit. There was, for example, the Dramont wreck, a Roman ship of the first century B.C. Found as a heap of amphoras 21 meters long by 8 wide, impacted in a protective covering of seagrowth, it was dynamited by skin divers in 1957. . . . A whole chapter in the history of navigation was blown to rubble by some mindless diver, perhaps hunting nonexistent gold, destroying not from malice but stupidity, like a bored child spilling the sugar on a rainy afternoon. . . .

The glory of the world must indeed pass away, but it seems wrong to speed its passage with dynamite and sledgehammers (Throckmorton 1969: 187–89).

It was not until the late 1960s that underwater archaeology in the Mediterranean emerged as a scientific and scholarly pursuit. Shipwrecks ceased being simply targets for casual looting by holidaying scuba divers and became archaeological phenomena, precious documents of the human past. The research project that introduced control and discipline to shipwreck archaeology in the Mediterranean is that of George Bass at Cape Gelidonya, Turkey (Bass 1966, 1967, 1975). As recently as 1960, few of the recording techniques now used routinely by hundreds of underwater archaeologists all over the world had even been devised. As indicated by Throckmorton (above), the situation in the Mediterranean area was particularly acute, and here Bass had to start at the very beginning to develop appropriate techniques:

The wreck was only ninety feet deep, which meant that each diver could work for forty minutes during the first dive and thirty during the second, with only five minutes of decompression for each dive, provided the dives were six hours apart. Bass drove the professional divers mad. A professional diver learns very early that time on the bottom equals money, and accordingly works with an eerie speed and efficiency. Bass often spent his entire dive contemplating a bit of rotten wood, deciding what to do with it, while the experienced divers wondered how long it would be before he lost his mind completely (Throckmorton 1969: 196).

Far from causing him to lose his mind, Bass's close study of the poorly preserved hull fragments and other remains on the sea bottom at Cape Gelidonya enabled him to recover an amazing amount of information about the anonymous craft whose voyage suddenly ended there some 3,000 years ago. The resulting archaeological report (Bass 1967) is a model of interdisciplinary scholarship and historiography, not just because Bass is a good scholar, but because he approached the shipwreck as a competent and thoroughly professional archaeologist would approach any archaeological site. In other words, he was the first person to demonstrate that Mediterranean shipwrecks—far from being helter-skelter heaps of debris—are orderly universes of archaeological data. He and his staff also developed, adopted, and refined a great many underwater recording techniques that have since become standard (and have themselves been modified and refined). In short, Bass's work revolutionized shipwreck archaeology in the Mediterranean, and, by removing it from the realm of sport diving and relic collecting, reclaimed it for mainstream classical archaeology.

Underwater archaeology in Europe and the New World, although for the most part independent of work in the Mediterranean, has also by now attained a high level of competence and precision (McKee 1968; Muckelroy 1978; Lenihan this volume; Murphy this volume). McKee characterizes British shipwreck archaeology as having had a strong historical emphasis from the beginning:

the British approach was strictly scientific and firmly historical, from the first; an attitude which has been maintained. . . . In brief, the attraction, the importance, the value of the Spithead wrecks was, that they were known, named ships, identified with important historical personages and events, which they brought closer and made more personal (McKee 1968: 75).

In the New World, however, underwater archaeologists still face enormous difficulties because of sport divers and treasure hunters.

I am sick to death of skin divers. . . . Personally I am tired of clearing sites of sunken vessels, and spending energy and money only to have a bunch of stupid people go under water by day and by night destroying simply for the fun of it.

I know that the problem Mr. Inverarity outlined exists. The wreck of the "New Hampshire" outside of Boston was torn to pieces by skin divers who removed brass nails made by Paul Revere and sold them for fifty cents and a dollar apiece. Skin divers have also ripped to pieces in Narrangansett Bay the first diesel-powered submarine (Inverarity 1963, with comment by J. Jenks).

The great intrinsic worth of many shipwrecks in the Atlantic off Florida, in the Gulf of Mexico, and in the Caribbean has resulted in the flourishing of vicious, multimillion-dollar salvaging schemes that ensure the unrecorded destruction of all known historical wrecks in these waters (Cockrell 1980; Lenihan this volume; Murphy this volume). It is extremely unfortunate that a recent article in *Science* (Wade 1981) condones the principle of treasure hunting among Florida's wrecks. The bewildering complexity of state, federal, and international legislation permitting legalized and unmonitored site destruction in Floridian waters is a sufficient nightmare for professional archaeologists and historians without the added burden of support for the looters from the most important scientific periodical in the U.S.

The unprecedented and unmitigated attack on the archaeological and historical record by profit seekers with no scholarly training is justified by themselves and their supporters on the grounds that the shipwrecks are disorderly scatters of detritus offering no archaeological information, that detailed contemporary plans of them exist so nothing could be learned from them anyway, and that they are prohibitively expensive for noncommercial enterprises to reach and investigate. These allegations are untrue, and are rightfully categorically denied by professional underwater archaeologists (Lenihan 1974a; Bass 1980, 1981; Cockrell 1980; and Lenihan and Murphy in this volume). To date, however, the profit incentive has triumphed over the scholarly one whenever the commercial salvors have been brought to court by the archaeologists. This ugly situation confirms—at least for this part of the New World—McKee's judgment that "the pattern in the Americas was, from first almost to last, that of treasure-hunting" (McKee 1968: 75).

Nevertheless, throughout much of the rest of the U.S., as in the Old World, the 1960s–70s phase of rapid development in methods and techniques has now given way to self-conscious and more abstract concern about the identity and goals of professional underwater archaeology. This concern is expressed by the British underwater archaeologist Keith Muckelroy (1978) and in a variety of New World literature (De Borhegyi 1963; Lenihan ed. 1974; Marx 1978; Shiner 1978; Cockrell, Lenihan, and Murphy this volume) and has stimulated the present seminar.

SHIPWRECKS AS HISTORICAL PHENOMENA AND SHIPWRECKS AS ANTHROPOLOGICAL PHENOMENA

It seems clear that shipwreck archaeology is at a critical and exciting juncture. The great logistical difficulties have been mastered to such an extent that underwater archaeologists can and must discuss, debate, and apply alternative research designs and alternative methods of approach to shipwrecks and shipwreck data.

As in any other variant of archaeology, there are two possible emphases with respect to the scope of research designs employed in shipwreck archaeology: a particular wreck may be perceived as a unique phenomenon and of interest primarily for its intrinsic characteristics, including the information it may offer about more general issues, or a general problem may require seeking out one or more particular wrecks in specific places dating from specific periods. Here the concern is primarily with the information the wreck provides about the general problem.

At present, Bass's Cape Gelidonya report as well as a variety of other accounts (Marsden 1967; McKee 1973; Wheeler et al. 1975; Arnold and Weddle 1978; Fenwick 1978) variously represent the first (idiographic) emphasis. These accounts range from rather minutely particularistic in scope (Marsden 1967; Fenwick 1978) to broader historiography (Bass 1967; Arnold and Weddle 1978), but all are characterized by a primary emphasis on the particular wreck or set of wrecks rather than on a general question or problem to which the wrecks were thought to be relevant.

There seems to be no good published example of the second (no-mothetic) emphasis. This is doubtless because the field is so young, and because in the early stages of its development so many of the wrecks were found by accident. For example, the several millennia of the Bronze Age in the eastern Mediterranean, a time range of great intrinsic and extrinsic interest for many people, are represented by only one well-excavated and well-published shipwreck (Bass 1967), found accidentally by Turkish sponge divers. But even on the basis of the small body of information now available, a generalizing or nomothetic emphasis could be profitably applied to shipwreck archaeology of the eastern Mediterranean Bronze Age. For instance, one of the most significant implications of Bass's findings from the viewpoint of an ancient historian is that Western Asiatics (Phoenicians or Syrians or Canaanites, as they are variously called) were acting as sea-going mid-dlemen and traders much earlier (by the latter second millennium B.C.) and apparently much more intensively than had previously been suspected. Prior to the Gelidonya work, scholars had inferred from available documents that the Mycenaeans monopolized maritime trade at this period in the Bronze Age. The respective roles of Syrian and Mycenaean merchants are thus brought into question by the Gelidonya research. This matter, together with the details of just how the trade was carried out—insofar as the Cape Gelidonya ship represents it—are, of course, fascinating to ancient historians. But these details also bear much of interest to anthropological generalists concerned with long-distance trade, with technological innovation and diffusion (the Gelidonya ship carried a considerable quantity of copper ingots and of scrap bronze with the equipment for working the metal on demand), or with the expression of ethnicity in material goods (the ingot shapes and the signs on them, morphological details of some of the bronzes, the pottery, the weights, the seals). Given the Gelidonya case, an anthropological generalist investigating technological innovation and diffusion in nonindustrialized societies, for example, might devise a research design that required detailed knowledge of the cargoes of several eastern Mediterranean ships, especially information on metal and metallurgical techniques, pre- and post-dating the Gelidonya wreck. This information could be compared with archaeological and historical evidence from terrestrial sites in the same geographic area, with ship-wreck and terrestrial data from, say, the Far East, where there was an equally early development of bronze and of maritime trade, and with data from some parts of Africa, where there was an emphasis on metal and metallurgy but no maritime distribution of the objects or the techniques. Practically speaking, it would take a great deal of time and money to locate relevant shipwrecks and excavate them, but it could be done. At least for the Mediterranean, there is sufficient knowledge of the routes these ships followed and sufficient technical expertise with search equipment to enable accurate predictions as to locations of wrecks, and then to find them on the sea bottom. But here our anthropological generalist squarely confronts the perennial archaeological dilemma: is the excavator justified in extracting only the information required for the specific research design being implemented? In this case, that could mean documenting and recovering the ships' cargoes in enormous detail but neglecting entirely or giving short shrift to details of hull construction, or of organization and materials in the noncargo part of the vessel. It might even mean ignoring the pottery and other artifact categories not directly relevant to dating the ship or to the transport and processing of the metal cargo.

I hope and believe that professional archaeologists would say the hypothetical Principal Investigator of the project just outlined would not be justified in completely ignoring all data categories other than those of primary concern, but I also believe there to be a very wide and essentially nongeneralizable spectrum of possible compromises for such an investigator. We return to this crucial matter of the confrontation between theory and practicality in field archaeology later in the discussion.

Another possible reason for lack of attention to the second emphasis listed above is the credibility problem still facing nautical archaeologists. A great many terrestrial archaeologists and other scholars do not regard underwater archaeology as a legitimate part of the profession because they fail to realize that excavation and recording at underwater sites has attained a completely professional level. Hence, outside the field of underwater archaeology itself, there are relatively few scholars who know or care about the potential information shipwrecks contain for a wide variety of topics ranging well beyond the particulars of a specific ship. One possible example was just outlined, and other papers in this volume address other such topics. An additional example is the comparative study of transoceanic colonializing processes (Spain in the New World and the Netherlands in the East Indies, for instance). The nature and quantities of goods carried are not always accurately portrayed in ships' manifests (Schmidt and Mrozowsky, this volume), and excavation of actual cargoes in wrecked ships furnishes vital detail supplementing and complementing that in historical archives. A final example is the study of the world system in ancient times. In the absence of historical documentation, shipwrecks are probably the best way to do this, and they are an invaluable supplement even in the presence of fairly detailed records.

The great potential shipwreck data have to alter our understandings of global communication networks and of resulting broad developmental trends in technology is clearly demonstrated by wrecks recently found on the Korean and Chinese coasts (Keith 1980). The Chinese ship (Sung Dynasty) found in the harbor of Ch'uanchou is built in a manner very similar to that of European carracks, yet it is 100 years older than any of the previously known European carracks that have long been credited with enabling the age of global expansion by the aggressive European traders and sailors who manned them. The ship that went down near Sinan on the west coast of Korea about A.D. 1310 is closely similar in construction to the Ch'uanchou ship. These finds cast considerable doubt on what was thought to be a well-established generalization about the evolution of ship technology. The older ideas are summarized in Muckelroy's book (1978: 136):

As in so many other areas of activity, the craftsmen of China developed their own designs and techniques, owing little if anything to outside influences and having surprisingly little impact on ideas in neighbouring lands.

Clearly, these earlier understandings about the isolation of the Chinese shipbuilding industry from world watercraft technology need to be reevaluated. Such reevaluation would have important implications for our knowledge of global communication dynamics: where the networks ran at particular times, how they functioned, and especially what the mutual effects of contact were on the societies in question.

As indicated by its title, a great deal of discussion during the seminar at Santa Fe was devoted to the question of whether or not shipwreck archaeology should be (or could be) brought into the anthropological fold to some significant degree, and what would be entailed should that occur. Opinions by seminar participants were, of course, varied, but the crux of the debate seemed to revolve about two points, each of which follows from our mutual understanding of anthropology as a broadly generalizing and cross-culturally comparative social science. Hence, to commit shipwreck archaeology to anthropology is to commit it to a basically nomothetic, or at least cross-culturally generalizing, approach. One node of debate, then, is the issue discussed in the immediately preceding pages (shipwrecks as providing data of primarily intrinsic interest vis-à-vis shipwrecks as providing data of interest primarily for their relevance to general problems). This issue is a variant of the "culture history vs. culture process" discussion in New World archaeology during the late 1960s and the 1970s (Flannery 1967; Watson 1973a), which is in its turn a variant of the perpetual tension between idiographic (particularist) and nomothetic (generalist) approaches in any field.

The logical response to the debate between generalists and particularists is always the same: both emphases are essential and both are present in everyone's work, although individual scholars usually stress one more heavily than the other.

Within the context of shipwreck archaeology one must conclude, now that a wealth of detailed and varied data are demonstrably retrievable at will, that those data can be used for any purpose whatever on the nomothetic-idiographic spectrum. And, as always, although the overall emphasis will differ depending upon the training, experience, and aptitude of the investigator, both perspectives are logistically essential, and, in fact, inseparable in any piece of research.

But in shipwreck archaeology as elsewhere, logic and practicality do not always go hand in hand. Shipwreck archaeology is an acute example of that perpetual archaeological dilemma already briefly illustrated. One's research must be problem oriented, but it must also be thoroughly justifiable as regards comprehensive data recovery, because whatever portion of a site is excavated is destroyed forever.

Logically speaking, as just noted, the empirical data from shipwrecks can be recorded and recovered for any purpose or set of purposes from the highly idiographic to the highly nomothetic. Practically speaking, the crunch comes because in archaeological excavation of any kind—where, by definition, that part of the site being investigated is irrevocably destroyed—some of these purposes are mutually exclusive of others. Probably the most extreme example of deliberate, single-minded destruction in the realm of shipwreck archaeology is commercial treasure hunting off the coast of Florida and in adjacent southern waters. Here the shipwrecks are being exploited (methodically destroyed by a variety of technologically sophisticated means) for a single purpose (monetary profit for a few individuals) that excludes any other form of data yield potentially present in the debris. At the nondestructive extreme is detailed video surveillance of an entire wreck (analogous to intensive surface mapping and tabulation without collection or excavation on a terrestrial site), as is being done in and on some of the historical wrecks in the Great Lakes.

Again practically speaking, the most desirable procedures to be followed depend a great deal on the nature of the wreck in question and on the context of the proposed work. If a small and/or unique wreck is threatened with destruction, then total excavation of all remains, as was done at Cape Gelidonya, is probably the best solution. But if the wreck is very large and/or very complex, then the excavation must be done in accord with some appropriate sampling design.

Or, once again practically speaking, if the question of how to attack a shipwreck arises in the context of management, as is the case for the hundreds of wrecks in the U.S. for which the National Park Service is responsible (Lenihan 1974b), then answers are constrained in yet other ways.

The individual charged with responsibility for these wrecks and for monitoring all research done on them must be informed of proposed work in sufficient detail to enable evaluation of the potential yield in historical, anthropological, sociological, or other information, and the manager must also be able to assess the impact of the proposed work on the total data corpus. The manager must then weigh the probable returns against the probable amount of attrition or destruction to that corpus. Reciprocally, proposers of research on such managed cultural resources must provide explicit research designs including clearly laid out work plans and honest appraisals of expected returns in knowledge gained.

But, to return to the central issue, other things being equal, what is the most fruitful and productive possible way to do research on shipwrecks? In my opinion the answer must be in an anthropological (meaning a broadly generalizing and cross-culturally comparative) framework within which the highest standards of fieldwork and scholarship are applied.

But there are many built-in complications even to this idealized

32

solution. For example, the nature of the particular data as they are recovered day to day will necessitate continual minor—and sometimes major—modification of the original, generalist research design. Another perennial and much more basic problem is that there are very few individuals who are able to function equally effectively as generalists and as particularists; it is nearly always the case that two or more scholars must cooperate, with all the attendant potential for conflict inherent in such collaborative arrangements.

The second node of debate is that of an anthropological approach as meaning not just a generalizing approach, but also a cross-cultural one. Although cross-cultural reasoning is second nature to anthropologists, who are accustomed to range freely through space and time, it may seem very dangerous to scholars whose training has not accustomed them to juxtaposing traits and trait complexes, or various portions of cultural systems, from widely separated chronological and geographical proveniences. Furthermore, such scholars may simply not be interested in, for instance, the insights attained by students of hierarchical, class-based social organization who compare officers' and crews' quarters on World War II Japanese warships at the bottom of Truk lagoon with those on American vessels sunk in Chesapeake Bay during the war of 1812 and those on fighting ships of the Spanish Armada.

ARCHAEOLOGY AS ANTHROPOLOGY, SHIPWRECK ARCHAEOLOGY AS ANTHROPOLOGY, AND ARCHAEOLOGY AS ARCHAEOLOGY

Historically speaking, in North America at least, archaeology has been anthropology for nearly a hundred years. There were good reasons for this, and nearly all of us presently practicing prehistoric archaeology in the Americas (as well as many who work in prehistoric periods elsewhere in the world) were trained as anthropologists first, archaeologists second. However, that situation is changing. In fact, the nature of American anthropology—if such a unitary field can even be defined now—has changed sufficiently that explicit secessionist rhetoric is appearing. Archaeologically oriented secessionists include Butzer (1975, 1980), Dunnell (1980), Gumerman and Phillips (1978), Meltzer (1979), and Wiseman (1980). Even ardently anthropological archaeologists

33

have realized they can no longer rely on ethnological or social anthropological colleagues to obtain the information from living societies that is crucial to comprehending extinct ones; hence the burgeoning of ethnoarchaeology. Indeed, it has lately become apparent to all anthropologists how inadequate and shaky much of the older ethnographic literature is because of powerful but unacknowledged colonialist, racist, and sexist biases. For example, Berndt (1981) methodically demonstrates how virtually all information about Australian Aboriginal women in the standard anthropological literature is doubly biased because they were automatically assumed to be inferior on two counts: first because they were Aborigines, and second because they were women. Influential writers like Malinowski (1913, *The Family Among the Australian Aborigines*), Roheim (1933, "Women and Their Life in Central Australia," *Journal of the Royal Anthropological Institute*, vol. 63), and Maddock (1972, *The Australian Aborigines: A Portrait of Their Society*) presented erroneous (sometimes wildly so) conclusions about women in every facet of Aboriginal life.

Another relevant issue is that, in these times of general economic retrenchment, many archaeologists have realized they are severely disadvantaged politically by unquestioning acceptance of subdisciplinary status to sociocultural anthropology, a status all too often interpreted as meaning second-class citizenship within a university departmental community. A strong argument can be made for the proposition that the future of archaeology—politically speaking at any rate—is not within anthropology, but in and of itself as an independently functioning, strongly interdisciplinary pursuit.

But is the "archaeology as archaeology" route the best solution to the difficulties indicated above? As just noted, it certainly offers many practical and political advantages. If all archaeologists could agree on an explicit, basic theoretical orientation (for instance, that the most productive use of the archaeological record is for advancing our scientific understanding of humankind, or, alternatively, for advancing our humanistic understanding of humankind), then archaeology could flourish independently as a special discipline with uniquely varied and demanding requirements for laboratories, equipment, and fieldwork. However, for the reasons noted in the previous section, it is quite unlikely (and perhaps not entirely to be desired) that such consensus on theoretical orientation will be achieved in any meaningful way. It is still essential for archaeologists who identify themselves primarily with a broadly generalizing, cross-cultural approach to the archaeological record to retain strong intellectual ties to anthropology, in spite of the practical difficulties that may sometimes arise from such association. In any case, what structures our inquiry is not the layout of contemporary academic boundaries, but rather the problems defined by archaeologists operating as generalizing social scientists.

Yet minutely particularistic data are not to be scorned by archaeological generalists. On the contrary, such data are essential not just to particularists but also to generalists in a variety of contexts beginning with chronology and including evidence for trade or other contact. The "direct historical approach" and other narrowly analogical and particularistic techniques (for comprehending nautical technology, for instance) are as necessary to shipwreck archaeology as they are to terrestrial archaeology. It must simply be realized that these are not ends in themselves. Rather, the very limited corpus of shipwreck sites can be most productively investigated when carefully designed and executed particularistic studies are employed in the pursuit of broadly conceived questions about processes generalizable to many human societies, regardless of their placement in time and space.

SUMMARY AND CONCLUSIONS

Since the end of World War II, shipwreck archaeology in the Mediterranean and the New World has developed from looting and unrecorded destruction of sites to archaeological respectability, except in Florida where it has gone from illegal or semilegitimate looting on an individual scale to legalized looting by multimillion dollar corporations—a sad exception to the preceding generalization. In Britain and in northern Europe, shipwreck archaeology apparently started and continues within the bounds of professional history and archaeology.

With technical and professional competence, uncertainty has come to many underwater archaeologists about the most effective use of the archaeological record contained in shipwrecks. On an abstract logical plane, the most crucial issue here, as with any archaeological site, is one of relevance. Were all shipwrecks safe from threat by looters, or from other direct and indirect impacts resulting from modern use of the seas, then there would be no justification for excavation of any of them except where they alone could furnish information relevant to solution of some important problem, be it primarily idiographic or primarily nomothetic. But this is not the case; many shipwrecks are menaced in many different ways, and hence the lines of debate and discussion are drawn, as was demonstrated in the seminar itself and in several of the papers in this volume.

Given that shipwrecks will be excavated, I would still advocate as little excavation but as much detailed documentation as possible to answer well-thought-out and well-justified questions of demonstrably general intellectual significance. Or, to rephrase using appropriate jargon, logically the ideal approach to get the most from a finite and rapidly dwindling data corpus of shipwrecks is to use nomothetically conceived research designs that guide but are modifiable by idiographically conceived implementation of those designs. Thus I stress the nomothetic approach, but I also stress the fact that that approach is worthless in the absence of careful scholarship.

A final sobering and complicating factor is that, at the present moment in the real world of shipwreck archaeology, the only thoroughly and comprehensively published work is idiographic; the generalists have yet to prove themselves by designing projects, carrying them out, and publishing them in detail so the results can be evaluated and used by interested experts and scholars of all kinds. Therefore, the discussion upon which the seminar focused—intensely interesting though it is to anyone concerned with archaeological theory—is academic, and must remain so until the generalists provide such results.

3
Rethinking Shipwreck Archaeology:
A History of Ideas and Considerations for New Directions

DANIEL J. LENIHAN

INTRODUCTION

The term *underwater archaeology* encompasses a number of very distinct research foci with only one unifying element—the use of underwater technology. This has created a semantic and a conceptual problem in terms of communication with the terrestrial archaeological community. The other subdisciplines of archaeology are distinguished by geographical area (e.g., Plains, southwestern) or subject matter (e.g., prehistoric, historic). The only exception to this rule is underwater archaeology, which is distinguished solely by technique.

This exception immediately creates a curious credibility problem with the rest of the profession. If any archaeologist can put on a scuba tank and do underwater archaeology, what then is an underwater archaeologist? It would seem this individual is either an archaeological technician whose only qualification is that he can dive, or a super archaeologist who can practice archaeology on Spanish shipwrecks, early-man sites, Mayan cenotes, Phoenician trading vessels, or Anasazi ruins submerged in southwestern reservoirs.

In reality, the individuals within the American archaeological community who are referred to as underwater archaeologists compose a group that encompasses a whole spectrum of highly variable skills and research interests. This ranges from well-established prehistorians such as John Goggin to classical archaeologists, historians, specialists in submerged cultural resource management, and treasure hunter-adventurers. It has been only in the last two years that papers by commercial treasure hunters were explicitly excluded from meetings of the International Conference on Underwater Archaeology.

The reason for this cognitive dissonance in the world of underwater archaeology is that the practitioners come from a host of different backgrounds with a host of different motivations. The activity existed well before any specific scientific rationale for doing it. Of course, most scientific endeavors, including terrestrial archaeology, have a somewhat similar history if traced far enough into the past; the anomalous aspect of underwater archaeology is that its identity crisis has persisted right up to the present time. This state of affairs has resulted in an unfortunate tendency for underwater archaeologists to spend much time speaking to each other, and only sporadically and uneasily communicating with their terrestrial colleagues. This is particularly true in the United States, as opposed to, for instance, the British school of marine archaeologists, perhaps because the overall philosophical foundation of the British archaeological community more easily permits integration of a subfield that has traditionally been dominated by historians. It is not within the scope of this paper to pursue the fascinating development of the whole field of underwater archaeology, but it was necessary to point out briefly the underlying confusion and cross-cutting of interests and abilities within the profession to set the stage for addressing shipwreck archaeology.

Shipwreck archaeology, as it exists today, derives from several distinct sources, including marine salvage, maritime history, classical archaeology, and cultural resources management. It has been almost totally disregarded, however, by traditional American archaeologists who are grounded in anthropology. This neglect probably represents a knee-jerk negative reaction to an aspect of the archaeological data base that seems to be tainted by "gold and glory" or that has been traditionally the domain of the historical particularist. The result has been a case of academic tunnel vision of amazing proportions.

Like many other new thrusts in American archaeology, the first serious efforts to consider shipwreck sites from an anthropological perspective have come from agency archaeologists responsible for cultural resources management. Archaeologists responsible for developing protection or mitigation programs for resources on submerged lands in marine parks, rivers, and harbors were forced by law to address this issue. Unlike others who had come up against the question of shipwrecks as data sources, these people were not historians, curators, or salvors, but rather products of anthropology departments.

As a result of this rather confusing past, proposals for new directions for underwater archaeology in the present must be predicated on an understanding of the complex ideational milieu in which it developed. In other words, in order to know where we are and what we can do, it is necessary to know where we've been. We will first examine the historical development of shipwreck archaeology, seeking an understanding of its isolation from the anthropological mainstream, then offer some thoughts on the anthropological potential of shipwrecks.

HISTORICAL DEVELOPMENT
OF SHIPWRECK ARCHAEOLOGY

It is probable that a greater number of monuments of the skill and industry of man will, in the course of ages, be collected together in the bed of the ocean than will exist at any other time on the surface of the continents (Sir Charles Lyell 1872, quoted in Hole and Heizer 1965:14).

Men of vision had no trouble over the years recognizing the unique historical importance of shipwrecks and other types of submerged sites. Those who have seriously applied themselves to the subject, however, have rarely been involved in the intellectual mainstream of their disciplines, especially in the United States. Perhaps the demands of the environment that surround shipwreck sites have tended to stir men of action more than men of contemplation, but whatever the reason, it is apparent that the activity in this area has far outdistanced the thought process.

The enterprise popularly termed *underwater archaeology* developed from two interrelated activities: the quest for sunken riches and the quest for antiquities in the extraordinary states of preservation that often characterize submerged sites. With regard to shipwrecks, the

39

specific disciplines that became involved in these activities were marine salvage, treasure hunting, marine history, marine architecture, classical archaeology, and museum collecting.

Marine Salvage

The first efforts at finding and exploiting sunken ships for any purpose were primarily motivated by commercial interests. The history of marine salvage extends back almost as far as the history of ships. The use of specially trained free divers to remove valuable cargo and apparel from sunken vessels is documented hundreds of years before Christ. Herodotus mentions using divers to salvage valuables as early as the fifth century B.C. (Marx 1971: 68). Such efforts usually took place as soon as possible after a sinking, but in many cases the efforts to salvage a particular vessel continued over decades. The preservation characteristics of shipwrecks are such that within a short period of time after sinking, the major impact of settling into a submerged context tends to run its course and the material remains stabilize within the new environment. In the case of certain more perishable cargoes, the rescue must be almost immediate, but with respect to precious metals and many inorganic cargoes, armament, and apparel, the intrinsic value remains for extended periods of time. Salvaging wrecks for non-utilitarian purposes, such as relics with symbolic historic value, is primarily a modern-day phenomenon. This latter type of salvage activity is the most closely associated with marine archaeology and is also the most destructive to the archaeological integrity of the shipwreck site. Although the cargo that contemporary salvagers remove is certainly an important element in a ship's story, it is one of the least fragile aspects of a wreck site because it is often possible to determine its nature even after most of it has been removed.

One of the earliest examples of shipwreck salvage for antiquarian purposes was the raising in 1822 of a sixteenth-century ship which had been found on the River Rother in Sussex. The remains were put on display near London. In 1863, a vessel, apparently from the fourth century A.D., was excavated from a peat bog in Schleswig and restored by the Danish archaeologist Conrad Engelhardt (Johnstone 1974: 7).

At the turn of the century additional discoveries from marine contexts prompted increased attention from classical archaeologists and art historians. In 1900, Greek sponge divers discovered off of Antikythera the remains probably of a Roman vessel dating to the first century B.C. (Rackl 1968: 14–24; Karo 1965: 35–39; Bass 1966: 79–83). The cargo contained a large number of exact copies of original Greek sculptures bound for wealthy Roman art enthusiasts. Between 1908 and 1913 the Greek government monitored salvage operations of more statuary and columns from another Roman ship at Mahdia, this one dating to the fourth century B.C. (Diole 1953; de Frondeville 1965: 39–52).

The harvesting of antiquities, rather than specie or unmodified materials of intrinsic value (e.g., mercury or copper), from wreck sites by salvors selectively focuses on the most subtle and archaeologically significant attributes of the resource. A beneficial result of these early twentieth-century incidents, however, was to attract the attention of serious classical archaeologists who eventually spearheaded a more scholarly involvement with sunken ship remains. The only other activities equally as, or more, destructive to the scientific potential of a wreck site are treasure hunting and, paradoxically, archaeological excavations. The damage caused by the latter activity is usually somewhat alleviated by a research report resulting from controlled data retrieval. Unfortunately, the trade-off between having the site intact and having the archaeological report is often a sad one indeed.

Treasure Hunting

This activity is being considered separately from marine salvage because its effects on the shipwreck data base are of a decidedly different nature. If treasure hunters simply dived down to the remains of a historic vessel and neatly removed the silver plates or gold coins from the hold, the effect on scientific data retrieval potential would be minimal. The standard procedure, however, is to "investigate" magnetic anomalies found as a result of a magnetometer search by deflecting propwash downward from the search boat, thereby denuding huge areas of the bottom of their protective sediments. Ship remains, which had until then been redistributed only through natural sea dynamics, are hopelessly jumbled over the seabed. Reconstruction of many attributes of the wreck and the actual act of sinking becomes totally impossible. The most tragic element of this scenario is that many historic vessels are destroyed in the search for those few that have enough intrinsic value to make the effort worthwhile. Unlike the

41

marine salvage community, treasure hunters have made almost no tangible contributions to even the technical development of the field of underwater archaeology. Their frequent claims to have introduced new technology can almost always be disproven with even the scantest of historical research on the matter.

The one inadvertent effect they have had on the development of shipwreck archaeology in this country has been in capturing the attention of the public. Their efforts have fired the imagination of the American public and have at least helped force many state historic preservation officers to recognize that marine sites are an entity to be considered. Unfortunately, state administrations have too often been prone to see wrecks much in the way that treasure hunters do—as just another economic resource in the unharvested sea. The involvement of powerful commercial and political interests in underwater treasure hunting has served to make it the focus of a major cultural-resources management (CRM) issue. By comparison, both monetarily and politically, the problem dwarfs the relatively low-key rape of Mimbres sites in the southwestern United States. That this issue has become a major CRM concern has directly contributed, however, to the recent stirrings of interest in the anthropological community because anthropology is the academic root of most archaeological resource managers who are responsible for the public submerged lands on which shipwrecks lie.

Marine History and Maritime Museums

The concern that marine historians have with historic shipwrecks is easily understood, as is the interest of maritime museologists. The unique preservation of underwater sites offers artifacts in excellent states of preservation, and the actual remains of a shipwreck offer much that is not known from the literature about ship construction, material culture, and unique events in history.

Reputable scholars in these fields have often taken part in or supervised excavations of shipwrecks, activities usually left to professional archaeologists when terrestrial sites are being investigated. Their frequent alliance with treasure hunters as a means to their ends has had predictable results. They have obtained the information and material specimens they have sought, but in so doing have precipitated the

42

destruction of many underwater archaeological sites. The treasure hunters have benefited from the symbiotic relationship by learning better archival research techniques (enabling them to discover more wrecks), and by gaining an aura of respectability for their enterprises. It is interesting to note that all of these practitioners—historians, museologists, treasure hunters—are commonly referred to as marine archaeologists when they are engaging in shipwreck excavations even if they have never had the slightest formal training or experience in archaeology. The questions the marine historians and marine architects ask of shipwrecks are different from, but every bit as valid as, those an anthropologist would ask. What has been unfortunate is the fact that rarely is there an understanding by the former that major nonrenewable resources are being destroyed for only highly focused data returns.

Classical Archaeologists

Some of the most professional and responsible excavations carried out on shipwreck sites to date have been by classical archaeologists. Their concern for accuracy and respect for detail has partly been conditioned by the fact that they often investigate changes in design and form over long periods of time which are variably documented. Perhaps what is more important is that they are archaeologists by training and choice, no matter how different their theoretical orientation may be from that of anthropologically oriented archaeologists.

English School of Nautical Archaeologists

The term *nautical archaeology* primarily refers to a British-dominated school that is attuned to questions of nautical history and seafaring. The popular *International Journal of Nautical Archaeology and Underwater Exploration* is the major forum for their field and analytic reports. Their approach to wreck excavation and interpretation is as responsible and professional as that of some of the classical marine archaeologists. The approach is again almost totally descriptive and oriented toward historic particularism, with one major exception discussed below. They, of course, do not all hail from the British Isles; there are major practitioners in Australia, Canada, and so on. It is a literary convenience to refer to them as the "British" school, probably stemming from an ethnocentric perception by American archaeologists of English-speaking non-Americans.

43

Demonstrating little interest, for the most part, in human behavioral problems, they operate almost totally without benefit of any demonstrable, explicit research designs, much like the classical archaeologists. A canvass of eight issues of IJNA covering the years 1978 and 1979 (Lenihan and Murphy 1981) indicated that in the thirty-nine "main articles," as defined by the publisher, and in the numerous short pieces, the concepts *research design, research strategy, theory,* and so on were never even prominently mentioned, let alone addressed.

Again, it must be emphasized that this criticism—and it is a criticism, not just an observation—is based upon a prejudice toward a scientific methodology which almost by definition involves developing an explicit rationale for research activities. Although thinking, planning, and background research are very much a part of the nautical and classical archaeological approach, we are forced to take on faith that this cerebration has transpired. The problem with evaluating the worth of much of the research of this genre on shipwrecks is probably best articulated by recalling an observation by Kluckhohn.

If the methodology and theory are almost wholly beneath the level of consciousness it is axiomatic that they are inadequate. For all aspects of intellectual procedure must be made explicit in order that they may be subject to criticism and empirical testing (Kluckhohn 1940).

Institutional Archaeologists in the U.S.

The issue was raised earlier in this paper that there has been a marked lack of interest shown toward shipwreck sites by traditional land archaeologists in the United States. For all intents and purposes the history of ideas in shipwreck archaeology has been totally devoid of input from that sector. The demands of the underwater environment are certainly not a sufficient reason for this neglect, because archaeologists tend to be a hardy lot, and it's difficult to imagine that after years of trudging through deserts and over mountains they would find the sea an insurmountable obstacle. It is understandable that prehistorians might be put off by the fact that we are dealing with what is primarily a historic data base, but what has happened to our historical archaeologists of the anthropological persuasion?

Perhaps the best clue we have is in the literature. The only publication we can find in *American Antiquity* that concerns underwater archaeology, besides the article by Jewell (1961) that discusses only

44

inundated sites in reservoirs and a very recent article by Cockrell (1980), is the classic article by John Goggin entitled "Underwater Archaeology, Its Nature and Limitations" (1960: 348–54). Goggin, in that article, articulately presented the state of the art as it applied to underwater archaeology at that time, but he overemphasized its limitations.

Reinforcing an already implicit dichotomy in the American archaeologist's mind between underwater archaeology and the rest of archaeology, Goggin made several authoritative statements regarding the nature of this aspect of archaeological enterprise which should be noted carefully. In the abstract of the article, Goggin states that

Archaeological remains in lakes, springs, rivers or the sea have considerable to offer. Perhaps their greatest value is the more complete condition of such artifacts in contrast to similar remains on land (1960: 348).

Because Goggin was a recognized authority in both prehistoric and historic archaeology, it is suggested that this widely read statement has had a significant effect on the role that underwater archaeology has assumed in the total New World anthropological spectrum in the two decades since its publication. This position contributed to the development of stock answers to queries regarding the value of underwater archaeology, such as the stereotyped response that, "yes, submerged sites have value, primarily as sources of museum specimens in superior states of preservation." Goggin also stated,

In general it can be said that stratigraphy will not be a major factor in underwater archaeology. I can conceive of situations where it would exist and with skillful work could be revealed. However, such situations are probably rare and opportunities to work them out even scarcer (1960: 351).

These views contributed to a lopsided appreciation of the limitations of submerged archaeological sites. Besides having completely ignored the fact that horizontal spatial relationships are almost always observable and usually meaningful in an underwater site, more recent research has shown startling examples of excellent, retrievable stratigraphy (Cockrell 1975b; Muckelroy 1978: 176). Goggin reinforces this view that underwater sites simply comprise repositories of artifacts in good condition by implying in that 1960 article that ease of access and ease

45

of artifact recovery are suitable criteria for judging the worth of a submerged site. Although factors such as visibility, siltation, and water movement (currents, etc.) are extremely important to the underwater archaeologist and must be taken into consideration for any site being excavated, these factors do not determine the archaeological potential of the site. Certainly land archaeologists would not base the value of particular sites on the presence or absence of such climatic conditions as the occurrence of heavy windstorms or rain. Specifically in regard to shipwrecks, Goggin once again demonstrates his perception of sites as only repositories of artifacts in the way he structures his site classification system. He classifies wrecks according to criteria that would determine the condition of remains rather than nature, period, or function of the vessel (i.e., ships that foundered, ships that sank after being driven onto an obstacle, and ships that sank as the result of a collision [1960: 352–53]).

The salient point for our discussion is that Goggin's views on the matter were presented in a highly visible forum to a group of colleagues with no firsthand experience in the underwater environment at a time when shipwrecks were first coming into general public and academic consciousness in this country. The legacy he left in this regard was probably an inadvertent one, but its effect was to encourage the relinquishing of this portion of the archaeological resource base to historians and museum curators. It is significant that only one article dealing with shipwrecks has appeared in *American Antiquity* since that time (Cockrell 1980). In other national anthropological journals only a token few dealing with submerged sites of any kind have been published. *The Journal of Field Archaeology* has printed a few (e.g., Clausen, Brooks, and Wesolowsky 1975), and a couple have appeared in *Historical Archaeology*. The possibilities of inundated terrestrial sites on the continental shelf has been broached (Emery and Edwards 1966: 733–77), but little effort has been made to act on that exciting potential.

It is ironic to note that Goggin's overall effect on the field of underwater archaeology may have been somewhat negative because he was one of the first anthropologists to recognize the potential of certain rather narrow aspects of submerged sites archaeology. One of his students eventually produced an unpublished, but well-circulated, master's thesis entitled "Underwater Archaeology—Theory and Method" (Gluckman 1967) which lightly touched on some of the major issues we are now addressing.

46

Cultural-Resource Management

To date, serious efforts at scientifically investigating shipwreck remains in the United States have been tied, almost totally, to cultural resource management programs on a state or federal level. The exception has been the work by George Bass and some of his colleagues, although most of their energies are focused on the Mediterranean.

The National Park Service was involved in one of the earliest scientific efforts in 1968 with the steamboat *Bertrand*. It was discovered not underwater but near Omaha, Nebraska, in a field that had been underwater before the Missouri meandered and left it to eventual burial by river sediments (Petsche 1974). Not long after the finding of the *Bertrand*, the remains of the U.S.S. *Cairo*, a Civil War gunboat that had been raised in 1964, were turned over to the care of the National Park Service (Jones and Peterson 1971). Probably one of the most ill-advised affairs in the annals of historic preservation was the raising of the *Cairo*, because it posed a conservation problem of proportions that would stagger any agency's budget. Nevertheless, the Park Service found itself once again in the shipwreck preservation business and has done a creditable job with the remains since then, considering the fact that the *Cairo* had already been severely affected by its removal from a reasonably stable underwater environment.

George Fischer, a National Park Service archaeologist, was probably the first to articulate in print the need for investigating submerged sites on federal lands within a cultural resources management framework (Fischer 1973: 4). A CRM approach has been gradually adopted by a number of coastal states and by other coastal land management agencies including the Bureau of Land Management on the outer continental shelf.

Major CRM-inspired research in the 1970s on shipwrecks in the U.S. has been concentrated in several East Coast states and Texas. Survey and excavations took place in Virginia (Broadwater 1981), South Carolina (Albright 1977), North Carolina (Watts 1975), Maine (Switzer 1978) and Padre Island, Texas (Arnold and Weddle 1978). The Florida Division of Archives and Records Management History monitored the activities of treasure salvors during that time and forced a modicum of data retrieval at certain sites, meeting with frustration at most others (Cockrell 1975a, 1980).

The National Park Service during that decade also pursued its involvement with shipwrecks, but chose to emphasize survey and inventory of the resources rather than excavation (Fischer 1974; Lenihan 1974a). The state of the art for conducting shipwreck surveys advanced markedly during this time and it was in this area, rather than through excavations, that the beginnings of an anthropological orientation became evident. Carl Clausen and Barto Arnold, through the Texas Antiquities Committee, pioneered an approach to shipwreck inventory that not only employed predictive models for site location but also identified remote-sensing signatures for wrecks and emphasized saturation coverage of tracts of submerged land. The latter is a particularly important point since their methodology was clearly one designed for survey and not for random search. The electronic positioning and plotting systems they used off of Padre Island generated data that could be used by archaeologists and land managers to understand not only where shipwrecks were but where they weren't.

Although it is evident that a fair amount of energy began to be directed by some CRM entities into controlled professional shipwreck research, the question of a theoretical grounding to these activities was still quietly circumvented. The issue was raised occasionally (Lenihan, 1974a: 32; Mathewson, Murphy, and Spencer 1974) but stirred little interest. It is only at the turn of the decade 1980–81 that we begin to see some interesting developments in that direction. The intimate association between Basque whaling ships and their Canadian home ports has been approached with an obvious degree of sensitivity toward anthropological questions by Robert Grenier (1981). The Army Corps of Engineers Tennessee–Tombigbee Waterway Project resulted in a steamboat survey that was tied into a total overview of cultural resources in the river drainage. The report on the steamboat research (Murphy and Saltus 1981 in press) has a decided anthropological overtone, with some discussion of theoretical aspects of shipwreck research.

Discussion

As indicated earlier, an analysis of the conceptual roots of shipwreck archaeology is less a history of ideas than a history of action looking for some synthetic intellectual milieu within which to operate. All of the above practitioners are lumped together and referred to in the literature as marine archaeologists. With the exception of the last three discussed—the classical archaeologists, the English school of nautical archaeologists, and CRM specialists—this is obviously a misnomer. However, among none of these groups of individuals has there been ample attention paid to either the development of explicit research designs or the whole range of problems that could be addressed of an anthropological nature. The only exceptions have been recent. A few of the British school, most prominently the late Keith Muckelroy, have begun to raise some very germane theoretical issues.

Muckelroy (1978) has done an excellent job of confronting theoretical issues in an almost complete vacuum. Besides proposing perspectives dealing with the ship as "machine" and as "closed community," he has developed models for extracting different natural and cultural dynamics that may affect cultural remains on the seabed, an underwater version of Schiffer's "N-transforms" and "C-transforms" (Schiffer 1976: 12–19).

Aside from Muckelroy's work and some rather useful manipulations of other shipwreck data (e.g., Bass 1972; C. Martin 1979b: 279–302), the returns from shipwreck archaeology have been almost totally descriptive in nature. When terrestrial archaeology was in a similar developmental stage in this country, Walter Taylor commented as follows:

Archaeological data, then, consists of the material results of cultural behavior, and the affinities—quantitative, qualitative, spatial, etc.—which can be found to exist among them, and between them and the natural environment. But mere description of these phenomena cannot satisfy the requirements of archaeological study if the archaeologist is bent upon writing history or studying culture. Description must be made, to be sure; but there is also the need for interpretation and synthesis (Taylor 1948: 112).

SHIPWRECKS AND ANTHROPOLOGY

Shoes and Ships, and Sealing Wax, and Cabbages and Kings

The time has come, the walrus said, to talk of many things—and indeed it has. We have discussed the curious indifference that American archaeologists in academic circles have shown to shipwrecks and proposed reasons why certain questions were never asked. Now it's time to present some that should have been asked.

As the walrus suggests, ships do not sail in a cultural vacuum; that is, if the kings did not want their cabbages, shoes, and sealing wax moved from place to place, there would be no need for ships. This is no revelation to either marine historians or classical and nautical archaeologists. A *History of Seafaring Based on Underwater Archaeology,* edited by George Bass (1972), illustrates well, as do numerous monographs by serious marine historians (e.g., Rackl 1968; Throckmorton 1969; Marsden 1974), that there is a strong sensitivity to the fact that ships are the material expression of more generalized cultural dynamics. In almost all cases, however, the publications are oriented toward presenting a sequence of design changes over time along with a recapsulization of historic particulars that are conjectured to have been relevant to changes in form. Aside from these works, there are the popularized accounts of modern-day dilettantes and adventurers which describe *ad nauseam* the use of air lifts, bubble levels, and portable grids. All of these works go under the title of underwater archaeology, maritime archaeology, or marine archaeology, but in no case are there major site reports that directly contribute to the anthropological data base in a nomothetic sense. The indirect contributions are fairly numerous; the technical quality of data recovery in many of these cases rivals or surpasses that to be found in terrestrial sites excavated by American archaeologists without benefit of well-conceived research designs.

We are at the point in our historical development where we must either put shipwrecks into an anthropological perspective or drop the matter once and for all. In many areas of the world, shipwrecks are an endangered species and all discussion may become academic in a few decades.

A Modern-day Analogue

Consider for a moment the nature of the social commitment involved when a sixteenth-century European nation dispatched a sailing ship to what was, in every sense of the word, a "new world." The closest modern-day analogue we could propose to an early exploratory vessel would be a manned space vehicle. The main difference would be that the spaceship is the quintessence of twentieth-century man's technological capabilities, and the astronauts' role is usually a negligible one in terms of decision making, whereas the emphasis in sixteenth-century exploratory ships was on the explorers' know-how, and the vessels were often second rate.

An exploratory ship, whether powered by wind or rocket fuel, is designed to be self-sufficient and to maintain a shipboard community for periods of months before a landfall. During the voyage, the shipboard stress factors may become enormous; the diseases associated with human beings living in extremely close quarters, coupled with poor hygiene and the whole range of malnutrition factors that accompany isolation from fresh food sources, all come into play. Scurvy played a major role in the success or failure of many early voyages. A highly stratified shipboard society during the voyage can be assumed—ships are rarely run by committee. The interaction between crew and officers would be largely dependent on the social norms of the ship's parent culture and the special requirements of the voyage. The crew may have been impressed, or volunteers paid on salary or commission. They may be primarily nationals, or specialists recruited from another seafaring nation.

The ship and all the material culture it is carrying are specifically selected for a narrowly defined purpose. Space is at a premium, and the ship's stores and cargo hold are not likely to be carrying a great deal that is not pertinent to the mission at hand. Yet men have needs past subsistence, and one may expect there to be many items on board that occupy only a modicum of space but that can be used to reestablish a cognitive link to the more familiar and less frightening world from which they came, for example, games, musical instruments, and charms. The golf clubs smuggled aboard a spacecraft bound for the moon are a famous modern example of this tradition.

The stress involved in long sea voyages is both physical and mental; releases may be sought in aggression which would have to be controlled by the officers through punishment, or in other ways such as writing diaries and logs, taking up carving, or perhaps practicing homosexuality. There may be a priest on board to deal with some of these stress factors and to act as a tool for establishing a spiritual presence of the parent culture in the New World.

The proxemics involved in this intense microcosm sailing across the ocean are also well worth considering. The personal social space required in their home nations may well have been entirely different for different crew members. These individuals now find themselves crammed into a world for months at a time that below decks would be functionally no larger than a Trailways bus. Within this area they must eat, sleep, keep warm, interact, defecate, and reflect on their condition with no relief from each other. All of these functions have some material culture associated with them.

Carrying our analogue to completion, let us suppose disastrous terminations of some of these voyages that result in archaeological sites separated by centuries. The exploratory vessel wrecks in uncharted waters well off course from its intended destination in an area that bears no relation to either the parent culture or the purpose of the voyage. Our unhappy astronauts meet a similar end on an asteroid that wasn't supposed to be there. We'll leave the latter-day voyagers for the archaeologists of the future and concentrate now on what the anthropologist of 1981 might do with the material remains of our sixteenth-century scenario.

The Shipwreck Site

The historians have already demonstrated what they would do with the material remains of our hypothetical voyage. The questions they would ask are geared toward appreciating the event, its significance in recorded history, and the information it could add regarding known linear progressions in changes of certain types of artifacts. They would be most concerned with armament, cargo, and navigational instruments used to negotiate that part of the world. The basic question they ask is, How do all of these material things fit into an existing picture of documented history? The classical archaeologist, working a similar wreck in the Mediterranean, may concentrate more on hull construction and other attributes of the ship's physical characteristics because many classicists are interested in the ship as a stylistic entity in transition over time. From an anthropological perspective, the above-mentioned factors are of less importance than what the site can suggest regarding questions of man at sea, societies extending themselves, human beings under stress, and the ship as a system of interrelated artifacts comprising a microcosm of human interaction. Further, how does this wreck site, in association with other shipwreck sites and written documents, afford us a glimpse of changes in classes of things over time? Instead of focusing narrowly on the evolution of deck guns, we could ask a broader question, that is, In reaction to what social and environmental stimuli does ship armament evolve over time?

To bring it down to the most direct and substantive level possible, let us now examine the components of some real and hypothetical sites.

52

Ship Construction

The architectural elements of a sailing ship, Great Lakes steamer, or nuclear-powered submarine represent a unique adaptive response to the demands for commerce, travel, exploration, or warfare which are internalized by a particular society. Influences on these design factors go well beyond a concern for hydrodynamics and performance. At different points in the history of a particular maritime culture, very different needs will be felt with regard to a ship's capability for speed, seaworthiness, and maneuverability. The deep-hulled, broad-beamed Spanish naos that lumbered across the Atlantic in the sixteenth century were slow, cumbersome, and not very sleek, but they were dependable, carried a good-sized cargo, and did not require a huge crew. The demands for great speed, during the late nineteenth-century gold rush in California, influenced the design of the clipper hull which was streamlined, but the square-rigged variety of clipper ship needed a very large crew to slave over thousands of square yards of canvas. These are obvious, historically documented external stimuli on the construction characteristics of vessels, but what of the more subtle factors—aesthetics, cultural identity with seafaring, and interpersonal dynamics such as social stratification? How do these manifest themselves in the ship as artifact?

The division of living space between crew members on the one hand and the captain and his officers on the other may be an interesting indication of status hierarchies in different maritime cultures. In confined quarters, space is a valuable commodity, and the amount of it allotted to a particular segment of the shipboard community can be a strong clue as to what value is attached to that societal niche by the shipboard culture. Certainly the extreme can be found in "blackbirders" or slaveships, in which allotted space may be the area one's body covers when lying down chained to the deck; the other extreme is the admiral's quarters on an eighteenth-century flagship in a Spanish flota. The study of proxemics as evidenced in ship remains has a great deal of potential. Even as late as World War II, we could hypothesize different attitudes about the value and quality of life as opposed to strategic advantage in Japanese and American warships. A comparison of the construction characteristics of the U.S. ships sunk during the air raid at Pearl Harbor with those of the Japanese navy lying at the bottom of Truk Lagoon could tell us much about what efforts were really made to see to the safety and comfort of shipboard personnel, as opposed to what we are led to believe from documents written in an emotion-charged era.

Simmons has pointed out (1981) that the trend toward increased compartmentalization of sailing ships had definite implications for shipboard hygiene. Deeper hulls with more enclosed, poorly ventilated decks caused serious health problems. Simmons observed that organic refuse consequently tended to migrate downward to the hold rather than overboard, increasing problems with vermin infestation and disease. This has more pleasant implications for the archaeologist, however, whose treasure is traditionally other people's trash. The unique preservation qualities of the underwater environment also come into play here. Work conducted on a 1554 shipwreck off Padre Island has even turned up fossilized cockroaches which had been unregistered passengers on the vessel (Arnold and Weddle 1978). Some of the most dramatic examples of organic preservation in an aqueous environment can be found in deep freshwater. Some of the early twentieth-century shipwrecks in Lake Superior still have intact human remains on them, including preserved soft tissues.

Modern man's innate compulsion to beat the system also had some curious effects on ship construction. Because tonnage, according to European standards, was figured by including a beam measurement (gunnel to gunnel at the widest part of the ship), it followed that the closer together the gunnels, the less duty paid. The Dutch response to this situation was to modify their carracks so they had an exaggerated sweep to the center, thereby giving a false impression to the revenue masters.

During the Industrial Age, what was an innovative design in one decade could be made totally obsolete in the next, as mass-produced support facilities became incompatible with vessel design. Such seems to be the case with the whaleback steamers produced for a brief period in the Great Lakes area. Their cigar-shaped hulls were ideal for meeting the special demands of the Great Lakes environment, which is one of the toughest for any vessel. Instead of plowing through the waves, they were constructed to allow the waves to wash over the decks, where tightly fitting small hatchways prevented the water from making its way below. This well-planned, highly specialized adaptation became obsolete in less than thirty years because newly developed automatic

54

loading and unloading facilities could not accommodate the tiny hatch-ways (Barry 1974: 155).

Adaptive change in design is far from the rational, step-by-step, upward evolution implied in many works on marine history. Industrial archaeologists on land have demonstrated the anxiety that using new materials causes in structural engineering. The first iron bridge (constructed in Shropshire, England) was mortised and pegged as if it were a wooden edifice.

> . . . Given the Darbys, with their immense confidence in the possibilities of iron, the Iron Bridge was inevitable. It would have been a professional betrayal for the Darbys to have built it of any other material. But, as we can see from the structure of the bridge, their confidence had its limits. They were only adventurous up to a certain point. The iron ribs of the bridge are mortised and pegged together, exactly as if they were made of wood. Ten years later, bridge builders, including the Darbys themselves, had abandoned this pseudo-carpentering technique and were going the whole way with bridges made of complete cast-iron sections (Hudson 1976: 94).

A similar mistrust of iron existed among nineteenth-century ship-wrights. It is a readily observable fact that most woods float and metal does not. Even though it became apparent that a displacement hull made of iron was superior in many ways to one of wood, an era of "composite" wood and iron hull construction was required on the Great Lakes before shipbuilders and the men who sailed them would trust themselves to metal hulls.

There was also a decided diversity in the receptivity of different cultures to the use of iron in shipbuilding, partly based on availability of raw material but probably also based on varying degrees of conservatism about ship design.

> European shipbuilders pressed ahead with iron in ship construction, whereas the Americans with great reserves of timber stuck to wood construction. Steam ships came quite quickly to iron plating but it was thought by seamen that the copper sheathing which was used to protect wooden ships from the ship-worm of tropical waters, was essential to reduce fouling during a long passage. Copper sheathing on an iron ship presents frightening electrolytic corrosion problems and therefore the early English clippers were built of composite construction. That is with iron, and later steel framing but planked with wood and sheathed with copper. Towards the end of the century, all sailing ships were built in iron; even the masts and spars were built of iron tubes and wire

rigging had almost completely superseded rope for the standing rigging (Marshall Cavendish Publications 1975).

Even more curious adaptive phenomena accompanied developments in locomotive power in ship construction. The change of focus from wind-driven sources of power to steam was a very tentative and drawn-out process. Steam was at first seen as simply an auxiliary power supply on early ships, to be employed when there was insufficient wind. There was much understandable resistance to converting to a system that relied totally on heavy machinery that consumed huge quantities of coal (which therefore took up room normally assigned to cargo) and that belched out hot smoke and embers to settle on the decks of what were initially wooden ships. Hybrid craft developed that used combinations of sail and steam or side-mounted paddlewheels. Perhaps the oddest mutant resulting from this period of rapid evolution was a vessel named *The Great Eastern*, launched in London in 1858. The vessel was not of composite wood and iron construction, but instead sported two iron hulls, one inside the other, 6,500 square yards of sail, and two engines—one to drive two fifty-eight-foot paddle wheels and one for another innovation, the screw propeller (Dugan 1953). Actually, the concept of the screw propeller had been around for quite a while but did not come into general usage until the latter part of the nineteenth century. The phenomenon of inventions having to "wait their time" is another aspect of technological innovation which might be the subject of an interesting study by anthropologists. Certainly, shipwrecks over time offer an excellent data base for getting at this question.

Marine historians and classical archaeologists have perfected techniques for reconstructing ship architecture from minimal remains. Richard Steffy at Texas A&M University is particularly adept at this (see Steffy 1978). National Park Service historic architects have been able to piece together the extremely deteriorated remains of the *Cairo* to such a point that an extraordinary scale model has been produced. The questions they have asked of the data have been straightforward, descriptive, and useful. It is time that additional, anthropological demands are made of this data base.

Cargo

A ship's cargo is another fundamental aspect of a shipwreck site.

56

Using the model of the Spanish exploratory or colonizing vessel developed earlier, one sees clearly that a ship's cargo can be a powerful indicator of the priorities that the parent culture sees in its overseas involvements. Because of the extreme commitments in time and capital for long-term payoffs, there is little room for frivolous cargo on a sailing vessel making a trans-Atlantic voyage. All of the goods on board intended for use at the target destination must be very selectively chosen. This might include a cross section of all the materials needed for subsistence in an alien and often harsh environment, or specialized cargoes for high-priority undertakings in the New World. A good example of the latter would be a shipment of mercury needed for refining precious metals, such as silver and gold, from the mines in Mexico and Peru.

The much-touted "time capsule" nature of shipwrecks has special significance when we consider ship cargo. A cross section of all the tools and implements thought most necessary for a colony's use in adapting to what it feels is a hostile environment found in the tightly dated context of a shipwreck has obvious significance archaeologically. It is particularly tantalizing to imagine what could be done with a comparison of these synchronic snapshots of material culture over a given period of time, for example, inbound Spanish colonial supply ships over three centuries. There is probably not a purer test-tube case for a processual study to be found in the archaeological record. Heretofore, this aspect of the time-capsule effect has not been developed, but rather the emphasis has been on establishing *terminus ante quems* for particular artifact types and on proving contemporaneity of various cultural expressions.

It should also be noted that the time-capsule effect is dependent on the shipwreck site being well defined in nature and on there being little chance of confusing later or earlier cultural activity with the wreck under study. Unfortunately, the real world does not always present such an ideal situation. There are many cases in the literature where shipwrecks have tended to cluster owing to a particular hazard that has been extant in the area for as long as there has been shipping (e.g., submerged reefs) or because there have been "wrecking" activities traditionally carried out in the region. The latter is a curious maritime phenomenon independently instituted in many parts of the world; inhabitants of a particular coastal settlement will attempt to induce ship disasters, usually by lighting false channel beacons.

Naturally or culturally induced wrecks, in specific high-risk areas, can precipitate ugly cases of contamination of delightfully pure time capsules. On a high-energy coast this can be particularly troublesome because various ship remains may be terribly jumbled through natural processes. The most startling example of contaminants in a scattered wreck site is a situation in Florida at 8SL17 where an early Spanish wreck may be resting on top of an inundated megafauna site associated with prehistoric artifacts (Cockrell and Murphy 1978).

Another interesting aspect of cargo found in a wreck site is the light it can shed on activities of different cultures. The marine historians were quick to note that large percentages of the valuables, particularly silver and gold, on outbound Spanish wrecks in the New World were not listed on manifests. The whole question of illicit transport of goods as an enduring cultural trait could be the subject of some very interesting papers by anthropologists. It is probably safe to say that the only reliable data base for this phenomenon is to be found on shipwrecks.

Ship Stores

As distinguished from the cargo, we are defining ship stores as those materials taken along expressly for the subsistence needs of the crew. This is sometimes a difficult distinction to make, except by inference from the nature of the material or by spatial provenience in the ship remains. But when these materials can be confidently isolated as to function, they hold significant value for creating a picture of shipboard life and developing insights into seafaring norms in a particular culture. A high level of understanding regarding diet and nutritional needs is also potentially retrievable from the remains of ship stores. These, coupled with the ship's surgeon's tool kit, should leave the medical anthropologist with useful data sources for reconstructing the actual level of medical and dietary awareness of a society rather than the perceived level evidenced in written documents.

The food stores on a ship are directly relevant to understanding not only nutritional variables but also what was available in terms of foodstuffs in the port of origin or at reprovisioning stops on the way to the final destination. These remains also indicate what was known, and more importantly what was practiced, in regard to food preservation on long voyages. Although organic food remains may or may not be retrievable, the casks or containers in which they were stored often survive along with residues, which have usually been ignored by those involved with shipwreck investigations. There is an unsettling tendency among marine archaeologists, just as among many land archaeologists, to be too quick to "clean" artifacts possibly bearing organic residues in an effort to get at the typology of the container. One extraordinary example of food preservation in a shipwreck comes from a freshwater context in the Great Lakes. A cask of cheese was retrieved in almost perfect condition from a wreck that has been underwater for exactly one hundred years (Hoffman 1974).

Ship Armament and Apparel

A Spanish merchant nao bound for the New World, whether or not it was accompanied by armed escort, would most likely still be carrying some armament. "Armament" on a colonizing vessel is defined here as primarily defensive equipment such as cannon, swivel guns (light, usually breech loaded, antipersonnel weapons), and so on. If the cannons are found neatly and imprudently stored on the ballast, we have a clue that the captain was less concerned with the threat of attack or the regulations of the Spanish House of Trade than he was with a high profit margin.

The type of armament a ship is carrying offers a basis for making inferences as to the ship's period, function, vessel class, and origin. On the basis of several ships, hypotheses could be generated about strategies of war and degrees of anticipation of hostile action at different points in history. An investigation of the ship's magazine yields additional clues in this respect. Besides gleaning information on level of technology, one may determine whether the intended reaction to attack was predicated on antiship or antipersonnel weapons, grappling or trying to keep the enemy at a distance. It should be remembered that the concept of sinking the enemy in action is a fairly modern one. Except when ships were used as rams, they were usually considered to be seaborne platforms for adversaries to employ in damaging and boarding the opponent vessel. The words *forecastle* and *aftercastle* derived from a literal meaning harking back to medieval times, when the bow and stern of European vessels were raised and designed to look and function like floating castles.

A dramatic example of how information obtained from underwater archaeological investigations can shed light on major historical events is "The Armada Shot Controversy" (Wignall 1973: 463–82). Shot removed from the *Santa Maria de la Rosa* showed indications of being improperly treated during the manufacturing process; if so, this could have made them too brittle to be effective against the English ships. Whether or not this was actually a significant factor in the battle, it is a clear case of the analysis of material remains from a specific underwater site having implications for a much broader cultural question. Industrial archaeologists could use this issue as grounds for developing testable hypotheses related to a comparative study of European iron-working techniques in the sixteenth century and the stress of exigencies of war.

The best way to conceptualize the term *apparel* in reference to a ship is to think of what the ship is "wearing." In addition to its architectural attributes and its armament, a ship has other permanent fixtures including rigging, lanterns, hearths, steering assemblies, linkage, and so on.

A consideration of a ship's apparel presents a whole range of possibilities for anthropological inquiry. The hearth or stove areas in a ship have no less significance than those at a land site. In older ships, the fired-clay linings from "cook boxes" may provide the potential for magnetic intensity dating since this type of analysis is not dependent on preserving the integrity of the orientation of these remains.

A ship's anchors, rigging, and even the sheathing and patchwork it might wear over its planking to provide protection from marine borers bear testimony to general cultural traits regarding sailing and seamanship. An array of anchors seaward of our hypothetical wreck site on a reef or shallow coastline may help the archaeologist reconstruct the actual event of sinking during a storm. As the storm anchors fail one by one, the ship is driven helplessly aground or onto a reef. The material jettisoned during a sinking can also offer interesting insights into the priorities of men from different cultures under stress. What went first? Gold may have been the heaviest thing on board but we can readily assume it was the last material jettisoned.

The Bilge

The bilge area of the ship in our shipwreck scenario is of limited interest to the historian but is probably the high point for the anthropologist. Besides the ballast and whatever clues it may offer regarding

60

origin and stopovers of the vessel (type of ballast used is subject not only to questions of what is easily available but also to those of cultural preference), the bilge is also a natural magnet for refuse. It presents the anthropologist with what is essentially a floating midden, much as if a nomadic group of hunter-gatherers had been considerate enough to carry most of their trash with them on a seasonal migration and left it neatly deposited in an overnight campsite. To complete the analogy to those shipwrecks with documented dates of sinking, the hunters would have also left a neatly inscribed plaque telling the year, month, and day they left their garbage.

The full spectrum of anthropological questions asked of refuse can be transferred to the shipwreck site. Inquiry can be made regarding normal subsistence activities on shipboard, and there may be specific indicators of stress such as degree of utilization of faunal remains, rat bones with butchering marks, and so on. Again, it should be emphasized that depending on local environmental variables, organic remains in a wreck site may enjoy excellent possibilities for preservation.

The traditional placement of cook boxes in many early trans-Atlantic wooden vessels was forward, directly on the ballast (Morison 1971: 130). Cooking refuse often accumulated in the bilge to the point that the obnoxious odors forced the captain to have the ship careened and the ballast cleaned. A vessel that wrecked while engaged in an ocean crossing will frequently be hosting bilge residues specifically related to the crew of that particular crossing.

The question of hygiene problems associated with the bilge also suggests other areas suitable for model testing in reference to different social concepts of dirt and pollution. For example, the structuralist approach offered by Mary Douglas in *Purity and Danger* (1966) could be applied to the cultural residues of a shipwreck.

Additional test implications could be formulated from bilge materials as well as general artifact assemblages throughout a wreck site, which would complement those generated from ship construction, about status hierarchies in the shipboard community. How great a distinction is there, for instance, between subsistence kits and personal items associated with officers' quarters as opposed to crew's quarters? There is reason for conducting useful ethnological studies on the same question in extant shipboard environments. One interesting study along these lines has already appeared in the *Journal of Anthropological Research* (Prattis 1973: 210–19). In "A Model of Shipboard Interaction

61

on a Hebridian Fishing Vessel," J. I. Prattis uses a transactional model developed by Barth (1966) to address the issue of "status incongruence" associated with the cook on a modern-day commercial fishing boat. It is doubtful that one could ever obtain data from the archaeological record that would permit an understanding of individual expectations as opposed to actual status conferred on a certain crew member, but there is certainly room for cross-fertilization between the ethnological and archaeological methodologies on this question.

Whether Pigs Have Wings

Some other issues the walrus has raised, like many raised in the archaeological community, are not terribly substantive. It would be well, in regard to the new focus on shipwrecks we are developing, to avoid much of the polemics and adversary rhetoric that has accompanied theory-building efforts in a great deal of American archaeology heretofore. Our purpose should simply be to examine ways in which different conceptual models more attuned to anthropology may be applied to shipwrecks.

Others (Deetz 1967; Clarke 1968) have warned us that we must be careful in seeing anthropological constructs as immutable laws; they should be seen as tools for understanding rather than as belief systems. Particularist descriptive systems for addressing social change over time are useful and meaningful in their own right. However, the jump necessary to bridge the gap between identifying historical event progressions and making generalizations about human behavior requires a very considerable leap of faith. Claude Lévi-Strauss directs criticism against the historians by stating that all history is "history for" (Lévi-Strauss 1962: 257), meaning that all history is written for a purpose by people with specific ideological preferences. This may be true, but some of the same weaknesses exist in a processual archaeological approach where we are trying to identify patterned impulses behind social phenomena in other cultures by studying their physical residues according to currently popular behavioral models.

The argument that archaeology is anthropology or it is nothing (Willey and Phillips 1958) seems rhetorical and somewhat specious in this light. The need is for amalgamation of effort, not methodological pureness of thought. Also, we must not read "true" anthropology as ethnology; archaeology works from a data base different from, not less powerful than, that of ethnology. In the words of Ferguson:

Archaeology need not, and should not be the handmaiden of ethnology, history or any other field of study. Controlling a special expression of human behavior, archaeology can go about the business of treating the problem that may be clarified by an examination of the material evidence of culture (Ferguson 1977).

CONCLUSION

It should have become apparent during this discussion that shipwrecks present an extraordinary data base for investigation by anthropologically oriented archaeologists. Some suggestions were made earlier offering possible reasons why involvement with this class of archaeological resource by anthropologists has almost never taken place, including the proposition that the influence of Goggin's classic article on underwater archaeology created among anthropologists a lukewarm reception to shipwrecks.

We might also consider another factor, which is the conditioned caution of American archaeologists to subject matter not sufficiently mundane. The field of marine archaeology deals with subject matter and technology that have considerable romantic appeal and that have been dominated by adventurers, historians, and particularists of a number of different persuasions. To a discipline that has been going through throes of a neurosis that Glassie would term "theory envy" (1977: 23) and that has been extremely defensive of its claims to being scientific, the thought of studying shipwrecks may induce an element of hesitancy. It is not beyond reason to assume that the fear of being seen as a closet humanist plays a small role, but one worth mentioning in the overall consideration of why anthropology has not contributed to the subfield of shipwreck archaeology.

If American archaeology has followed the stages that Willey and Sabloff have proposed in *A History of American Archaeology* (1974), we can place contemporary work with shipwrecks solidly in the "classifactory-historical period." To be sure, the historically oriented researchers conducting marine archaeological investigations would have no qualms about admitting this, nor should they. The burden of aggressively pursuing the filling of this anthropological vacuum lies with the anthropologists, although it should be noted that the data base is suffering heavy attrition at the present time primarily from commercial exploitation. It appears the National Park system and certain areas designated by the National Oceanographic and Atmospheric Administration offer the only real sanctuary in any legal sense from this sort of depredation, but even there protection is often hampered by inadequate funding and insufficient personnel.

With a decreasing number of historical shipwrecks available in future years, it is incumbent on all serious researchers to get maximum returns from any wreck sites disturbed. Consequently, two primary developments need to take place: research on ships should be conducted with the benefit of well-planned, explicit research designs no matter what orientation is used; this is presently not the case. And, there must be a much more interdisciplinary nature to the studies carried out on shipwrecks, especially when heavy impact to the site (i.e., excavation) is anticipated. Areas of interest that should be represented in research designs for ships include, in addition to history and marine architecture, analytical archaeology, marine biology, maritime ethnology, industrial archaeology, archaeometry, ethnohistory, and cultural-resource management.

Cultural-resource management specialists have been forced into a sensitivity regarding an eroding archaeological resource base. The concepts of conservation archaeology (Lipe 1974) and minimal impact archaeology (Judge 1979) have real application to the future of shipwreck research. The basic tenet of this approach is that even the best-controlled total excavations of a site are totally destructive to that site, meaning it has been removed for all time from the archaeological record.

We have no choice but to embrace a conservation ethic in regard to shipwreck research in the United States. We hope that an archaeologist fifty years from the present who is writing a "History of Ideas" paper on shipwreck archaeology will be able to reflect on a development that took place in the latter part of the twentieth century wherein shipwreck studies were characterized by rich, interdisciplinary efforts conducted with the benefit of explicit research designs and a strong sensitivity for the fragile, nonrenewable nature of the resource.

4

Shipwrecks As Data Base for Human Behavioral Studies[1]

LARRY MURPHY

National Park Service
Submerged Cultural Resources Unit

Waterborne craft have been basic human tools since prehistoric times. Many societies rose or declined as a direct result of whether they successfully utilized ships for subsistence, transport, and protection. Ship production and deployment have been the focus of intense human cooperation and organizational efforts for several millennia. Ships have been, and still are, the largest and most complex mobile structures produced.

Maritime endeavors have resulted in a continual historical progression of technological development, rivaled in duration only by the production of weapons, tools, and dwellings. The seabed contains a virtually complete record of this progression. However, only in the last few decades has intellectual inquiry been directed toward a systematic understanding of this aspect of human activity.

The data base for such studies includes rich documentation ranging from prehistoric art to contemporary plans and bills of lading, sites of

1. The final version of this paper benefited considerably from the comments of Pat Watson, Dan Lenihan, W. A. Cockrell, Larry Nordby, Roger Smith, and Joy Roots.

terrestrial maritime support facilities, ethnographic data, ship models, and, of course, the ships themselves, whether in current use, preserved as historic relics, or as shipwrecks. This last element is the concern of this paper, although complete understanding of maritime traditions must include integration of all these factors. The purpose of this paper is to examine some ways shipwrecks may be approached so they may contribute more to the understanding of human behavior.

SOME CONCEPTIONS OF SHIPWRECKS

Shipwrecks have been many things to many people. Immediately after a disaster, they were a resource to be exploited by the contemporary salvors. Wrecks are often serious hazards to navigation, because they tend to occur in heavily traveled sea lanes. They have become popular as mines of historic relics and as fodder for the investment schemes of the modern-day treasure salvor. Shipwrecks are repositories of period artifacts for museum curators and sources of data for maritime historians. Most important, they are archaeological sites worthy of concentrated scientific research that have only recently been seriously considered for the insights they yield into past human behavior.

Shipwrecks have been described as "time capsules." However, this simile is somewhat limited conceptually, because time capsules are created by human intent, whereas shipwrecks are seldom deliberate. A time capsule usually results from the intentional, protected deposition of items thought to represent the present to the future. Such material shares characteristics with historic documents, principally in that these interments or recordings do not necessarily represent what actually was, but what was thought to be significant for posterity.

With the exception of the purposeful scuttling of vessels, a shipwreck is rarely the result of human intent. A shipwreck is more properly analogous to the destruction of Port Royale, Jamaica, or perhaps to the fiery conflagration of an inhabited, prehistoric pit house. In these instances, a viable, functioning social group and its material was frozen in time by disaster. The full spectrum of the group's activities at the location, represented by the material culture in use at the time, is deposited as a discrete unit. This is rare in the archaeological record, and contrasts sharply with the complex and disarticulated depositions characterizing the more common chronologically ordered archaeological sites. It becomes apparent that a shipwreck as an archaeological entity has special value because of its distinctly synchronic nature.

It is well known that shipwrecks provide a concentrated collection of tightly dated artifacts in use at the time of deposition, as assemblages of cargo, ship-related material, and the personal possessions of those on board. Ivor Noël-Hume (1969: 189–90) recognizes this peculiar aspect of the shipwreck and its significance: "Unlike the trash that the archaeologist must make the most from on land, wrecked ships contain cargoes of complete objects, all irrefutably associated and possessing an unimpeachable *terminus ante Quem*. Each wreck may be a miniature Pompeii and deserves to be treated accordingly." The potential contribution of shipwrecks for the comparative study of artifacts is certainly great, but the potential of shipwreck study goes far beyond this limited aspect. Shipwrecks can properly contribute much to the study of human behavior in many areas, and the only limits are imposed by the nature and scope of the questions developed by researchers. Attention should be focused on the development of this potential, as the discussion of shipwrecks continues within the discipline of archaeology.

Shipwrecks have also been described as microcosms of a particular maritime society (Lenihan 1974a: 32). One possible weakness of this perspective is the implication that the full range of patterned behavior in the sponsoring society is represented in shipboard life, a proposition that has not been demonstrated. More accurately, a ship is a cultural component that shares some conventions with the parent culture, but is also a cultural entity in and of itself. Shipboard life is composed of behavioral patterns designed to effect a common, techno-intensive goal: the successful operation of a ship, completion of the mission, and survival at sea. The shipboard community can be considered to be composed of groups with defined roles and duties, in a probable chain of command which establishes hierarchy and certain patterns of interaction. The ship provides a relatively defined group with minimal outside contact for study of social interaction. Productive approaches to this study would include examination of changes in behavioral patterns longitudinally on ships of a specific social group and comparative study between groups and perhaps between classes of vessels such as naval vessels, privateers, and merchantmen.

A further course of inquiry potentially productive would be the exploration of questions involving contrasts of maritime culture, as represented by shipwreck remains, specifically opposed to the archaeological reconstruction of the parent culture. For example, to what extent does the individual member of the shipboard subculture replicate any role analogy in the parent culture, or the shipboard subculture of other societies? Does a Spanish sailor have more in common with a Dutch seaman than with a fellow countryman who is a peasant? Questions of this nature contribute to more general anthropological questions about the nature and extent of the influence of environment on social groups, and the efficiency and effectiveness of the organization of specialized task units. The shipwreck offers a complex, multifaceted site for controlled study. Although it could be argued that more diverse interaction is represented within the assemblage of a shipwreck than in any other site of comparable size, shipwrecks also offer many opportunities for studying single-purpose specialty group interactions.

SHIPWRECKS, DOCUMENTS, AND ARCHAEOLOGY

Early shipwrecks, especially European vessels, are often well documented. This fact has resulted in a common but rather curious assertion by treasure salvors that little or nothing is to be gained from a shipwreck site that is not better found in the historical record. Some of these individuals, knowledgeable in archival research and archaic languages, point out that complete vessel histories, bills of lading, and passenger lists are extant in libraries and provide data not available from even the best archaeological excavation of a shipwreck. In some instances, this has become a justification for salvage work with minimal or no archaeological control and no useful results. Although shallow and self-serving, this argument raises certain considerations regarding the relationship of archaeology and history to the study of shipwrecks.

"History, that is the study of history, involves an interpretation of the past by the selection and manipulation of facts which have been filtered through the mind of the original recorder" (McKay 1976: 93). "It [history] denotes an abstraction or a set of abstractions from actuality, not that actuality itself" (Taylor 1948: 29). Historians, then, are often concerned with the printed word, the "curious obsession of historians" (Burlingame 1959: 14), which is in most cases an aspect of the mental process of the recorder and is subjective from its incep-

68

tion. Much historical documentation was recorded by persons who were compelled by some authority to record. The conceptions (or misconceptions) held by the compelled recorder were those believed to be relevant to and congruent with the desires of the compelling authority; as a result historical documentation more often reflects the attitudes of the authority group or recorder than those of lower-ranking persons in the general society.

The archaeology of shipwrecks should be not merely the embellishment of the maritime historical record, but the elucidation of otherwise unattainable aspects of human behavior. The combination of shipwreck archaeology with the methodologies of other disciplines will result in the authentic reconstruction of behavior patterns, and will permit the formulation of generalities regarding maritime lifeways and human social processes. Generally, New World archaeologists have claimed the end product of their study to be "the elucidation of the nature, the processes, and development of culture" (Taylor 1948: 35).

Though both history and archaeology are concerned with the study of social life and share much, one should not simply be the amplification of the other. Archaeological research is often concerned with aspects of human behavior undocumented by written history and provides the only means of study of the unwritten data base. The seaman throughout most of seafaring history has been illiterate; hence, historical documents, useful as they may be in some areas of research, reveal little of the lifeways of the seaman, and much of that by inference. Most historical documents are not normally concerned with ships operating outside official sanctions. Buccaneers, pirates, smugglers, and privately owned merchant traders are often addressed only peripherally in contemporary documents, although modern-day popular historians have paid much attention to them. Many aspects of seafaring have long preceded historical recording or have eluded contemporary documentation; consequently shipwreck archaeology is often the only means by which much maritime activity may be investigated.

A move toward developing archaeological research within more scientific parameters has been evident in the recent literature, and it is specifically concerned with developing general laws of human behavior through a problem-oriented approach. This nomothetically oriented archaeology is contrasted with the particularist approach in that it attempts lawlike generalizations of relationships between sets of variables.

It is an explicit search for regularities (i.e., hypotheses to be tested) concerning the relationships between the cultural debris and the extinct society responsible for it. This behavioral data is then potentially available to persons seeking broader regularities about human societies existing anywhere in time (Watson 1973: 119).

This approach in archaeology has been critical of the particularist approach which is primarily interested in describing various elements in a historical event progression.

Shipwreck archaeology to date has been primarily historical description and implicitly based on the premise that, with an unbiased approach, one can collect a large amount of data which can then be used for different interpretive analyses by the investigators and other researchers. This was the approach of most terrestrial archaeology until recently, but that approach has altered as a result of detailed criticism over the past decade: "when faced with a potentially infinite amount of data we are forced to make choices as to what to collect; these choices are determined by ideas held a priori—i.e., theories, problems, and so forth. The inductivist program of making thorough, unbiased data collections is not possible" (Hill 1972: 72).

The principal limitation of the contribution of shipwrecks to the body of data on human social processes has been the approach of investigators. Most shipwreck archaeology has been intensely particularistic and without a problem orientation. In the few instances where a problem orientation has been attempted, only problems very narrow in scope were addressed. For example, Mathewson (1977) develops hypotheses regarding the identity of a shipwreck and its distribution scatter pattern in an effort to find the main wreck concentration to expedite commercial treasure salvage operations. Shipwreck archaeologists need to develop and implement broadly conceived research designs asking significant questions of a general nature about human social behavior, or the contribution of shipwrecks to knowledge will only be the generation of historical detail.

THE SHIP AS ARTIFACT AND CULTURAL CARRIER

Ships themselves may be viewed as artifacts and, as such, they have morphological and technical attributes reflective of the culture of the builders and designers. These traits are to be found in the architecture

70

and construction techniques of the vessels. The ship is a cultural carrier, consisting of techniques, equipment, and knowledge which allows travel over bodies of water that would otherwise be barriers to cross-cultural contact. The vessel is a product of the technical abilities, materials, and use intent of the parent culture.

Their development has been conditioned by the geography of the local water; climate; purpose for which the boat was needed; availability of materials for construction; tradition of craftsmanship which grew up among the shipbuilders and the general state and nature of the culture of the people building them. Different types of boats developed in different environments (Greenhill 1976: 25).

Considering the importance of ships to all maritime societies and viewing them as vectors for the spread of technology, ship construction and shipboard patterns of interaction also are important in contributing to the diffusion of general cultural traits as well as to maritime technology. A chronology of development and refinement in ship construction as evidenced in shipwreck studies will expand knowledge of the spread of ideas, technology, and trade patterns, as well as many other areas of social interchange.

The developmental history of the design and construction of vessels is not complete, and often the only means of study is the archaeological record. Few prehistoric craft have been located, and the vessels of many non-Western societies have received little study. Riverine and lake vessels have also been comparatively neglected.

The use of ocean-going vessels has been postulated as enabling prehistoric contact between the Old and New worlds, and between South America and the Pacific Islands (Heyerdahl 1979). For instance, drifting Japanese fishermen are thought to be responsible for the introduction of pottery into the Valdivian culture of Ecuador some 4,500 years before the arrival of Cortez (Meggers and Evans 1966). This would mean the Jomon voyagers would have had to survive an epic trans-Pacific voyage of 8,000 miles. The use of rafts 7,000 years ago to island-hop the Caribbean Island chain from Central America to Hispaniola during a lower sea-level stand seems the most logical hypothesis for the appearance of the late Paleo-Indian Casimira people on that island (Cruxent and Rouse 1969). It is most probable these examples were not single voyages, hence there may be many early prehistoric craft preserved underwater.

71

There are great gaps in our knowledge of vessel use and construction even in the more recent past. Medieval ships, for instance, are less well known than earlier Viking ships, since few remains of the former have been examined. The rapid development of the ship in Europe from essentially a land-based, short-hop craft to a vessel capable of extended voyages will ultimately be found in the archaeological record.

Prior to the early years of the sixteenth century, there were no ship plans and very few models. The knowledge of ship construction comes indirectly from written descriptions (often by unknowledgeable observers) and artists' conceptions, and directly through investigation of the extant structure of shipwrecks. By 1700 it was normal for both a model and plans to be produced for the building of ships in the English navy, though few are available before 1740 (D. Lyon 1974: 67). It is only from this point on that historical documentation becomes very useful in augmenting the archaeological record of European ship design and construction.

There has been discussion of the relative importance of shallow-water shipwrecks when there are deepwater wrecks known which are virtually intact (Bascom 1976). While it is true in some cases that deepwater wrecks are more intact, they are fewer in number than the shallow-water wrecks in coastal waters, and they offer a biased sample for study which requires high technology and sophisticated equipment for site access. The attrition of the data base of shallow-water shipwrecks is increasing, while that contained in deeper sites remains more protected. Attention should not be diverted from developing techniques for maximizing data retrieval from shallow-water wrecks. Development and refinement of methods and techniques of testing and excavation on shallow-water wrecks will ensure maximum return on the more complete deepwater wrecks when they are studied. A fine example of the development of techniques to maximize returns from ship remains is the work of Richard Steffy, a noted ship reconstructionist, who has been able to extract useful information on ship carpentry and tool use from single disarticulated pieces of vessel structure (Steffy 1978a).

Deepwater wrecks may provide more complete structure for analysis, but shallow-water vessels have significantly contributed to the data base, both from more complete sites such as the *Amsterdam* (1749) (Marsden 1972, 1974) and from fragments of vessel remains such as the *Kennemerland* (1664) site which contained few structural members but produced data on treenail patterns and the type of wood used in construction (Price and Muckelroy 1977).

Study of the lower hull remains of shallow-water shipwrecks can produce evidence of modification to the vessel after construction as signs of repair, such as that found in the *Dartmouth* (1670) which was thirty-five years old when sunk (Martin 1978). During certain periods of ship development, the lower hull—that part of the ship most often preserved in shallow water—was the most innovative aspect of design, and yet the least represented in contemporary plans and drawings. This area of the hull often made a considerable difference in the speed and maneuverability of the vessel.

Intact lower-hull construction can be very well preserved in shallow water under certain conditions, as indicated by the 1733 Spanish Plate Fleet vessel *San Jose* (8M0130) sunk off the central Florida Keys. The entire lower-hull construction from the turn of the bilge was complete when located. (These remains, unfortunately, received little examination because they were torn apart soon after discovery by commercial treasure hunters.) A large portion of the rigging hardware material is often present on shallow-water sites, allowing possible reconstruction of this aspect of the ship, even where little organic material remains.

One fruitful approach for these studies may be the comparative study of function and design differentiation through time of certain classes of vessels. The development of merchant and naval ships is an example of such a study. The differentiation of these classes predates Roman times.

Rowed galleys were apparently the forerunners of naval vessels and were derived from the Roman *Liburnian*, whereas the merchant vessels were ultimately derived from the *Oneraria*. The merchant vessels were primarily moved by sail and were of a round, tubby design. The influence of the design of cogs from northern waters resulted in the carrack, which carried both lateen and square sails (Scandurra 1972: 213, 214). The shift from Mediterranean commerce to the Atlantic trade altered the design of merchant ships and resulted in the combination of useful attributes of both slender galleys and the round merchant ships to produce the armed merchant galleon which assumed the role of capital ship late in the sixteenth century.

The approach to this sort of study of ship design and construction development should focus on the human behavior responsible for the changes, rather than merely on the development of historical sequencing of vessel types. Much of the material for a comparative study of merchant and naval ships will have to come primarily from archaeology. The historical documentation on merchant vessels is relatively sparse compared to that on naval vessels, as a result of private ownership. The merchant ships, less restricted by official regulations than were naval vessels in Europe, often were the testing ground for innovative design and construction techniques (McKee 1972: 236).

A complete understanding of the developmental progression of vessels depends on placing the sequence of vessel forms within the larger cultural context. Morphological and constructional technique changes over time were prompted by many more factors than technical efficiency, and these factors will come to light only when the study of vessel development expands beyond mere description and begins considering the human behavioral component. For example, many important social and cultural hypotheses may be developed from the observation that "a first class frigate carries a complement of 470 men, while a merchant ship of the same tonnage would be handled by twenty" (Davis 1929: 90).

Careful study of the material remains of the ships themselves should produce many behavioral insights. The changes of compartmentalization of vessel space over time and between classes of vessels could be quite fruitful if approached cross-culturally. Whiting and Ayres (1968) demonstrated a correlation between building floor plans and certain cultural traits as determined from the Ethnographic Atlas (Murdock 1967). The implications of such studies, when applied to ship design and organization, may prove useful in making cross-cultural tests of a wide range of anthropological propositions concerning human spatial orientation.

Shipwrecks have been seen as synchronous snapshots frozen in time (Lenihan 1974a: 39). There are, however, some diachronic elements present. The ship itself has an individual history, unless it sank on its maiden voyage, as did the Swedish *Wasa*. The ship will show material evidence of structural changes, repairs and alterations, and multiple use, sometimes in different social groups, during its period of operation.

The nature of repairs can show developments in ship technology and carpentry, or may reflect change of ownership or use of the vessel. For instance, a Spanish prize of the British may be repaired and refitted according to British tradition, or the decks of a merchantman may be

74

strengthened for the placement of gun batteries while being refitted as a vessel of war. It is not necessary to have the majority of hull structure present to make interpretations of this nature. Anomalous concentrations of different fittings within a site may point to repairs or modification.

The life of a ship and its use will often be reflected in material remains. Alteration of ships, necessitated by different application, may be discernible. An example is the *Falls of Clyde,* now a museum ship in Honolulu Harbor. It was originally a four-masted ship, rerigged as a bark. Built in 1878, the vessel played a prominent role as a commercial square-rigger in the U.S.-Pacific island trade (Gibbs 1977: 106). At various times the ship was a merchantman, a freighter, and a lumber carrier, then was dismasted and pumps installed so it could be used as an oil barge. It was finally rerigged as a four-masted bark museum vessel. Examination of this vessel reveals evidence of its many uses.

Examination of the diachronic aspects of shipwrecks from a processual perspective leads to problem orientation and to hypothesis formulation and testing. There are innumerable examples, but one hypothesis potentially worth examining is that the more economically stressed a ship-producing/using social group becomes, the more extensive are the repairs performed on a vessel, ultimately extending the ship's use life beyond sensible retirement. An example of the "one more voyage" syndrome can occasionally be found in the Great Lakes, where iron and steel vessels have long use-lives (40–50 years is not uncommon) because vessels are less prone to rust and corrosion in freshwater and can be maintained until metal fatigue and failure cause the loss of the vessel from virtual disintegration. A study of the causes of sinking of Great Lakes vessels would be an example of nondestructive archaeology which could be done through an examination of the stress fatigue in the metal plates of these vessels. There is much to be gained from the incorporation of questions relating to human behavior when the wreck remains of a vessel are studied.

THE SHIPWRECK AS AN
ARCHAEOLOGICAL SITE

The shipwreck possesses parallels to terrestrial archaeological sites. The spatial dimensions of shipwrecks vary from widely scattered, perhaps even jumbled, situations to compact, essentially whole, discrete sites, much like historic buildings. The analogy to a building illustrates an important point. Historic building sites often produce a great deal of information, even when the structure is absent. What the wreck site lacks is a stratigraphical sequence reflecting different periods of occupation. However, as mentioned above, a shipwreck may exhibit diachronic dimensions.

The nature of dispatch and deposition are important in the formulation of the wreck site. Transformational factors of both natural and cultural kinds have been recognized for terrestrial sites (e.g., Schiffer 1972, 1976) and shipwrecks (Muckelroy 1978). The first suggestion of the application of Schiffer's (1972) site transformation model to shipwrecks was in 1973 (Schiffer and Rathje 1973: 175). Schiffer speaks of N-transforms and C-transforms. N-transforms are noncultural site transformation processes. An understanding of these processes on the seabed would allow the archaeologist to predict their impact and, when seeking a certain kind of data from a shipwreck, limit the environmental situations that allow data survival to a manageable number of possible locations for study (Schiffer and Rathje 1973: 171).

C-transforms are cultural transformation processes, such as salvage efforts on a wreck. The development of an understanding of transformational factors, both cultural and natural, is necessary before the two can be separated for analytical purposes. The importance of this understanding in shipwreck archaeology is maximized when one considers the conceptions and presuppositions held in a "common sense" attitude regarding the nature of data possible to retrieve, and, by implication, the extent of productive knowledge obtainable from a shipwreck site. These common-sense notions contribute to the relatively low level of development of theory and results in shipwreck archaeology thus far.

A cursory comparison of deepwater vessels and shallow-water shipwrecks readily produces the "common sense" assumption that it would be more productive to concentrate on deepwater wrecks because they are more intact and therefore more capable of producing usable archaeological data than the scattered shallow-water vessels, which tend to become increasingly jumbled with each passing wave or storm. The question is one of the relative importance of provenience; the quick answer is that provenience in shallow-water shipwreck sites is of minimal importance due to the pervasive impact of natural forces.

The complex issue of the extent of natural environmental impact on shipwreck remains has been raised by various researchers (Dumas 1962, 1966; Clausen and Arnold 1976). The most sophisticated approach to date has been the work of Muckelroy (1977, 1978: 160–65), who attempted to classify twenty wrecks in British waters by isolating environmental attributes relevant to wreck preservation. More work in this vein is needed before predictions as to the potential data returns obtainable from vessels of particular regions and environments can be made. The end product of this research would be a valuable aid in assessing which questions can be answered by examination of specific wrecks. The ability to isolate regions containing vessels capable of producing the data relevant to certain questions will allow a judicious use of the resource base. If we had a clear understanding of critical environmental conditions in different geographic areas, it would not be necessary to disturb a site that is concentrated and well preserved in order to answer questions or to test hypotheses that could be investigated by use of less well-preserved sites located elsewhere. The comparison of excavations of relatively complete and the more scattered sites will contribute greatly to maximizing the methodology used on both. To dismiss scattered sites because of preconceived notions about the information they may contain is a serious and unnecessary mistake that will compromise the amount of information ultimately obtainable from the shipwreck data base.

There are numerous examples of misconceptions regarding environmental impacts on shallow-water shipwrecks becoming "common sense" laws. The 1715 Spanish Plate Fleet, lost during a hurricane off the east coast of Florida, was discovered in the 1960s when beachcombers began finding Spanish coins on the beach after storm erosion. The finders logically assumed they were being washed up from offshore, and set out to discover the wreck sites themselves. Later excavation of the wrecks showed them to be scattered; one was reported to be covering some four acres of bottom, although the main concentration covered only two acres. Clausen (1965: 27) had to rely on minimal provenience information provided primarily by the commercial treasure salvors, who used uncontrolled prop-wash deflectors to excavate the site under very crude positioning controls. He declared the site to be "jumbled and scattered," and said, "There was little if any discernible spatial relationship between the recovered items." An examination of the site map included in his report (Clausen 1965: 4, Fig. 2) does not seem to bear this out. The assumption was held by the treasure salvors and others that the wrecks were so scattered and jumbled that the maintenance of provenience was an absurdity, likening it to, as one salvor said, "trying to reconstruct a watermelon dropped from a car going 60 miles an hour." However, recent work (Cockrell and Murphy 1978) on these wrecks has shown that artifact concentrations are not randomly distributed and the jumbling that has apparently occurred has been more the result of modern salvage attempts, poor provenience control, and sampling bias, than the result of natural forces. Apparently, stabilization occurred fairly rapidly after the wrecks settled. The heavier artifacts evidently migrate down through the disturbed sediment rapidly during the initial deposition and immediately afterward, then are little affected by subsequent wave and storm activity. The depth of sand over these sites averages about one and a half meters in most places. It should be noted that examination of hundreds of gold coins and pieces of jewelry from these sites has revealed no traces of sand-wear abrasion, as would be expected if the material was indeed being moved about. The coins found on the beach were probably carried to shore intermixed with wreckage during the original storm or as a result of Spanish salvage activities. Coins and other dense artifacts, when located during the 1978 excavation in areas not subjected to modern salvage (prior to 1977) on the site, were invariably found at the base of the sand overburden on the top of a soft, sandy clay stratum. Salvage prior to 1977 utilized the prop-wash deflector and uncontrolled techniques. The more controlled and careful excavation in 1978 allowed stratigraphic determination of the site and stratigraphic observations.

An initial attempt (Cockrell and Murphy 1978) to quantify data on artifacts in specific categories recovered from the 1715 Spanish Plate Fleet sunk off Florida addressed the question of whether there is significant patterning by artifact class on a wreck assumed to be jumbled.

The field method was to record artifacts on clear overlay sheets according to categories, such as armament, glass, precious metal, coins, fasteners, lead, ceramics, and so on. Each artifact received a numerical tag and was recorded on a separate form with provenience data recorded to the nearest meter. Artifacts recovered in prior years with provenience data were added to the overlay maps. The data were recorded in a way compatible with computerization. This effort demonstrated the existence of nonrandom distribution of artifacts on these 1715 Spanish Plate Fleet sites. Although there were definite clustering trends, the effects of cultural and natural sorting were not separable at the time. It became apparent that this effort did not go far enough, but it should serve as a basis for future investigation.

Additional questions for this study should be posed, such as: Can modern salvage efforts be defined by means of provenience data? Can certain aspects of shipboard organization be inferred from cluster patterns? One specific method that may contribute to answering these questions would be selection of artifact categories reflecting behavior developed from hypotheses of shipboard organization and activity. The situation in Florida is one where multiple Spanish Plate Fleet sites have been worked for a number of years by commercial salvors using few or no archaeological controls. As a result, there is a large backlog of unanalyzed artifacts with no provenience; obtaining any systematic information from these would be an important contribution to the development of shallow-water shipwreck archaeology.

Occupational specialization aboard these vessels should be discernible with proper analysis of the patterned artifactual assemblage. The use of social-functional shipboard groups as an investigative tool would allow cross-cultural, intraregional, and intersite comparisons of behavioral elements. In lieu of studies demonstrating clustering resulting from human behavior, these artifacts have been invariably viewed as isolated data useful for little more than historical amplification and museum display, or at best for comparative study.

Although the study is incomplete, the only responsible conclusion to be drawn at this point in the development of shipwreck archaeology is that meaningful distributional data exist within all sites. This assumption should serve as methodological guide on all sites unless proven inappropriate for a particular site.

To develop the research potential of shipwreck artifact patterning, one must at least make the following assumptions: (1) Regularities of shipboard life occur and will be reflected in the archaeological record. (2) Specialized activities will produce artifact patterns relative to those activities. (3) Shipboard activity may overlap in certain areas. (4) The data will be skewed relative to discard patterns. (5) The record may not be complete because whole portions of activity loci (vessel structure) may be completely absent from the record. (6) Data from comparative sites have been collected consistently.

The first three assumptions are self-explanatory, but the latter three should be clarified. Discard behaviors aboard ships may be widely

79

varied. The shipwreck may not contain the whole record of discard and consumption because the side of the vessel provides handy trash disposal. Discarded material often found its way to the bilge and other recesses, although this disposal behavior may be dependent on the size of the trash items and their place of origin aboard the vessel. Vessels were sometimes stripped and reballasted between voyages, a practice which would reduce trash buildup on board.

In assumption (5), the nature of wreck dispatch is important. Obviously a vessel lost as a result of fire would produce a different record from one that foundered at sea. It was not uncommon for the upper decks to be swept from the hulls of vessels run aground in heavy seas. Analysis of the site environs and consultation of historical documents when available will enable more accurate site assessment and interpretation.

Assumption (6) highlights the severe limitations of comparative studies. Analyzing existing shipwreck artifact collections without discerning the nature of collection and conservation biases makes the formulation of productive hypotheses of human behavior difficult.

Some collections reflect strong biases as to what was recovered or conserved. Often only artifacts of certain categories are collected and only the spectacular or unique conserved. This is frequently the case on "treasure" wrecks where few "base" artifacts are recovered. The Spanish wrecks of Florida worked by commercial salvors are a prime example. The state normally retains a 25 percent sample of what the salvors decide is worth collecting in their effort to turn a profit, despite the state's attempt to control the work. The salvors' portion of the artifacts is quickly sold or divided among the investors, usually before the assemblage can be subjected to any archaeological study. The rapid and irrevocable dispersal of the collection has seriously hampered comparative study and the formulation of research questions which could have otherwise been easily answered by the study of a more complete assemblage recovered under appropriate archaeological controls. Most unfortunately, the state and federal courts have in recent decisions supported the plunder-for-profit approach to historic shipwrecks (Cockrell 1980) and, as a consequence, jeopardized future research possibilities offered by the long-term study of curated collections.

The application of a multidisciplinary approach to the assessment of environmental aspects of shipwrecks is long overdue. Little is known about the environmental impact on wrecks, and, conversely, about the impact of wrecks on the environment. Recognition of environmental anomalies which result from the presence of wrecks may be an aid in site location to both in-water direct search and aerial remote-sensing techniques. An initial attempt to determine the interaction of fluvial processes with wrecks was recently carried out as part of a cultural resource management survey of the Tombigbee River (Murphy and Saltus 1981). To develop a reasonable perspective in the rational utilization of a limited resource base, one must understand the effect of natural forces on wreck deposition.

The most devastating impacts to wreck sites may well be human, yet effects of contemporary salvors should be separable from natural and environmental impacts. Assessing disturbances of any kind is critical. Often wrecks must be partially uncovered for survey-evaluation purposes. This subjects a stabilized site to a renewed period of deterioration before equilibration with the environment recurs. Every effort should be made to develop minimal impact techniques for survey, sampling, and assessment, and partial excavation of sites only to the point necessary to answer specific research questions should be the rule. Research questions, whether particularistic or general in nature, should be formulated to be cumulative, both for the individual researcher and for the discipline at large.

Uncertainty about the significance of vertical provenience may be met by comparing the shipwreck, again, to a historic building site. Stratigraphic excavation can reveal the construction levels of such a building even when the actual structure is not present. Vertical provenience data have rarely been collected on shipwrecks, and consequently little can be said regarding their importance. Before a decision is made not to control for vertical location within shipwrecks, a body of empirical data must be accumulated regarding it. Stratigraphic excavation may be useful in determining ship structure and organization, and should prove important in separating particular wrecks when multiple wrecks are present in an area. The latter case is an ideal test for the extent of impact of natural forces on vertical deposition in a particular environment. Vertical provenience control of more intact vessels may reveal the order of cargo stowage and enable the reconstruction of the order of port visitation during the final voyage of the vessel (Bass 1966: 94).

It should be remembered that although the stratification of terrestrial sites may become blurred through animal burrows or solifluction, the archaeologist does not usually despair and cease recording context. It has been recognized that the soil matrix of terrestrial sites is not a static body, but rather a dynamic, active system that may distort original provenience in many directions. In land sites, the recognition of the distorting forces at work in the soil and their role and impact on site formation are becoming more important in interpreting cultural remains (Schiffer 1972, 1976; Wood and Johnson 1978; Stein 1981). The history of natural impacts on terrestrial sites is as long as the time span since original deposition. Shipwrecks, however, may be deposited in environments wherein they experience initial traumatic impact, then stabilize quickly. Once equilibration occurs, the site may be relatively free of further natural impacts in certain environments. Deep sand is at least one such stable environment for shipwrecks. Once stabilized, wrecks are not normally subjected to such impacts as faunal disturbance, freeze-thaw cycles, mixing from floral processes such as root growth or tree fall, swelling and shrinking of clays, gas, air, and wind, growth and wasting of salts, or erosion from surface runoff. Hole (1961) recognized nine pedoturbation processes potentially present on terrestrial sites (Wood and Johnson 1978), most of which are absent on submerged sites. It is clear that shipwrecks, even in shallow water, have exceptional preservation and contextual integrity when compared to many terrestrial sites.

In some cases a site widely scattered during deposition may have the added advantage of a more completely retrievable artifact assemblage than one less scattered, because of the added difficulty posed to the salvors contemporary with the wreck. A broader cross section of material culture may be present than in a more consolidated site which would have been easier to salvage.

The difficulty of defining what constitutes an archaeological site is a recognized problem in archaeological site surveys due to the variability injected by different individuals and crews on land surveys, but there are no studies specifically addressed to this problem (Plog, Plog, and Wait 1978: 413–14). The problems of site determination during shipwreck survey are rarely as complex as those on land. Shipwrecks are often located in otherwise culturally sterile situations. Difficulties do arise when multiple sites are located in the same area or when the site is in an area not culturally sterile, such as an anchorage, harbor, or river landing. It is technically possible, however, to find and recognize virtually any shipwreck.

82

Shipwrecks, whether in deep or shallow water, scattered or intact, are important archaeological sites which contain much data pertinent to human behavioral studies. New approaches to data collection and interpretation can generate perspectives and insights into the social processes of the past available from no other source. Today, shipwrecks face unparalleled threats from modern treasure salvors and looters, augmented by a lack of concern from the professional archaeological community. The rapid attrition of the data base, without active response from the archaeological community, may well result in a situation where archaeologists of the future will have to make excuses for the shortsightedness of the archaeologists and cultural resource managers of the present. The discussion of shipwrecks as archaeological sites will then be academic.

THE SHIP AS PART OF A CULTURAL SYSTEM

While perhaps not correctly termed a microcosm, the ship does carry and represent aspects of the parent culture, which can produce analytically useful perspectives on social processes if the proper questions are posed during wreck excavation and analysis. If patterned behavior and organization indeed characterize shipboard society, then the organization of shipboard components should reflect facets of the larger society as a whole. Higher organizational elements such as merchant fleets and navies should mirror societal organization also.

The ship structure is both a result and a component of an ideational system, and is based upon principles and rules which are the products of that system. Single ships embodied the design norms of their culture to the extent that they could be differentiated by nationality, much the way present-day aircraft are.

There were certain characteristics by which sailors could recognize the nationality of a sailing ship almost as far as they could see her. The French vessels had shorter yards which gave a high-narrow appearance to the sails on each mast. The Swedes generally had very short lower masts and fairly long yards, which gave a more squatty look. Such nationalities as the Swedes, Danes and Hollanders were referred to by seamen under the one general term of "Dutchmen" (Davis 1929: 84).

Ships form the primary element in exchange systems of most so-

83

cieties with coastal access. The analysis of ships and their cargoes, therefore, can contribute much to the reconstruction of the economic systems of these societies. Comparisons of ship design and social organization, coupled with analysis of cargoes, will add to the understanding of the exchange of ideas and the flow of influence and power, as well as trade goods, between societies. The parent culture is reflected not only in the design, construction, and organization of the vessel, but also in the cargo, which was deemed socially important enough to warrant the expense and risk of transport by sea.

One of the many possible examples of productive wreck research would be a study of the economic development of a particular social group, such as the Spanish. The operations of Spain as a cash economy, after New World exploitation began, profoundly affected the development of internal industrial production, while providing impetus and markets for the industrialization of other nations. A comparison of technology, products, shipboard organization, vessel design, and so on between contemporary British and Spanish vessels can be phrased in productive behavioral hypotheses useful in the comparison of shipboard material culture in order to discern parallel and differential economic and technological growth of the two societies. The implications of this effort relate directly to more general statements about world-market economy formations and the societal impacts of uneven development of monoeconomic countries in today's world-market system. Appropriately designed studies of shipwrecks can contribute much to the understanding of worldwide processes such as colonial expansion, the development of capitalism, and imperialism.

Methodologically historic sites archaeology, and other branches of historical archaeology, should be the most sophisticated archaeology. It is the least sophisticated. Historic sites archaeology should be making major contributions to our understanding of the expansion of Europe and the world wide impact of that expansion, rather than adding marginal footnotes to historical research (Schuyler 1978: 30).

"Shipwreck archaeology" could be substituted for "historical sites archaeology" in this quote without any change of meaning or import.

The shift from considering ships as discrete time capsules to viewing them as integral aspects of a larger parent culture can produce methodological and theoretical developments heretofore not readily apparent. The use of a regional research design is one methodological approach that would be productive in some areas of shipwreck study. The study of the Great Lakes maritime tradition lends itself particularly to a regional approach (Murphy 1981; Hulse 1981). Vessel types were specifically adapted to the socioeconomic requirements of the lakes, and their study could only be reasonably analyzed on a regional basis.

The development of vessel types, and their adaptation to river systems, is another possibility for regional analysis. The development of a unique vessel type, the western river steamboat, was a response to the environmental and social demands of the Mississippi and Ohio River drainage systems. These were highly specialized craft, and quite different from the steamboats produced for the eastern river trade. A study of a smaller river within the general area of western river steamboat use, such as the Tombigbee River of Alabama and Mississippi, would be most productively carried out as part of an overall regional research design (Murphy and Saltus 1981).

Although it is frequently asserted that the final location of a wrecked vessel is an accident, in a more general sense wreck concentrations represent patterns of human activity in an area over time. Surveys of areas to locate the wrecks contained within them (as opposed to a search for specific vessels or types) can be most productive when carried out from a regional perspective. The concentration of wrecks at Fort Jefferson National Monument and the Cape Hatteras National Seashore are good examples. A total survey of vessels in this area, coupled with systematic sampling, can yield much information on the interaction of the social groups whose ships were in the area, and how they changed over time. The location of a number of burned English trade ships of a certain period in the Dry Tortugas, for example, may be a result of smuggling activity and the attempt of the Spanish to suppress it. There can be many hypotheses tested within an area which require only minimal disturbance of a site. Development of methodological approaches such as this will assure a maximum return of results for all phases of shipwreck examination and excavation. In many areas, a regional approach is a viable alternative to the discrete single-site analysis current in shipwreck archaeology.

When considering ships as part of a cultural system, it may be profitable to view them as similar to hunting-gathering or trading parties. These groups are organized and sent out for the benefit of the parent society and are normally composed of, or at least led by, individuals experienced in and prepared for the task. The advantage of the hunting-gathering/trading analogy is that it focuses on the social nature of the effort and forces corollary considerations such as the interrelationship of the parent and satellite groups. The material and labor efforts expended by the parent group stem from conscious decisions and should naturally reflect the technical and economic capabilities and goals of the society, as well as its organizational concepts.

The culture aboard a ship may be considered as a specialized statement of the way a society relates to other societies. The manner in which a society sees itself in relation to others is evident in ship design, fittings, and deployment and shipboard lifeways. Aspects of the social dynamics of the parent culture will be found in crew composition, organization, and control, as well as in status and role hierarchies aboard a vessel.

Another level of cultural organization of which a vessel may be a part is the fleet. There have been cases of entire fleets of vessels being lost at the same time under similar circumstances. The Spanish Plate Fleet losses of 1554 in Texas and the 1622, 1715, and 1733 fleet losses in Florida offer a remarkable opportunity for comparative intrafleet and interfleet analysis of some forty vessels and their contents. Synchronic archaeological deposits of this magnitude are unparalleled. Fleet-sized losses have occurred elsewhere, such as the 1588 Spanish Armada defeat and the Japanese Fleet losses in Truk Lagoon during World War II. The earlier fleets probably represent the largest focused human effort of that period, and still await scientific study directed at the human behavior of which they are a product.

THE SHIP AS A CULTURAL SYSTEM

The ship can be viewed as a cultural system, basically a closed community (Muckelroy 1978: 221). The ship is not a totally closed community, however, because it can be "open" on both ends of a journey, during visits to numerous ports on a voyage, while in contact with other vessels at sea, and also by discarding material overboard. Normally aboard a vessel during a voyage there is little activity not directly related to ship operation and mission objective. The nature of activity aboard would vary according to the purpose of the voyage. Very different artifact assemblages would be expected from a merchant ship, passenger ship, exploratory vessel, research vessel, troop transport, or naval vessel. Few human activities expected of a viable terrestrial community or fort will be totally unrepresented in the material culture of a ship. Ceremony, death, care of the sick, killing and butchering, construction, modification, repairs, and so on may be present. Kinship ties may be one element absent in ships other than passenger or coastal fishing vessels. Colonizing vessels may carry the full range of what is considered necessary for survival in a new territory, and closely parallel what would be found on a contemporary land site, including evidence of agriculture.

Archaeology has more than a century of experience studying behavior through material remains. Until recently, there has not been an expressed concern for determining the linkages of material remains to human behavior. Modern material culture studies are concerned with determining the interactions between material culture and human behavior by observations of contemporary societies. The testing and validation of archaeological principles is the rationale for some current ethnoarchaeological analyses of small communities (Gould 1978). Examination of the material culture of shipwrecks, coupled with analysis of parallel modern shipboard behavior, seems particularly appropriate to these studies. The closed nature of ships means there is little need to consider ecological aspects of the context, as required in terrestrial communities, except in the most general way; thus the archaeologist can focus directly on comparative human behavior aboard ships. The hypotheses generated from ethnological examination of material culture aboard vessels, and their testing in shipwreck sites, will offer much data for statements concerning the human behavior responsible for material remains and their patterns and anomalies. Results of this testing will contribute to the unique knowledge to be gained from archaeology: that of human behavior in relation to material cultural objects.

Discard practice is an aspect of material behavior that lends itself to investigation aboard a ship. Examination of cultural correlates to shipboard discard behavior and their variations cross-culturally can contribute to the growing body of data on this aspect of human behavior, and provide closed community tests for general hypotheses.

Modern material culture studies are also interested in the social context of technology (Rathje 1979: 17). This emphasis has stemmed from a desire to understand the impact of increased human involvement with technology, and how people function in an increasingly manufactured modern environment. Shipwrecks can provide a testing

87

ground for general principles of human interaction with technology. There is virtually total involvement with technology in the manufactured environment aboard a ship.

CONCLUSIONS

Shipwreck archaeology is in the pioneer stage of development. The study of ships through time has been mainly the task of the historian relying on documents. To date, the study of the physical remains of ships has been in a historical context. Archaeologists are only beginning to view shipwrecks as important sites which can contribute greatly to the knowledge of human social processes.

American archaeology has traditionally been focused primarily on chronology, developed through an emphasis on artifacts rather than on their cultural contexts. Shipwreck analysis has paralleled this focus by concentration on typological descriptions, historical research on the vessel when possible and, perhaps, more generally, the history of technology. Recent terrestrial archaeological research has been centered on the environment, settlement patterns, subsistence, and to a lesser degree, the sociopolitical aspects of society, but is shifting concern to more specific questions of general human behavioral importance. Shipwreck archaeology has much to contribute to this newer emphasis within archaeology.

The nature of the sea and of most rivers has changed little over time. Humans constructing a vessel to survive the conditions of the North Sea in 1000 B.C. faced the same environment we observe today. Ships offer insight into the mind of the seafarer of all ages. However, it is when these insights are placed in a broader cultural context that they become important to the elucidation of human behavioral processes and variables. Archaeological research greatly increases the number of societies available for study and provides the only truly long-term longitudinal perspective on human behavior. The use of waterborne craft has an extremely long history and provides an extensive cross-cultural human behavioral data base for study.

The potential contribution of shipwrecks to the study of human behavior will be limited so long as the use of an explicit research design formulated to speak to broader behavioral questions is avoided. Terrestrial archaeology is still greatly concerned with the nature of data return possible from an archaeological site; this concern has pointed out methodological shortcomings as responsible for limited returns from archaeological sites. Regarding the amount of sociocultural information available from the archaeological record and the limits imposed on knowledge of past societies, Binford (1972: 96) has stated:

The practical limitations on our knowledge of the past are not inherent in the nature of the archaeological record; the limitations lie in our methodological naivete, in our lack of development for principles determining its relevance of archaeological remains to propositions regarding processes of events of the past.

For shipwreck archaeology to assume its correct role as a principal contributor to the knowledge of human social processes, it must initiate research formulated to answer broad questions of human behavior. Some of these questions can be answered by complete excavation, but many can be answered by systematic survey and sampling as well. The time has come for anthropologically oriented archaeologists to approach shipwrecks as a data base for the study of human behavior.

5
A Plea for
Historical Particularism in
Nautical Archaeology

GEORGE F. BASS

Texas A&M University

As a nautical archaeologist I have been on the defensive for more than twenty years. I have spoken rapidly, smiling, trying pleasantly but desperately to pack as much information as possible into a few minutes' conversation, words tumbling on top of one another as I watched the knowing smiles of those opposite me over desks or dining tables— classical archaeologists, anthropologists, historians, geographers, and laymen. Was I simply paranoid?

Not when a leading classical archaeologist spoke to me about this "silly business you do under water." Not when anonymous anthropologists reviewing my grant proposals wrote that it "sounds like fun but has nothing to do with anthropology," or "as the current literature shows underwater archaeology has contributed nothing to our knowledge of ancient trade or economics." Not when an ancient historian dismissed a junior colleague (since chairman of the department of Near Eastern studies at a major university) after his first job interview by saying: "We want a historian—not a skin diver!" Not when a student told me that her anthropology professor, now holding one of the most prestigious archaeological chairs in England, would not allow her to write a thesis on anything to do with underwater archaeology because it was "not serious." Not when the major news magazines print articles on the looting of Spanish galleons in their "Science" sections, and even *Science* (July 29, 1981) has praise for the archaeology of blatant treasure hunters.

I think that nautical archaeologists finally have won the respect of most classical archaeologists, probably because we have been most closely associated with them, have given papers at their conferences, and have published in their journals. Now the struggle is with the anthropological community and the public at large—the latter group simply is ignorant of what archaeology really is, but the former is not only ignorant of but frequently hostile to underwater archaeology.

This puzzles me. I am puzzled why the "seafaring revolution" has not been studied as intensely as the "urban revolution" by archaeologists. Seafaring and river travel both antedate the emergence of food production, metallurgy, and urbanization (Bass 1980: 137–38), and surely played a major role in the direct and indirect contacts which spread them and thus fundamentally transformed the human socio-economic system. Watercraft provided the most economical means of moving goods from one place to another (Bass 1972: 9) and carried ideas with these goods. "Being swift and silent," they "are an ideal way of moving warriors around, and their presence has assisted the development of warfare in hunter-gatherer contexts . . ." (Orme 1981: 174). And, "being the largest and most complex objects produced in most societies before the industrial revolution," they "formed the 'leading edge' of the technologies of most preindustrial societies from the Mesolithic period onward" (Muckelroy 1980: 24). I can only presume that anthropologically oriented archaeologists have paid so little attention to watercraft because they are unfamiliar with the rapid strides taking place in nautical archaeology, for crucial to a systemic understanding of culture is a delineation of the way in which systems communicate and modify one another through contact. No true understanding of the cultural ecology of the Mediterranean basin, or similar basins, now or in the past, is possible without a detailed knowledge of seafaring.

Perhaps I should not be puzzled, for one should profit from his own experiences, and mine stem from my days as student and faculty member at the University of Pennsylvania. I remember well the day when the editor of one of the major anthropological journals in the United States said at a meeting of all the archaeologists in the Philadelphia region: "Now we anthropologists, unlike you classical archaeologists who are just interested in royal tombs and gold treasures . . ." and he glanced pleasantly around the room, not realizing his ignorance or noticing how the classical archaeologists looked at their shoes, embarrassed for him. Certainly some classical archaeologists are especially interested in classical art, particularly how art reflects the constantly changing societies in which it is made, just as there are anthropologists with special interest in African or Eskimo art. On that day, however, most of the classical archaeologists present were not inclined toward art history.

One of my students, who had worked on a Byzantine shipwreck with me in Turkey, took a course in the anthropology department. He said that his professor indicated to him that we were good at tagging and mapping amphoras and other artifacts on the seabed, but that our interests seemed to lie mainly with techniques of excavation and with the artifacts simply as artifacts.

Shortly afterward both this professor and I gave illustrated talks to museum members on our most recent fieldwork. I remember telling what we had learned of Byzantine ship construction and what we· thought were the socioeconomic causes underlying this ship's construction, of the economics of the ship's last voyage, and of shipboard life. I do not recall showing the slide of a single object simply for its beauty.

Then the anthropology professor spoke. Slide followed slide of jade masks, jewelry, and other striking objects from Guatemala. The talk was filled with words like "lovely" or "gorgeous." It was a display for aesthetes, a brazen show of glittering treasure.

Certainly nautical archaeology is best known by the public from glamorous color photographs and films of underwater scenes, but that is no excuse for anthropologically oriented archaeologists perceiving it as a technical exercise at best and a frivolous pastime at worst. The main thing the public knew of the museum's Iranian excavation at Hasanlu, directed by still another anthropology professor, was a decorated gold bowl which received much notice in the press and was studied and published and republished by art historians. This did not lead me to suppose, however, that the director was simply digging for treasure.

I recall these events not to condemn anthropologists, but to condemn the mutual misunderstanding that existed and still exists between various branches of archaeology. I cannot deny my own guilt. I perceived my fellow graduate students of classical archaeology as grinds—there is no better word—whereas the anthropology students seemed to live in the coffee shop, talking, talking, talking endlessly, often joined by their professors, rather than reading thoughts on the subjects under discussion that had been written by the best minds of, at least, the Western world. When I took my single anthropology course (in which, I must add, I received the highest grade I ever received at the university), I was appalled at the fuzzy thinking of the anthropology students who constantly tried to form theories without the discipline to learn detailed facts. When I later joined the classical archaeology faculty, I had to make special reading assignments for the anthropology students in my seminars on Aegean prehistory, for English was the only language which most knew. Did they not care what French and German and other scholars thought about things?

My early prejudice, I admit, had made me as ignorant of anthropology as most archaeologists seem to be of nautical archaeology. I prepared for this seminar, therefore, by reading as much as time allowed on theories of archaeology proposed by anthropologists, using where possible anthologies prepared by those better able to select articles than was I (Deetz 1971, 1977; Watson, LeBlanc, and Redman 1971; Leone 1972; Flannery 1976; South 1977; Clarke 1978; and Muckelroy 1978). I read also reports by anthropologically trained contract archaeologists, works on cultural resource management (McGimsey and Davis 1977) and historic preservation (King, Hickman, and Berg 1977), and a number of successful proposals to the Anthropology Program of the National Science Foundation.

This limited crash course could not, of course, substitute for a degree in anthropology. I was, however, exposed to some surprisingly thoughtful and intelligent work, more than a little of it beyond my intellectual grasp. But just as I have no desire, or perhaps ability, to become an astronomer, criminologist, or athlete after enjoying books on astronomy, criminology, and sports, even the most stimulating of the anthropological readings did not make me regret that I am not an anthropologist. The farmer digs into the ground for a different reason than a miner, and a classical archaeologist digs for different purposes than does an anthropologist. All have valid goals. One should not condemn the farmer because he is not trying to explain human behavior and cultural change. And this leads to the main objection I found to my anthropological readings.

I found the readings often disturbing, primarily because of the frequency with which authors intimated strongly or stated categorically that there is a "right" and a "wrong" approach to archaeology. These statements seemed based on limited knowledge, reflected in the almost total lack of cited references by other than American and British colleagues, of what other professionals are doing and trying to do. In the readings I was struck, too, by the apparent fear on the part of many of the authors that they would somehow suffer if they did not "toe the party line" closely enough; they protested their purity too loudly, using nearly identical phrases of jargon over and over again. It was surprising to me to see how often authors felt compelled to quote a very few authorities, as if the statements of these authorities had become unquestioned dogma and by quoting them they were expressing their undying loyalty. This may explain why no group of young anthropologically oriented archaeologists has yet created for the New World what classical archaeologists created for the Old World in nautical archaeology two decades ago: they are afraid that whatever they do will be criticized by the archaeological Falwells whose thundered "archaeology is anthropology or it is nothing" echoes through the pages of nearly everything they read. Since an anthropological approach may well not be the right approach for many New World wrecks, these young archaeologists are caught in a bind and thus have done nothing. This concerns me, for the statements that have caused this situation smack of the kind of close-minded arrogance which in my view endangers the open society in which most of us would like to live: "Christianity is Catholicism or it is nothing!"

In the very first chapters and articles in Leone's *Contemporary Archaeology*, each author repeats the same premise, which is certainly open to question. Paul S. Martin says, "I make two assumptions and if they are acceptable, then much of the rest will follow. 1) That anthropology, and therefore archaeology, is a social science" (Leone 1972: 6), and "archaeology is a part of anthropology" (Leone 1972: 8). Leone, himself, states that "most ignore what no archaeologist will deny: archaeology is part of anthropology" (Leone 1972: 16).

If a classical archaeologist excavates and publishes with care an ancient theater simply for a better understanding of Greek architecture and drama, is he not still an archaeologist? I do not think he is immoral or misguided.

My concern over this matter in the selection of articles I read was eased slightly when I noted that Walter W. Taylor wrote that "archaeology in the United States has long been considered a subdiscipline of anthropology" (Leone 1972: 28), and both Lewis Binford (Leone 1972: 93) and Kent Flannery (Leone 1972: 102) felt compelled to quote Willey's statement that "American archaeology is anthropology or it is nothing." So it was only *American* archaeology that most of the authors were talking about. Why hadn't they said so? Still, if an American community wishes to use archaeological techniques in examining and restoring an old house simply because it is old, so that the children of the town may be exposed to the material culture of their ancestors, then who is to say that the community does not have the right to do this? Who are these self-styled judges of the only purposes of archaeology? Most archaeologists today, whether anthropologically oriented or classical or biblical, find it fashionable to condemn simply antiquarian interests, but I find such interests neither wrong nor immoral, although they happen not to be my own.

I read again some of the selections in *Contemporary Archaeology* and then realized that generally the authors were discussing *prehistoric* American archaeology. One more modifier. Why had they not been more careful of their terminology? American archaeology presumably includes Spanish galleons wrecked off the coasts of Louisiana or Florida, as well as Civil War blockade-runners sunk off North Carolina. I hope that none of the authorities had meant to engrave in stone that archaeology of Civil War submarines is anthropology or it is nothing.

Once I understood that the authors were in general discussing prehistoric, and in particular prehistoric American, archaeology, I better understood what had seemed at first to be flaws in their statements. Leone, for example, said that "archaeologists will soon realize that two of their aims are outworn. One, the reconstruction of events in the past, is nearly complete; it offers little in the way of challenge today" (Leone 1972: 26); other authors repeated the lack of challenge they faced after spending years categorizing stone implements and pottery. This lack of challenge, however, is not true in nautical archaeology. Before our excavation of a shipwreck of ca. 1200 B.C. in Turkey (Bass 1967), our knowledge of the mechanics of the copper and tin trade in the Late Bronze Age Aegean probably was not more than 2 on a scale of 1 to the present 10; almost every dive or every day of subsequent research brought some totally new information about ancient smelting, smithing, metrology, trade, or seafaring. Every wreck we excavate surprises us anew with how very little we know of early ships and shipping. The categorizing of stone tools by the land-based American prehistoric archaeologist may have become boring or pointless after a time, but nautical archaeology desperately needs decades of cataloging and categorizing shipwreck remains, for we have so few comparative data with which to work.

This last point was reinforced vividly when I recently had to dive off Jamaica, at the request of the Jamaican government, in order to prevent still one more wreck from being destroyed by treasure hunters. (Why must I leave my Mediterranean work to solve the problems of American archaeologists, those anthropologically inclined scholars who still, after twenty years, are only talking about what approach they should take to shipwrecks instead of doing anything concrete to save them?) During my stay in Jamaica, I learned how very, very little is known (or at least published) on the particulars of New World shipwrecks. We found complete rims of more than a dozen olive jars, and find that we cannot date any of them to within less than two hundred years by published studies of olive jars. We cleaned, photographed, and drew in detail two cannons on one of the wrecks we located. Why is there not a catalog of cannons as precisely written as works on Greek pins or Roman lamps? It is usually possible for us to date a Mediterranean shipwreck to within one or two decades, even without the discovery of coins or other artifacts with dates on them, and yet there is no published body of material which will allow us quickly to decide the date or even the nationality of the major artifacts we uncovered on our Jamaican project. Similarly, a cannon raised from a Mexican shipwreck site last year by a joint team of Mexican and American archaeologists has not been properly identified as to date or place of manufacture, although it may represent the oldest bronze cannon yet found in the New World, making the site important for our understanding of early seaborne contacts with Mexico. How can archaeologists of any persuasion make meaningful suppositions about this ship or the people who sailed her or the people who built her or the people who financed her if we don't yet have any idea when and where these people lived? It is, to me, a shocking state of affairs. Yes, there are treasure hunters and others who have seen photographs of the cannon and say, "Oh, I can identify that easily," but what kind of word-of-mouth scholarship is this without published evidence?

While anthropologically oriented archaeologists continue to talk about what they plan to do next, perhaps drawing up research designs, I plan to train a number of nautical archaeologists of particularistic persuasion to begin the careful excavation of New World shipwrecks before the best are all destroyed by treasure hunters—and this is happening at an alarming rate. I expect these new archaeologists to set examples similar to those we set in the past two decades in the Mediterranean where most countries would now not ever permit research of a lesser quality, and certainly not treasure hunting. I hope to inspire some of these students to begin the often dull but essential task of beginning major catalogues of materials, on which some may spend large parts of their lives, so that in future years archaeologists will be able to identify ceramic containers or cannons within a matter of days instead of years or never. Only then can they make meaningful hypotheses about otherwise mysterious wrecks.

The anthropologically oriented archaeologist unfamiliar with the work of Old World nautical archaeologists may sneer too quickly at the suggestion that one of the greatest present needs is almost blind and thoughtless cataloguing of types of artifacts frequently encountered on New World shipwrecks. I am certain, however, that this thankless task will be of more importance to nautical archaeology twenty years from now than any other single act.

The second archaeological aim that Leone considers outworn, a picture of past lifeways, he says is a scientific impossibility (Leone 1972: 26), stressing that archaeologists produce the artifacts for picture-book reconstructions of the past, but not the artistic syntheses. We, on the contrary, work closely with our own artists to depict the ships that we spend so many years to reconstruct, and the resultant illustrations are the only reliable pictures of seagoing vessels from the ancient Mediterranean. A shipwreck is unlike most land sites other than Pompeii and Thera, for if it has sunk deeply enough to have avoided salvage in the past, much of its hull and contents, including normally perishable material, will be preserved in a remarkable state, often lying in their original positions. After more than a dozen years of research following our excavation of a seventh-century Byzantine shipwreck, we know for the first time exactly what implements a Byzantine boatswain used, and where he kept them (as opposed, for example, to the carpenter's tools, which were sufficient for building an entire new ship); we know where the helmsman stood to man his giant steering oars, and where the ship's cook stooped over a low, grilled firebox on the port side of the small, tile-roofed galley. We learned this, and much, much more about shipboard life, including mercantile and religious aspects (Bass and van Doorninck 1982). Models and pictures made of the interior and exterior of the ship are not based on some artist's imagination, but on hard archaeological evidence.

One of our most important discoveries was that the seventh-century ship had been built in the Greco-Roman "shell-first" manner up to the waterline, and then in the modern "frame-first" manner above that line. More recently, between 1977 and 1979, we excavated an eleventh-century shipwreck, chosen from seventeen we located off the Turkish coast during a 1973 survey, partly so we might learn if the evolution from ancient to modern shipbuilding methods had been completed by that time (Bass 1979). The eleventh-century ship was, we learned, constructed entirely in the modern, frame-first manner. In order to understand better the causes for this development, however, we not only must excavate other wrecks, especially a known ninth- or tenth-century wreck which will fill the gap between the seventh and eleventh centuries, but we must understand the nationalities of these wrecks. If the eleventh-century ship was an Arab merchantman, for example, what role did Islamic seafaring tradition, or lack thereof, play in the development of modern ship construction? What role did deforestation, or technical advances, or economics play? It will take many years to determine simply the nationality of the ship, for its cargo, cooking and eating wares, coins, official documents, and food-stuffs all seemed to be somewhat evenly divided between Islamic and Byzantine Christian sources. Because timber was exported widely, not even a determination of the source of wood for the ship's hull can tell us where the ship was made, or who sailed her on her final voyage.

This basic identification is necessary before other conclusions can be drawn about eleventh-century shipboard life. We excavated in one area of the ship wooden combs of the type used by women in the medieval Islamic world, as well as bone spindle whorls. Do these suggest the presence of women on board? In order to make eventual hypotheses about this, we are studying from written records the role of women on both Byzantine and Islamic ships. We are learning how women have traveled on recent and contemporary Mediterranean ships of various cultures. We are trying to determine, partly by a study of fiber remains among the nine hundred lead net weights excavated, if there is evidence for male sailors using spindles to make thread for fishing nets or lines, or for sail repairs. Perhaps something about the location of these finds in relation to others on the ship eventually will suggest that they were trade goods rather than implements used on board.

What we learn from just the spindle whorls and combs, therefore, will not result from a specific research design, but from a desire to learn everything possible we can from the site and its tens of thousands of artifacts. In this we naturally are working with art historians, ethnoarchaeologists, paleobotanists, Islamic and Byzantine historians, metallurgists, glass specialists, zooarchaeologists, naval historians, numismatists, conservators, ship reconstructors, dendrochronologists, weapons experts, and a host of similar specialists. To obtain as complete a picture as possible at this time of this medieval merchant venture will occupy a substantial team for the next ten to fifteen years, but it deserves no less or the site should not have been touched.

One of the reasons for the lack of understanding of Old World nautical archaeology by anthropologically oriented archaeologists may be that we in the Mediterranean who have done so much have not used *formal* research designs, although clearly our research is not random. I find formal research designs restrictive rather than expansive, and choose to ignore them. When I talk to New World colleagues, trained to work within the strictures of research designs, I find that it is difficult for them to think expansively of everything that a wreck can yield: archaeological and historical interpretations in scholarly publications, as well as popular books and articles and films and reconstructions and museum displays—in other words, everything that, say, Michael Katzev accomplished with the total excavation, salvage, conservation, and restoration of the fourth-century B.C. Kyrenia ship off Cyprus, whose final archaeological publication is now being completed by Katzev and his team (Katzev 1981). Katzev not only restored the ancient hull, but made a full-scale replica of part of it to test construction techniques and theories of labor, a fifth-scale model to test sailing characteristics, and other models to understand better details of the hull. When I talk about *all* the things one site can yield, more than one anthropologist has looked at me quizzically and said, "But that's not in the research design." Yet when I find them trying to formulate a design—Can you distinguish contraband from cargo on a wreck? Can you determine if women were on board?—I find it rather pathetic. My sadness was reinforced by my reading of a number of successful anthropological research proposals to the National Science Foundation, for if each was rewritten in plain English it would describe exactly the type of work those of us in classical archaeology are doing. (I myself had a rejected NSF proposal simply reworded in current bafflegab by a friendly "new archaeologist," and it was then accepted!)

Let me give but one example out of thousands about why I choose to work in my old-fashioned, unrestricted way. On the shipwreck at Cape Gelidonya, Turkey (ca. 1200 B.C.) I found in the living area at one end of the site (presumed to be the stern) a knucklebone or astragal. My immediate thought was that this represented remains of a meal taken on board, especially as the bone was found near olive pits. A French diver working with us, however, suggested that the bone might have been used to play the game of knucklebones he had played as a child (he later gave to me a set of plastic knucklebones made recently in France). This was a distinct possibility, especially as we since have found archaeological and representational evidence of games being played at the sterns of later ships. By that time I had begun to suspect that the Cape Gelidonya wreck represented the remains of a Near Eastern (probably Canaanite) ship rather than a Mycenaean Greek one; however, I found that knucklebones were excavated in the Near East in quantities and in contexts that nearly precluded them all from having been used as gaming pieces in antiquity. Could there be another explanation?

Through library research I discovered that knucklebones were used in antiquity for astragalomancy, a kind of divination. That sailors depended on signs from the gods before charting their courses was already known from at least Homeric references. Thus, I concluded that the Cape Gelidonya knucklebone might have been almost an early type of "navigational instrument," and that it may have held a significance for Bronze Age sailors far more than as remains of a meal or for playing a game.

I did not draw this conclusion from a research design, but from a desire to learn as much from each object as possible so that I can understand the *details* of the past before trying to theorize vaguely about it. Had the knucklebone been found and studied by my anthropologically oriented students, it is probable that they would not have reached the same state of knowledge: they probably would not have been familiar with the Homeric passages, although they might have stumbled on them, and they would not have learned about astragalomancy since all the references I originally found for it were in French or German works which few if any of them could consult.

At any rate, I had concluded, without a research design, that the astragal held a religious significance for Bronze Age sailors. The following years I purchased a number of ship's stoves, or braziers, from local Turkish spongers and gave these to the Bodrum Museum. Two of these were decorated with astragals in high relief, a startling coincidence if one notes that only one other type of decoration was found in the growing collection of braziers in the museum (Leonard 1973). Why did sailors from a much later period—the decorated braziers seemed to be Hellenistic—show an interest in knucklebones? I did not find examples of similarly decorated braziers in publications of land sites. Once more I assumed them to be shipboard talismans.

Many years later we were given by a fisherman part of a classical Greek anchor stock on which were two knucklebones in high relief, and we also saw a photograph of another lead stock, complete in this case, with four knucklebones in high relief; in the latter case the knucklebones were shown in all four possible positions, the so-called lucky cast of Aphrodite (Bass 1972: 58–59).

Almost certainly, then, the astragal had come to be some type of good-luck charm for ancient seafarers, and we hope one day to place this in the context of the religious beliefs of ancient mariners.

I could, of course, repeat this story dozens or hundreds of times. Almost all of the iron of eleven anchors on our seventh-century Byzantine wreck had corroded away centuries ago, but not until after the anchors had been coated with thick seabed concretion. Frederick van Doorninck studied the interiors of these natural molds of concretion carefully, making accurate reconstruction drawings of the original anchors based on his measurements. Later he calculated the volume of each anchor and, without a formal research design, decided to multiply these by the density factor he had obtained from one small remaining deposit of unoxidized iron in one of the concretions. He was surprised when he realized, perhaps unconsciously at first, that the anchors and their stocks were based on rather exact 50-unit multiples of a Late Roman pound of 315 grams, suggesting an arithmetic progression and, therefore, the possible source of later maritime statutes which specified the numbers and weights of anchors used on ships of various types and sizes. This increase in our understanding of how the ancients thought about seafaring was derived from van Doorninck's prior knowledge of such esoteric details as Roman weight systems. There was no reason for him to have set out to prove that weights of Byzantine anchors were carefully controlled, although in retrospect it is easy to formulate the necessary research design.

Based on the above, as well as on the excavation reports published by anthropologically oriented archaeologists who must hire archivists and historians to interpret their catalogues of finds, I suggest strongly that wrecks of all periods be left to particularistic archaeologists who have a proven record of gaining the most knowledge from wrecks. I would not like to see what might happen to wrecks were they attacked by the quantitative sampling techniques advocated for land sites by anthropologists. I would hate to see wrecks excavated by those ignorant of the languages, histories, and cultures of the people who built and financed and sailed the ships. I urge my own students who wish to specialize in New World shipwrecks to study such things as Spanish colonial history and Spanish paleography so that they may conduct their own archival research; it was extremely important to our Mediterranean results that many of us who worked on the seabed also knew ancient Greek.

I admit that I have presented an extremely unbalanced picture, but as the theme of these papers is Shipwrecks as Anthropological Phenomena, and as I am the only author who is not an anthropologist, I felt it necessary to present a biased case. An experienced colleague said to me recently, after seeing them fight tooth and nail to obtain excavation permits for Caribbean shipwrecks so that they might be better paid, that contract archaeologists rather than treasure hunters would be the chief enemies of scholarly nautical archaeology in the near future, especially as they have the credentials to make their work seem scientific. And contract archaeologists are not in general trained by departments of classical, Near Eastern, medieval, Islamic, biblical, Egyptian, or Far Eastern archaeology, whose interests are scholarly rather than financial.

In conclusion I submit that the major discoveries concerning ancient seafaring have been made and will continue to be made by historical particularists. Experience over more than two decades has shown me, in addition, that some of the most brilliant insights into ancient sea-faring have, at first, been intuitive rather than the results of prior research designs. Instead of further theorizing about approaches to shipwrecks by those who oppose historical particularism, I would like to see concrete results which can be compared to ours.

6
The Archaeology of War:
Wrecks of the Spanish Armada of 1588 and the Battle of Britain, 1940

RICHARD A. GOULD

Wrecks and wreck sites afford a unique opportunity to observe the material by-products of human conflict. They provide the signatures of particular kinds of behavior associated with such conflict if one is willing to examine the relationships that exist between behavior and material residues. As "documents," wrecks and wreck sites are subject to various kinds of alterations arising from circumstances of deposition (what Schiffer 1976: 15–16 refers to as N-transforms) as well as human behavior (Schiffer's C-transforms, 1976: 14–15) which differ significantly from the literary and ideological editing processes that affect historic documents. At the present time, shipwreck archaeologists are paying close attention to recognizing and controlling for various natural factors that affect the deposition and preservation of wrecks (Goggin 1960: 352–53; Muckelroy 1978: 157–213), but along with this there is also an urgent need to examine the relationship of specific kinds of behavior to the materials that are deposited at wreck sites. This paper represents a first step in this latter domain.

What are the archaeological signatures of war as evidenced by wrecks? First, let us understand what is meant here by "archaeological signature." This term should not be confused with stylistic signatures that archaeologists have sometimes identified as hallmarks of particular prehistoric craftsmen and artists or schools (i.e., aggregates of such artists or craftsmen). This is a useful idea, but it is not what is intended here. The "signature" referred to in this case is more akin to what might appear as a particular configuration of sounds on sonar or other underwater listening apparatus to identify a particular submarine or class of submarine and what it might be doing. Such distinctive patterns are recorded by antisubmarine forces in modern navies and are used to identify underwater sound contacts (Wit 1981: 33–34). They serve as unambiguous indicators and identifiers, and the same should be true of archaeological signatures. That is, they should serve as unambiguous indicators and identifiers of the particular kinds of behavior that produced them.

In order to begin to deal with this question, I have chosen to examine two parallel case studies in the history of war: the Spanish Armada of 1588 and the Battle of Britain of 1940, with emphasis on the former. Since this study relies heavily upon secondary sources and historic documents it must be regarded as tentative and exploratory rather than conclusive. My purpose here is to draw attention to general relationships that may exist between particular kinds of behavior of combatants in situations like those represented by these cases and the archaeological residues that these kinds of behavior can be expected to produce. Relationships thus posited should be regarded as hypotheses, to be subjected to further testing through the examination of further primary historic documents and actual collections of archaeological materials and notes pertaining to these battles and others like them.

I hope, too, to show how archaeology can deal most effectively with the wreckage of war from an anthropological perspective. This comparative study of the Spanish Armada and the Battle of Britain should indicate what kinds of questions are best answered by means of wreck archaeology and how satisfying answers to such questions are arrived at. Perhaps, then, this study can be viewed as a first attempt at wider efforts to explain the behavioral processes that account for different kinds of wrecks—in other words, an organized approach to what we might call the science of "wreckology."

HISTORIC PARALLELS:
COINCIDENCE VS. CAUSALITY

A span of 352 years separates these two historic episodes, yet they bear so many specific resemblances as to revive the old question of whether or not history repeats itself. Mattingly (1959: v–vi) notes how the events of both 1588 and 1940 represented "total war . . . transcending national boundaries," while McKee (1963: 10) refers to the Battle of Britain as "a real parallel to the story of the Armada." Was the constant reference to "armadas" and "air armadas" by the British on both occasions simply a literary device of Elizabethan and Churchillian prose? Or does it imply resemblances based upon something more than mere coincidence?

In each case the English faced the prospect of invasion by what was then the most powerful and consistently successful land army in Europe. In 1588 this was the Duke of Parma's Army of Flanders, with its core of Spanish professional soldiers, while in 1940 it was the German Wermacht, fresh from its victories over Norway, the Low Countries, and France. England's land armies were clearly smaller and less well prepared to fight, and it was apparent in both cases that the best defense lay in disrupting the invasion in its amphibious phase—that is, before troops could be landed on English soil. For their part, the Spanish and Germans each recognized the same problem and sought to attain local superiority over the cross-channel approaches before attempting to load their troops into barges and ships for the assault.

In each case, defensive preparations for meeting this threat were similar, involving both active and passive components. Active components were the Elizabethan navy on the one hand and Fighter Command of the Royal Air Force on the other hand. In each of these cases we see well-designed weapons together with hastily recruited and assembled but well-led sailors and fliers. Although the ships of the Elizabethan navy represented a careful development of naval architecture suited to fighting under North Atlantic conditions and representing innovative tactics in naval warfare, the immediate preparations and deployment for battle were surprisingly *ad hoc* in nature, according to vicissitudes of the royal purse, weather, shipboard diseases, and other conditions of warfare under sail in the sixteenth century. Opinions vary among historians as to Elizabeth's wisdom in holding her fleet in harbor during the winter and spring of 1588 instead of following Drake's advice and using it to attack the Spaniards in their home ports as they struggled with the task of assembling the Armada. Mattingly (1959: 197–200) regards this as a wise move, since it spared ships and crews the stress of a winter at sea, noting that they were healthy and well provisioned when the time came to meet the Armada. Lewis (1960: 104), on the other hand, saw this as a tactical failure to seize a priceless opportunity to obviate the need to fight the Armada at sea, and, as it turned out, the English later ran short of powder, shot, and other provisions anyway. Similar tactical difficulties were experienced by Fighter Command in 1940. The need for adequate single-seat monoplane fighter aircraft had been underestimated by the RAF until 1937, when belated efforts were made to place the Hurricane and Spitfire in production (A. J. P. Taylor, in Deighton 1977: xvi–xvii). Even more critical were shortages of trained fighter pilots, despite expanded training programs begun in the late 1930s (Deighton 1977: 46). At the beginning, too, Fighter Command faced a decision similar to Elizabeth's at the start of the Armada campaign, which was whether to allow large numbers of fighter squadrons to operate overseas—in this case, with the British Expeditionary Force in France, which was clearly becoming a lost cause. The meeting of the War Cabinet on May 15, 1940, was critical to preserving a sufficient number of Hurricane fighter squadrons in England to ensure an adequate home defense. Dowding, chief of Fighter Command, regarded fifty-two Hurricane squadrons as the minimum needed for home defense, and he sought to restrain Churchill and the cabinet from sending more to France, where they would probably be lost (and, in fact, most were). He was only partly successful and had to make do with roughly half of the minimum number of squadrons he had argued for (Deighton 1977: 47–51). So, as with the case of Elizabeth's navy on the eve of the Armada campaign, preparations related to the active military forces of Fighter Command were marked by compromise and *ad hoc* arrangements.

Regarding more passive components of defense, we see additional parallels. The English armies were smaller and less well trained and equipped than Parma's, and it was essential to deploy them effectively and quickly if invasion occurred. So a system of beacons was established to alert the English land forces once the Armada was sighted and to enable them to assemble at key points like Tilbury. This system worked well, although the armies never actually fought. For the RAF and Fighter Command, the key was radar, which had been developed rapidly during the 1930s. Radar itself and the complex system of communication and tactical control that went with it worked well during the battle and can safely be regarded as decisive in the outcome. In

108

each case, early warning was an essential part of England's defensive preparations.

For the Spanish and the Germans, too, historical parallels abound. Despite their military successes on land, neither Parma's army nor the Wermacht was prepared for the final overwater assault, and their belated attempts have the appearance of a token effort to satisfy the ambitions of their authoritarian leaders, Philip II and Hitler, respectively. Hastily assembled barges at relatively insecure embarkation points were a far cry from the level of organization and planning required. Compromises and *ad hoc* arrangements characterized the offensive preparations and conduct of these two campaigns to at least as great a degree as with the English. In the case of the Spanish, the plan was for the Armada to act partly as a covering force and partly as transports, by sailing from Spanish ports to Parma's embarkation point at Dunkirk, linking up with his army, which would travel in a mixed flotilla of ships and barges, and escorting it to England. It would have been better for the Spanish to carry the army directly across the channel in a single assault, but there simply were not enough ships to accomplish this. The vulnerability of this complicated plan to changes in wind and weather, disease, and, of course, the intervention of the English navy became apparent from the beginning and brought about the serious consideration of alternative approaches such as invasion of the Isle of Wight during the course of the campaign. For the Germans in 1940, the invasion plan was even more changeable. Hitler repeatedly postponed the embarkation date from August through September, 1940, despite the fact that enough barges and ships had been assembled at the embarkation ports between Ostend and Le Havre as well as Rotterdam and Antwerp (Fleming 1957: 287; Wheatley 1958: 108). German invasion planners found it especially difficult to ensure local air and naval superiority over and around the channel owing to their inability to overwhelm the RAF and their relative weakness against the home units of the Royal Navy (Wheatley 1958: 129). By the end of September unfavorable tides and weather made the risks too great, so the final postponement meant, in fact, that invasion was no longer a possibility in 1940. As one writer puts it: "A contrast is inevitable between the Germans' feeble preparations to cross the Channel in 1940 and the vast, highly-trained machine that proved necessary to enable the Allies to do so in 1944" (Deighton 1980: 78). In each case, lack of serious recognition of the practical difficulties inherent in any amphibious assault of this magnitude caused the plans to be abandoned before they were even put into action.

The Armada and the Luftwaffe, respectively, were assigned the task of achieving localized sea or air supremacy over the English Channel, and both failed. The battles themselves, ill defined and inconclusive as they sometimes were, achieved the cumulative effect of keeping that local supremacy in the hands of the English. Thus they were English victories in a defensive sense, and one must keep in mind that the fighting continued in each case, sometimes with even greater ferocity. Unlike most land battles, these were protracted engagements, each extending over an entire summer and early fall. When one historian refers to "The Spanish Armadas" (Graham 1972) he is making the point that the campaign of 1588 was but one in a series of large-scale and bitter engagements between England and Spain that continued into the years that followed, just as the war in Europe continued for five more years after the Battle of Britain. So in each case we are looking at long, stressful engagements that were as much battles of attrition as they were tactical encounters involving direct combat, and it will be essential to consider the relative effects of such attrition upon the combatants and the archaeological residues that resulted from their responses to this problem.

Finally, it should be noted that each of these campaigns was the first of its kind, representing a clear break with earlier traditions of warfare. The Armada campaign marked the beginning of naval warfare based upon bombardment rather than boarding (Lewis 1960: 61–80; Martin 1979a: 15), despite the fact that sixteenth-century gunnery was less effective at "ship-killing" than the combatants expected (Lewis 1961: 203–4; Guilmartin 1974: 37). Similarly, the Battle of Britain represented the first decisive military engagement in history based entirely upon air power, despite the fact that the results failed to fulfill the expectations, shared by a majority of both combatants, of the Douhet doctrine (as echoed by Stanley Baldwin in 1932) that "the bomber will always get through" (Deighton 1980: 14–15).

Historians dealing with both campaigns have tended, understandably, to emphasize the particular elements of combats and personalities involved. Individual battles are analyzed, usually in chronological order, and the outcomes are evaluated in relation to tactics, weapons, leadership, and other factors. Should we expect archaeology to do the same? Now that the archaeology of Armada and Battle of Britain wrecks

110

is being pursued with gusto, we must consider just what it is that we expect archaeology to tell us about these events. When one Armada historian states:

Although arguments on technicalities, such as that concerning Armada guns, might even now be resolved by undersea exploration, a field of research much neglected by students of maritime affairs, only Sir Francis Drake in person could settle authoritatively those discussions which concern tactics (McKee 1963: 10),

he may be missing the point of doing underwater or other kinds of archaeology on wrecks. Admittedly archaeology can probably tell us little about tactics, but neither should archaeology's domain be restricted to arcane matters of technical detail. To do this would be to relegate archaeology to a kind of footnote status in relation to history, whereas in fact archaeology offers information and interpretations of a unique sort not always afforded by documentary history.

One can, of course, regard the above-mentioned parallels as "accidents of history"—that is, as coincidences involving essentially unique events. Yet there seem to be enough of these "coincidences" to warrant a closer examination for possible causes. Could there be necessary relationships between the circumstances under which these military campaigns were conducted and the behavior of the combatants? If such circumstantial-behavioral linkages exist, can we identify them through the archaeological study of their most characteristic and visible residues, namely wrecks? Finally, can the discovery of such relationships help us to define the appropriate domain for the archaeology of wrecks and identify archaeological signatures that apply more generally to the wreckage of war?

BEYOND RELICS AND TREASURE: THE NATURE OF THE EVIDENCE

Although treasure hunting and relic collecting have occurred in connection with the wrecks from these two historic events, we are fortunate in having substantial bodies of data obtained from careful and, in some cases, highly systematic excavation. Much of this has resulted from the efforts of amateur organizations of archaeologists, such as the Derry Sub-Aqua Club and the Essex Aviation Group, but in each case the enthusiasm of amateur investigations has been com-

bined with systematic record keeping and careful preservation of specimens. At times professional archaeologists have directed or been directly
involved with these excavations, although this was more characteristic
of the work done on Armada wrecks than on Battle of Britain wreck
sites. One reason I chose to compare these two historic events in
particular was the relative availability of published reports and other
materials based upon systematic excavation and recovery. I hope my
efforts here will encourage further work along these lines by indicating
the "payoffs" that are possible when this kind of information is available.

Armada Wrecks

Aside from such fragmentary and incompletely documented wrecks
as the "Tobermory Argosy" (Hardie 1912), now identified as that of
the *San Juan de Sicilia* (Martin 1979a: 13), we must rely at present
upon evidence from four major wreck sites, all of them well excavated
and reported in varying degrees of detail. Good published summaries
of these wrecks are available (Martin 1975; Fallon 1978: Appendix 3;
Muckelroy 1978: 98–105), so my remarks here will serve only to
provide a general orientation to the work that has been done and the
results so far.

La Girona   This unique wreck was discovered by Belgian diver and
marine archaeologist Robert Sténuit in the vicinity of Port na Span-
iagh, near the Giant's Causeway in northern Ireland, in 1967. Although the ship itself had largely disintegrated, three seasons of work
on the wreck site produced an astonishing collection of roughly 12,000
artifacts including 1,276 coins, assorted jewels, rings, gold chains, and
crucifixes along with more mundane objects such as five nautical
dividers, two astrolabes, three sounding leads, two bronze cannon,
188 iron and stone cannonballs, and numerous fragments of muskets,
swords, daggers, spoons, plates, flasks, and ship's gear (i.e., pulley
blocks, ballast plates, etc.). The ship itself was a galleass—an unusual
and relatively short-lived design representing a combination of features
of both the galley and galleon. *La Girona*, a Mediterranean design
like the other three galeasses in the Armada, was square-rigged for sail
but also was rowed under calm conditions. Historic documents provide
strong circumstantial evidence for the identification of this as the site
of *La Girona*, since the ship was commanded by a notable Spanish

captain, Don Alonzo Martínez De Leiva, who attracted a following of noblemen whose presence was well documented. It was possible to identify many personal items belonging to these individuals from among the items recovered, especially the jewelry (Sténuit 1971: 209–31).

Santa María de la Rosa   Working under the extremely difficult conditions of Blasket Sound, near Dingle in southwestern Ireland, Sidney Wignall and his team discovered this wreck in 1968 after "the most exhaustive and largest underwater search by divers ever recorded anywhere in the world" (Fallon 1978: 219). The lower timbers of the ship, a large merchant vessel converted into a temporary warship, were found under a mound of ballast rocks and artifacts, including roundshot, lead ingots, muskets, but no cannon. Positive identification of the wreck was made possible through historic documentation of the wreck in 1588 by eyewitnesses aboard another Spanish ship nearby and by the discovery of a set of pewter plates bearing the name of an infantry captain (the famous Matute plates) known to have sailed with the Armada on board the *Santa María* (Martin 1975: 98–135). This was a big ship, displacing 945 tons and carrying 26 guns, according to historic documents, and this wreck has proved important for understanding the details of shipbuilding methods that characterized many Armada vessels. Important, too, were several sixteenth-century Spanish anchors discovered in the vicinity of the wreck site and identified with circumstances surrounding the loss of the *Santa María*.

El Gran Grifón   This was the flagship for the Armada's supply hulks and was of Baltic origin and heavily armed. *El Gran Grifón* narrowly escaped being lost on the Irish coast but eventually was driven ashore on Fair Isle (between the Orkney and Shetland islands) in a rocky cove called Stroms Hellier. A team led by Colin Martin worked on the wreck in 1970 (Martin 1975: 156–87). Twelve guns (or gun parts) and ninety-two pieces of cast iron shot were recovered from the wreck. Assorted lead ingots, a bronze pulley-wheel, hull bolts, a wrought-iron rudder pintle, a cooking pot, a pewter flagon, and a silver coin were among the other artifacts found at this wreck site, but it is the guns and ammunition found here that give special importance to this particular Armada wreck. Identification of the wreck was based largely upon circumstantial evidence as it related to historic documents and local traditions and is less definite than that of the other Armada wrecks, although the attribution of the wreck is almost certainly correct (Martin 1972: 61).

La Trinidad Valencera   Work on the wreck of this Venetian merchant ship of 1,100 tons has been in progress by the City of Derry Sub-Aqua Club since 1971. The ship was wrecked at Kinnagoe Bay in northern Ireland and has been positively identified on the basis of two large bronze siege cannons, along with remains of three spoked wooden wheels from their gun carriages, that were mentioned in historic documents connected with this ship (Martin 1979a: 19). In addition to four ship's guns, *La Trinidad Valencera* is notable for the remarkable preservation of wooden and organic materials including ship's timbers, arquebus stocks, scaling poles, leather and hemp-soled shoes, cordage and fabric, and wooden barrels. Preliminary indications are that this may be the richest Armada wreck yet found, at least in terms of the information it can provide. Extraordinary efforts are being made by the Ulster Museum, Belfast, and Magee University College, Londonderry, to preserve these organic remains. *La Trinidad Valencera* was heavily armed with both cannons and troops, and, according to Spanish documents listing the contents of various Armada ships prior to sailing, the equipment loaded included three forty-nine-pounder siege cannons with both sea and land carriages (Martin 1979a: 14). Details of this wreck are well known to the public through two recent BBC-TV documentary films, *La Trinidad Valencera* and *Shipwreck*, and the edited American version of those films presented in the "Odyssey" series on Public Television (Odyssey 1980; Pollock 1980).

Battle of Britain Wrecks

Wrecked aircraft from the Battle of Britain are less fully reported than their Armada counterparts. Aside from some general references on the subject (Robertson 1977; Deighton 1980: 221), the best information I obtained was in publications by the Essex Aviation Group and the recent summary published by Ramsey (1980: 319–713). Unlike the Armada materials, which included only Spanish wrecks (there being no English ones), these publications describe wrecks belonging to both of the principal combatants. The Essex Aviation Group excavation reports provided information about the nature of each dig and detailed historic background, whenever possible on the aircraft and its involvement in the actual battle. They are, in fact, a good sample of the kind of work presently taking place in aviation archaeology. But less-detailed information is available concerning the natural factors affecting the deposition and preservation of each wreck, nor is there much in the way of analysis of the wreck materials, such as one finds in Armada wreck reports. Thus, for the purposes of this paper, many of my arguments and conclusions will be based upon other sources of information, with the aim of seeing how these wrecks might be analyzed more effectively. The wrecks summarized below are simply intended as a sample of this approach to compare with the Armada findings.

Hawker "Hurricane"   Numerically, the most important day fighter used by Fighter Command during the battle, this type is represented by two wrecks, No. P3115 of 253 Squadron based at Biggin Hill and shot down near the base on August 31, 1940, and another, less positively identified aircraft shot down in August, 1940, onto a mud flat along the River Colne. This latter Hurricane may have belonged to 257 Squadron based on Martlesham Heath (Richmond 1979: 4–5), and substantial parts of the airframe were recovered along with some guns and ammunition. In the case of P3115, only the engine, a Rolls Royce Merlin, was recovered.

The most complete example of any Battle of Britain aircraft excavated so far is Hurricane No. P3175, recovered in 1972–73 by G. Rayner and a team from the local Air Training Corps from the Essex shoreline near Walton-on-the-Naze (Ramsey 1980: 400–401). This find received much public attention and is now on exhibit at the RAF Museum in Hendon.

Heinkel He 111   An example of this important type of German bomber from the Battle of Britain was discovered at Hutton, East Anglia, in 1978 in a farm drainage ditch. It has since been positively identified as No. 5709, flown by the 2nd Staffel of Kampfgruppe 126 and shot down during the night attack on London of October 15–16, 1940 (Hiscock 1979b: 9–10). One of the engines, a Junkers Jumo, along with instruments, cockpit controls, seat armor, magazines, and ammunition were recovered along with a complete navigator's bag containing map cards, flight computer, and other essentials. Another He 111 was recovered from Storvatnet Lake, Norway, in 1974. Originally it was believed to be from an aircraft lost during the German occupation of Norway in April, 1940, which thus played no part in the Battle of Britain. But closer examination suggests this was a later model aircraft that might belong with our Battle of Britain sample once it is positively identified. In this case there is a complete Junkers Jumo engine along with propellor, tail fin and rudder, and other wing and airframe components (Essex Aviation Group 1978: 30).

Messerschmitt Bf 110   Used as a twin-engined escort fighter by the Germans during the battle, this type is represented by the wreck of No. 3246, belonging to I Gruppe of Zerstoreregeschwader 2, which was shot down and came to rest in heavy clays at Noak Hill, Billericay, Essex, on September 7, 1940, following a raid on Thameside docks and oil-storage tanks. It was excavated in 1971. Unfortunately, no details have been published concerning the materials recovered from this wreck.

Dornier Do 17   Another important type of German bomber widely used in the Battle of Britain, this is represented by the wreck of No. 3294, of IV Gruppe of Kampfgruppe 3 shot down at Gladstone Road, Laindon, on September 15, 1940. The aircraft was badly burned when it was shot down, so only a single engine, a Bramo 323, was recovered, along with the propellor boss and reduction gear. Later models of this type and its derivative, the Do 217, have also been recovered in various parts of southern England (Essex Aviation Group 1978: 19–23) but were not involved in the battle and therefore lie outside the scope of this paper.

Junkers Ju 88   As the result of a major excavation, which, among other things, involved bomb disposal experts and a stoppage on the railway line nearby, remains of this important type of twin-engined light bomber were recovered and identified in 1979 by the Essex Aviation Group. The airplane was No. 3168 belonging to 111 Gruppe of Kampfgruppe 77 and was shot down over marshland at Pitsea, Essex, on September 18, 1940. Extensive remains of the airframe and parts of both engines and propellor assemblies were found along with assorted ammunition and a navigator's bag with plotter, maps, and other items. Like the He 111 and Do 17, this type of bomber was widely used by the Germans during the Battle of Britain.

Perhaps the most detailed and comprehensive summary to date in this field appears in Ramsey (1980: 317–713), beginning with "Aviation Archaeology and the Battle of Britain" by Peter Cornwell. It describes wrecks of both the Royal Air Force and Luftwaffe in the chronological order in which these aircraft fought and were wrecked. All of the aircraft types described above in the summary of wrecks found by the Essex Aviation Society are also described in the Ramsey volume, along with numerous additional examples and some of the more unusual types of aircraft that fought in these engagements, like the Westland "Whirlwind," No. P6966, excavated in 1979 in Stenhousemuir (Ramsey 1980: 340).

What emerges most vividly from a review of materials obtained so far by aviation archaeology is its strongly relic-oriented emphasis. They are excavated and researched mainly because of their association with important events in English history, and the materials are displayed with these associations in mind. This is, of course, an acceptable goal and closely resembles the historically oriented goals of much of Armada wreck archaeology. In England, such historical particularist goals clearly have led to high standards of excavation and historical research in wreck archaeology. Now the question is: Can anthropologically oriented studies add anything substantial to this body of archaeological evidence?

HISTORICAL DEBATES AND
ARCHAEOLOGICAL SOLUTIONS

Accurate and detailed historical accounts of both the Spanish Armada and the Battle of Britain, describing the chronology of events, tactics, personalities, and politics, are readily available to the interested reader and will not be summarized here. Perhaps the best of these on the Armada are Laughton 1895; Mattingly 1959; Lewis 1960; McKee 1963; Marx 1965; Graham 1972; and Fallon 1978, while on the subject of the Battle of Britain the reader is advised to consult Wood and Dempster 1961; Deighton 1978, 1980; and Ramsey 1980. As one might expect, historians differ in their views and interpretations of many of the events and actions that took place. Here I would like to look at a few selected debates based upon historic documents in order to discover the explanatory potential of archaeology in such cases.

These issues include the character of the Duke of Medina Sidonia,

117

commander-in-chief of the Spanish Armada, essential differences in shipbuilding between the combatants, and differences in armament as they affected the outcome. Each of these issues concerning the Armada has its counterpart in the Battle of Britain, and some of these will be compared briefly. Differing historical interpretations can be regarded as a source of alternate hypotheses, with archaeological evidence being used to test each alternative. Throughout this discussion there is a recurrent theme addressing the relationship between the use of historic documents and archaeological evidence.

Was the Duke of Medina Sidonia Incompetent?

For the Spanish, the Armada of 1588 was a monumental disaster. It not only failed in its objectives, but it also accrued losses estimated at 51 ships and at least 20,000 men out of the 130 ships and 30,656 men that departed from Lisbon in May, 1588, on the "Enterprise of England." As one historian puts it: "It is a grim thought that barely one out of every three who started in May was alive by the end of the year"(Lewis 1960: 209). By the time Medina Sidonia arrived back in Spain the extent of the catastrophe was becoming known in the country, and he encountered hostility from local citizens and found it necessary to return to his estates in Sanlúcar by way of a devious route, keeping clear of towns. Most historians, like the Spanish citizens of 1588, have judged Medina Sidonia as incompetent and even cowardly. How far should we go in accepting this judgment?

The original commander of the Armada was the Marquis of Santa Cruz, aging hero of the Battle of Lepanto. As Lewis (1960: 51) describes him, "Santa Cruz was . . . much more than a battle-winner. He was the father of the whole Spanish Navy, and of its war effort: he was to Philip's Spain what von Tirpitz was to Wilhelm II's Germany . . . the whole Armada idea was his special child." After working doggedly to prepare the Armada, Santa Cruz died in February, 1588, and Philip immediately appointed Medina Sidonia as commander in chief. The fact that Philip II acted so quickly indicates that he had already picked Santa Cruz's successor and that his choice was a careful one. Yet historians have had reason to wonder about this choice ever since (Thompson 1969: 197). Medina Sidonia was not a war hero. Indeed, his only important military activity had been to head the militia whose prompt arrival at Cadiz in April, 1587 prevented Sir Francis Drake from doing even more damage than he did on that occasion (Thompson 1969: 207). However, he was acknowledged to be diplomatic and effective in his ability to organize, as he had shown in preparing the defenses of Andalusia against the English, French, and pirates (Mattingly 1959: 204). Lewis (1968: 48) saw the choice of Sidonia for this command as a crowning blunder. Even Mattingly, whose view of Medina Sidonia is probably more sympathetic than that of any other historian, admits upon viewing his portrait that "he does not look like a lucky man" (1959: 205). This is surely one of the great understatements of all time.

Self-doubt, coupled with genuine lack of ambition, appears to have been one of Medina Sidonia's character traits. Upon hearing of his appointment, his first act was to write a now-famous letter to Philip II asking to be relieved of his command on the grounds that he was in poor health and prone to seasickness, had little in the way of financial resources, knew nothing of Santa Cruz's preparations, and lacked experience in war or at sea. Mattingly sees in this letter indications of intellectual honesty, self-awareness, and even some courage (1959: 206), while McKee regards this letter as "pathetic" and sees in Philip's choice the desire to have a subordinate without military experience who would not presume to oppose either Parma, now assembling his armies in Flanders, or the instructions he would send to him himself (McKee 1963: 27). As another historian puts it:

the duke's defects were exactly what Philip wanted in the man for this post. Philip judged that such a man would obey his instructions much more closely than an experienced seaman, would not fight unless necessary, and would not embark on rash adventures. All the king wanted from the duke was to get the Armada to ports where Parma's troops were waiting, then Parma could command even the Armada from that point on (Marx 1965: 49).

One thing which all historians agree upon, however, is that Medina Sidonia possessed one essential attribute for the post—high rank as a nobleman. This was vital for command in any sixteenth-century Spanish military venture, and, as a cousin of Philip II, Sidonia was extremely well connected and in a position to require the loyalty of his officers and men.

Medina Sidonia's first task was to prepare the Armada for sailing, and here, too, historians disagree. While Lewis (1960: 96) claims that Santa Cruz had succeeded in making everything virtually ready by

February, Mattingly points out that there had been a mad scramble to put men and supplies aboard the ships in Lisbon during the few days preceding Santa Cruz's death (1959: 206). After the marquis's death, there resulted a kind of "frozen chaos" (Mattingly 1959: 206) until Medina Sidonia arrived to straighten things out. So it is true to suggest, as McKee does in somewhat disparaging terms, that Medina Sidonia began his campaign on a mundane level (1963: 45), concerning himself with bringing order out of the chaos caused by the delay following Santa Cruz's death. Mattingly describes the scene:

In the mad week or so preceding the marquis' death, guns and supplies had been tumbled helter-skelter on the ships and crews herded aboard with orders to stand by for instant departure, and on no account to go ashore. There were soldiers and mariners on most of these ships without money or arms or proper clothing. There were crews—who had practically no food. Some ships were laden far too deeply for safety; some floated practically empty. In the wild scramble towards the end, every captain had apparently grabbed whatever he could get his hands on, particularly in the way of additional ordnance. Some ships had more guns than they had room for; others had almost none. One galleon had several new bronze pieces stowed between decks amidst a hopeless clutter of kegs and barrels; one Biscayan scarcely bigger than a pinnance had a huge demi-cannon filling most of her waist. Some had guns but not cannon balls; some had round shot but no guns to fire them (1959: 206).

Even Lewis admits that dysentery was rampant in the Armada at this time, but he blames this on Sidonia's "placid regime" which bred disease in the hot holds of the ships (1960: 96). In fact, evidence in the form of numerous letters to Philip at this time shows that Sidonia's regime was anything but placid, as he struggled to get his fleet organized and under way. The Armada finally sailed on May 18 but was beaten back by contrary winds and further outbreaks of dysentery. It took over a month to reassemble the fleet and repair the damage, and once more the Armada embarked on July 12. During this time the officers Sidonia had appointed as his staff worked effectively to remedy the Armada's defects in a manner Mattingly describes as "more harmonious than it had ever been under Santa Cruz" (1959: 207). As Mattingly has hinted, the biggest task facing Sidonia and his staff during this eleven-week grace period was to redistribute the guns and ammunition which had been frantically ordered by Santa Cruz. The old admiral had convinced Philip to increase the Armada's complement of big guns more along

120

the English model, but he died before this process was complete. Medina Sidonia continued the efforts to increase the percentage of big "ship-killers" in relation to the smaller, man-killing weapons that still prevailed throughout the Armada, and he also sought to distribute them effectively among his ships. He could probably have used more and better guns against the English, but there is no doubt that we shall need to evaluate these efforts in any judgment concerning Sidonia's competence. Incidentally, one of the ships that needed major repairs at this time was the *Santa María de la Rosa*, whose mainmast had collapsed and had to be restepped. This item was specifically mentioned by Sidonia in a letter to Philip II on July 10, 1588, along with other matters intended to convince Philip of the need to delay the departure until these essential tasks were completed.

The pros and cons of Sidonia's handling of the different segments of the battle have all been argued elsewhere. In general, it appears that he succeeded in maintaining the essential formation of the Armada in its unwieldy progress up the channel until he reached Calais. The engagements up to that point were indecisive in the sense that the strong defensive armament and tactics of the Armada pretty well kept it intact. They suffered some losses, but these were relatively minor, especially when one considers the amount of shooting done by the English. It was clear from the start that the English ships could out-perform the Spanish ones in every respect, so it was the English who could choose when to engage. Pitted as he was against resourceful and aggressive commanders like Drake, Howard, Frobisher, and Hawkins, it was no small accomplishment for Sidonia to have made it as far as Calais with his fleet intact. Much of the credit thus far goes to his officers, to whom he deferred in most matters of tactics. Probably his worst decision during these early encounters was to abandon the *Nuestra Señora del Rosario*, flagship of Pedro de Valdez and the Andalusian squadron, after the ship was damaged in a collision. This clash of honor tainted Sidonia's subsequent efforts to assert his authority even though, technically, he did the right thing. Historians agree that this abandonment not only demoralized the officers and sailors of the Armada but also provided the English with a prize containing a supply of powder and shot at just the moment when they were running short.

The real debacle began at Calais, when the English launched fire-ships against the Spanish ships while they lay at anchor awaiting word of Parma's arrival. Until this point, the Spanish losses were only seven ships (three of them galleys, which was no great loss), and the basic order of the fleet was intact. The fireships caused the Spanish ships to cut anchor and attempt to escape individually. Even so, the Armada, led by Sidonia, did form up well enough off Gravelines to fight, and what followed was a battle that differed from the previous engagements in the close range at which the English guns were brought to bear. Now the English guns did serious damage, sinking three ships outright, causing serious damage to numerous others, and killing around 600 Spaniards. This fierce encounter, shortened by a lack of powder and shot on both sides, convinced Sidonia that he would not be able either to collect Parma's army as planned or to return via the channel (he did not realize the English were out of ammunition). In all, the Armada had expended 123,790 rounds of great shot without sinking or seriously damaging a single English ship. The English suffered fewer than 100 sailors and officers killed in battle. From the Spanish viewpoint, it had been a dismal performance, and it was a thoroughly dispirited Armada that Sidonia ordered to return to Spain by sailing north and then via the open sea to the west of Ireland.

Interestingly, no one has accused Sidonia of cowardice in making this particular decision, which is perhaps some measure of how thoroughly beaten the whole Armada was at this stage. Indeed, Sidonia's sailing instructions showed good sense, since he emphasized the importance of keeping well to the west of the Irish coast and of maintaining formation. But battle damage and shortages and spoilage of stores, combined with storms and headwinds in early September, caused individual ships to become separated or to sink. Ship after ship fell out of formation or was wrecked. Most of those Spaniards who came ashore on the Irish coast were summarily executed by parties of English soldiers or handed over for execution by Irish who were under English control. A few hundred Spaniards escaped, mainly to Scotland. Like many of his officers and crew, Medina Sidonia was exhausted and seriously ill when he finally returned to Spain. He struggled ineffectively with the problems of his ships and crews upon their return, but was finally relieved of his command and allowed by Philip, who, unlike his other contemporaries, did not heap recriminations upon him, to return home to Sanlúcar.

What is archaeology's answer to the question of Sidonia's competence? In this case, the key seems to lie with the wreck of *El Gran Grifón*, which produced the best sample of guns of any of the four principal Armada wrecks. It will be recalled that this ship was a large merchantman that was converted for use as escort and flagship for the Armada's supply hulks. It was a second-line fighting ship and, according to historic documents, was intended to serve a purely defensive role. Martin's analysis of the cannons and other materials recovered from *El Gran Grifón* supports this view. He points out that her armament consisted entirely of relatively small guns such as *medias-culebrinas* and *sacres*, long-range weapons using light shot, rather than real ship-killing guns such as *pedreros*, which fired heavy shot at close range (Martin 1972: 69). According to the standards of their day, these guns were obsolescent at best and could not match the firepower of the first-line fighting ships. While documentary evidence pertaining to the period immediately following Santa Cruz's death and Sidonia's initial efforts to organize the fleet is spotty and inconclusive, the guns recovered from the wreck of *El Gran Grifón* led Martin to conclude:

The armament of *El Gran Grifón* is clearly tailored to a defensive, second-line role, with protective rather than offensive firepower as the paramount consideration. The front-line ships of the fighting squadrons, on the other hand, were equipped with formidable and aggressive armaments. . . . So clear and sensible a policy of distributing armament according to role implies deliberate and closely considered strategic planning before the Armada sailed. . . . The urgent reorganization which took place between February and May, when the fleet sailed, was clearly due to the energy and administrative genius of Medina Sidonia himself (1972: 69).

In this case, archaeology has furnished circumstantial evidence to support those historians like Mattingly and Thompson who have regarded the Duke of Medina Sidonia as a competent planner and leader who made the best use of the resources available to him. If archaeologists were to find large, ship-killing types of cannon from the wreck of *El Gran Grifón*, this hypothesis would be effectively disproved, but so far no such guns have been found there. Perhaps history has judged Medina Sidonia too harshly. If we accept Thompson's view that

what was required, then, was not an admiral, possibly not even a field-marshal, but a quartermaster-general someone who could guarantee that the Armada would sail in 1588, or the whole thing might as well be written off.

As an administrator there was nobody more suitable than Medina Sidonia
. . . (1969: 206),

then we must conclude from the archaeological evidence available
that he was competent and did his job well.

"Atlantic" vs. "Mediterranean" Ships

How did the ships of these two combatants compare? Here, too, we
have a major topic of historical discussion and debate. Myths abound
concerning what one historian describes as "the legend of the Elizabethan Galleons, lively little vessels with big guns and sharp-shooting
gunners which blasted the gigantic Spanish Armada away from England's shores" (Glasgow 1964: 177). Traditional accounts have emphasized the idea that the Spanish great ships were bigger than the
English ones (Carr-Laughton 1958: 151). Since the Spaniards failed
to sink a single English ship during the battles of 1588, we have no
wrecks to study in relation to historic documents about the English
ships. Such documents are available and furnish details about the
development of English galleons under Hawkins (Mattingly 1959: 195–
96; Glasgow 1964) and the efforts made to equip them before and
during the battles of 1588 ("List of the Fleet" in Laughton 1895: 323–
42). These documents present an overall picture of a refurbished fleet
of fighting ships designed to combine elements of speed and seaworthiness under the prevailing conditions of the English Channel and
north Atlantic waters.

The English never adopted the Mediterranean tradition of what
Lewis (1960: 64) terms "Long Ships" like galleys for anything besides
coastal and river defense. In 1588 the English possessed only one war
galley. It was based on the Thames and saw no action in the Armada
battles (Lewis 1960: 62). Galleys were light because they were rowed
into battle, and they were long for the sake of short bursts of speed
needed to ram and to engage at close quarters for boarding. They
performed badly in the open sea, especially outside the Mediterranean
where large waves and poor weather were the rule rather than the
exception. Instead, the English concentrated their efforts at naval architecture on the "Round Ship," larger, rounded-hull vessels depending entirely upon sails for propulsion and used in the Mediterranean
as long-range cargo ships rather than for inshore fighting. The galleon,
used as the principal fighting ship on both sides during the Armada

124

battles, was the culmination of an evolution in design based upon the "Round Ship" (Lewis 1960: 64–65).

Through a process of trial and error as well as design, the English during Elizabeth's time developed the fastest and most maneuverable galleons in the world, and the core of their fighting fleet consisted of eighteen of these in 1588. These ships achieved a shape that optimally combined speed under sail with carrying capacity for long voyages (Glasgow 1964: 186–87), and they had a lowered center of gravity thanks to a reduction in the height of the "castles" in the bow and stern. This lowering of bow and stern castles had the combined effect of reducing rolling in heavy seas and the sail-like effect of a high hull in strong winds, and it gave greater stability to ships as gun platforms. Thus the front-line English ships could outrun and outsail even the best of the Spanish ships under nearly all sea conditions. They were the epitome of an Atlantic tradition of shipbuilding.

The sailing and fighting advantages of these English ships and their superiority over the Spanish galleys were noted by Philip II, particularly after Drake's attack on Cadiz in 1587, when he realized that "some four-fifths of his established battlefleet was obsolete!" (Lewis 1960: 63). One reason for all the haste and confusion attending Santa Cruz's efforts to ready the Armada in 1587–88 was Philip's belated determination to change radically the composition of his fleet by replacing his war galleys with galleons and other round ships adapted for fighting. When the Armada sailed, only four galleys and four galleasses (one of them being the *Girona*) were included in the fleet, and none of the galleys even reached the channel. This downgrading of the galleys must have been difficult for Santa Cruz, who was an old fighter steeped in the tradition of Mediterranean galley warfare.

The Mediterranean shipbuilding tradition, however, affected the round ships as much as it did the galleys, and here lay some of the Armada's greatest weaknesses. While Philip had the right idea about altering the composition of his fleet, he could not match the qualities of the English front-line galleons on such short notice. Instead, he was compelled to ransack European ports for round ships that would serve either as warships or transports. It is one measure of the political and military dominance of Spain in Europe at this time that he was able to assemble such a large and cosmopolitan fleet in such a short time. Philip's final arrangements included twenty-four true galleons (i.e., large sailing ships designed for fighting) and forty-one great ships—

mainly big merchantmen packed with heavy artillery—improvised to serve as warships. The rest were lighter craft and hulks for carrying stores, as well as the four galeasses. About the latter, Lewis comments, "It was half-galley, half Great Ship, and it would, they hoped, combine the advantages of both" (1960: 66). As it turned out, the galeass combined only the worst features of both types and performed badly. The galeasses came from Naples, while the galleons were drawn from Spain, Portugal, and Italy. Other large ships converted into fighting vessels came from these areas as well as the Baltic, while the four galleys were Portuguese. Miscellaneous cargo vessels were drawn from as far away as the Baltic, Venice, and Ragusa (Dubrovnik). So on the eve of the Armada battles, Spain's navy was really a two-ocean fleet consisting mainly of galleys within the Mediterranean and large fighting ships under sail outside the Mediterranean. The question, then, is, how well suited were the great ships of Philip's Atlantic fleet for the task they were assigned?

Historical accounts on both sides agree that the English ships were faster and more maneuverable, but the belief that the Spanish ships were bigger has been effectively challenged (Carr-Laughton 1958). Obvious differences in shape have been noted, especially the reduced fore and aft castles on the English ships. Historical sources have provided details on armament and tonnage, but they do not provide commensurate information on details of ship construction. For this we must turn to the archaeological record.

Archaeologically, the best information so far on Armada ship construction comes from the wrecks of the *Santa María de la Rosa* and *La Trinidad Valencera*. Sometimes the details of this information are remarkably specific, as, for example, the discovery of the splintered rectangular box constructed along the keel thirty-five feet from the bow of the *Santa María*. This box appears to be related to the mainmast step—a point of heavy mechanical stress on sixteenth-century ships of this kind. In this case, the break and the efforts to repair it are clearly visible thanks to the preservation of the timbers along the keelson, and the excavators were quick to note that the *Santa Maria* had required urgent repairs to her mainmast immediately following the Armada's abortive attempt to depart in May, 1588. One senses the urgency of that moment when reading Martin's comment:

It is of particular interest to compare the makeshift appearance of the shoring

126

around the step with the solid shipwrightry of the other components, for it will be recalled that the Santa Maria underwent a remasting operation not long before she sank. It is therefore not unreasonable to see in this shoring a temporary arrangement intended to clear the stepping area of ballast in preparation for the new mast which was fitted at Corunna (1973: 446).

This particular detail assumes greater significance when one realizes that large ships constructed in the "Mediterranean" shipbuilding tradition of that time favored light construction, with most of the hull strength concentrated in the interlocking of many close-fitting components to form what Martin refers to as "a relatively solid self-stressing 'shell' " (1973: 449). "Atlantic" ships, on the other hand, derived their strength from an internally stressed frame consisting of fewer but more massive components. Martin (1973: 449) notes that it was the Castilian Squadron, with its ten new "Atlantic"-type galleons, that suffered the lightest casualties in the Armada (10 percent) while the Levant Squadron, whose ships are positively known to have been of Mediterranean origin, suffered the heaviest casualties (80 percent). The *Santa María de la Rosa* was clearly not of "Atlantic" construction, and one could regard her as overstrained by her mast, which could give way in high winds or heavy seas and cause the kind of "cracked egg" damage that may well account for the rapidity with which she sank upon striking Stromboli Reef in Blasket Sound.

La Trinidad Valencera was not a warship but an armed transport of Venetian origin. As in the case of the *Santa María*, portions of the ship's hull have been preserved. These consisted of oak planks held together with iron fastenings. While iron fastenings would have been quicker and easier to attach than wooden ones, since unskilled workers could attach them, their working life was not great—generally ten years or less. The use of these iron fastenings was related to mass production of merchant ships by the sixteenth-century Venetians at a time when their commerce was under pressure and in decline (Martin 1979a: 34). Venetian merchant ships then were designed for relatively intensive but short use-lives, and the reliance upon iron fastenings resembles the modern practice of welding instead of riveting on supertankers (Mostert 1974: 75–77) in the interests of rapid production combined with short-term but intensive use. Other indications of sixteenth-century mass production, in this case directed specifically toward the provisioning requirements of the Armada, appear in the form of pottery recovered from all of the major Armada wrecks (Martin

1979b). In this case, the iron fastenings found by archaeologists on the wreck of *La Trinidad Valencera* represent both a "signature" of the exigencies of mass-producing ships in the Venetian merchant marine (and the state of the Venetian economy in the sixteenth century) and a further insight into construction methods for Mediterranean ships of that period. Such were the ships that fought and failed.

Their greatest failure came not in battle but off the west coast of Ireland during the Armada's attempt to return to Spain. Although relatively few ships had been sunk outright during the battle off Gravelines, many ships were seriously damaged by the close-range fire of the English (Fallon 1978: 20). All of the weaknesses of the "Mediterranean"-type ships in the fleet became apparent as the fleet rounded the northwest coast of Scotland in late August and faced the contrary winds and usual storms of September–October in the north Atlantic. Battle damage on ships basically unsuited to the waves and weather of the north Atlantic was clearly an important factor, along with poor provisions, illness, and confused navigation. In all, twenty-six Armada ships were lost in Irish waters (Spotswood Green 1906: 430; Fallon 1978: 213), to which we may add the galeass *Zuñiga* which eventually reached the coast of Le Havre in shattered condition after a harrowing voyage in the north Atlantic, *El Gran Grifón*, wrecked on Fair Isle, the *San Juan de Sicilia* (often referred to as the "Tobermory Galleon") on the west coast of Scotland, and finally, the hospital ship *San Pedro el Mayor*, which ran aground on the south Devon coast, England. The fact that so many of the Spanish ships were "flimsily built and eminently unsuited to northern Atlantic conditions and prolonged gales," and that these "frail ships . . . were easily holed by shot" (Fallon 1978: 20), as evidenced generally by the Elizabethan State Papers and specifically by the archaeology of *La Trinidad Valencera* and *Santa María de la Rosa*, helps to account for the magnitude of the disaster.

The Cannonball Controversy

No other aspect of the Armada battles has been dealt with in greater detail by historians than armament, meaning, in this case, ships' guns and ammunition. *Armada Guns* (Lewis 1961) is a classic and provides the starting point for any comparative analysis of guns and gunnery tactics of the combatants, augmented by further information in Guilmartin (1974: 277–91), the information and references contained in

Appendix C, "The Secrets of the Use of Great Ordnance" (Laughton 1895: 350–51), and the brief review essay "Ships that Fought the Armada" (McKee 1964: 331–32). Although the Spanish had tended to rely upon boarding as the principal tactic in ship-to-ship battles, retaining the high bow and stern "castles" and large number of soldiers on board each ship to that purpose, they also recognized the growing importance of big guns at sea and made a determined effort to obtain heavy ordnance.

Santa Cruz began the process for Spain, seeking new cannons, demi-cannons, culverins, and demi-culverins from the arsenal in Madrid, as well as from whatever foreign ships were in Spanish harbors, and from Italy, Germany, and Flanders. Medina Sidonia continued this effort at procurement and, as noted earlier, rationalized the distribution of these weapons throughout his fleet. But throughout this period English guns were generally regarded as the best in the world, and the English government succeeded in keeping its gun-manufacturing processes secret (Lewis 1961: 191). Bronze guns were generally favored during the sixteenth century, although the English were successful in producing superior cast-iron guns and shot (Wignall 1973: 466–67). On the eve of battle in 1588 the Spanish fleet possessed a total of 1,124 ships' guns, averaging 9.0 guns per ship and an average weight of shot thrown per gun of 17.2 pounds. The English had a total of 1,972 ships' guns, averaging 11.5 guns per ship and an average weight of shot thrown per gun of 7.4 pounds. The Spanish had 163 of the heavyweight cannon and demi-cannon to the English total of 55, while the English fleet carried a preponderance of lighter but longer-range culverins (Lewis 1961: 190–91).

In other words, the Spanish relied upon heavyweight ship-killers at short range while the English depended more upon longer-range but lighter-shotted guns. Given the superior sailing ability of the English galleons, English tactics, not surprisingly, consisted at first of engaging only when within culverin range but staying far enough away from the Spaniards to avoid their heavy cannon. After much shooting by both sides, the results were inconclusive. Until Gravelines, Spanish losses were due mainly to collisions and factors other than English gunfire, while the English were almost completely unscathed. Even at Gravelines, where the English closed in to cannon range, thereby gaining greater destructive effect with their culverins, the results were not always immediately apparent. And again, the English ships emerged

129

virtually undamaged, despite five hours of point-blank firing by both sides. The battle ended when the English, as well as the most heavily involved Spanish ships, ran out of ammunition.

As an aside, it is worth noting that the RAF had much the same experience against the Luftwaffe in 1940. Deighton (1977: 136–37) notes that English pilots during the Battle of Britain became aware that their Browning machine guns were relatively ineffective at the regulation firing distance of 650 yards, and they often harmonized their guns for much shorter firing distances, down to 250 yards. Eventually these closer firing distances were officially approved, and, as with the English at Gravelines in 1588, their gunnery became more effective.

Considering the huge amounts of shot fired by both combatants, even at close range, it seems odd that the effects upon the English ships were so minor. For example, McKee argues that it is "inherently impossible" to assume that "the Spaniards fired off all their ammunition when out of range, as an explanation of why the English suffered such negligible damage" (1964: 332). Archaeologist Sidney Wignall asks: "Could it be that the Spanish 50-pound and 32-pound cannon shot, when fired at point-blank range, was ineffective against the sides of a well built oak ship?" With this question in mind, Wignall carried out a study of Spanish gun and shot making to see what factors could account for this anomaly. In particular, he noted the poor quality of Spanish iron casting in relation to guns, shot, and anchors, as alluded to in historical sources. As the numbers cited earlier indicate, the Spanish were in no sense under-gunned. While it is possible that the quality of their gunnery was poorer than that of the English, this would not have mattered much at the close range of the Gravelines battle.

Moreover, other battles between English vessels and Spanish ships had produced similar results. Spanish gunnery was equally ineffective against the English in the fight between Hawkins, in the *Jesus de Lubeck*, and Spanish galleons in the port of San Juan de Ulua in the Caribbean in 1568; in the fight by the English galleon *Leicester*, captained by Edward Fenton, against three Spanish warships off the coast of Brazil in 1583; and in similar encounters in 1589, 1591, and 1593 (Wignall 1973: 473–75). In all of these cases, as in the Armada battles of 1588, Spanish shooting was impotent, with the result that "in over thirty years of face-to-face gunnery battles between English and Spanish ships not one of Elizabeth's galleons was sunk by the Spaniards" (Wignall 1973: 475).

Wignall's archaeological research on the *Santa María de la Rosa* could provide only a partial test for the hypothesis that poor iron-casting techniques led to the failure of Spanish shot to penetrate English hulls. The shot from this wreck had decomposed under water into a mass of iron oxide and was useless for analysis, but there were broken anchors associated with the *Santa María de la Rosa* and accompanying ships that attested to the poor quality of the cast iron used in their manufacture. And it was noted that the wreck site of the *Girona* had also produced a broken iron anchor (Sténuit 1975: 79). But the question remained: Were the iron cannonballs of the Armada as poorly made as the anchors?

The best evidence so far for this hypothesis comes from the wreck of *El Gran Grifón*, which produced cannonballs that could be analyzed for possible signs of weakness. These were studied at the Royal Armaments Research and Development Establishment at Sevenoaks and showed minimal deterioration. Together with at least one analyzable piece of whole cannon iron shot from the *Santa María* (Wignall 1973: Fig. 1), the *El Gran Grifón* sample showed:

All examples of Armada shot examined proved to have been quenched, that is, they had been rapidly chilled from the hot state immediately after casting. This was shown by masses of concentric rings, which gave the appearance of a shot within a shot. . . . This process would make the ball brittle (Wignall 1973: 465).

Brittle cast-iron shot fired at fairly high velocity, which was definitely a possibility for the Spaniards, since their gunpowder was of the fine-corned variety that produced strong propellant forces, would be likely to burst upon initial contact with the side of a ship (Wignall 1973: 465).

Archaeological work in this case had produced a valuable hypothesis, although it still remains to be proven that the low effectiveness of Spanish gunnery in the late sixteenth century was due to brittle cannonballs that burst upon contact. This hypothesis can and should be tested. One could design a by-product experiment involving quenched and unquenched cast-iron cannonballs of similar weight and fired or otherwise propelled at wooden targets to see if the quenched projectiles burst at the predicted velocities. Perhaps the greatest utility of this hypothesis is not so much in its truth, which remains to be demonstrated, but in its amenability to further testing. Further archaeology of Armada wrecks clearly should focus on recovering implements of cast iron, especially shot, and should delve more deeply into the subject of ferrous technology among the combatants.

THE STATE OF THE ART IN ARMADA ARCHAEOLOGY

The archaeological responses to each of these historic debates on the Armada reveal both the advances and limitations of archaeology as it has been applied to this body of shipwreck material. Wreck materials have provided a body of circumstantial evidence in the context of a set of physical associations, each of which represents the final locus of discard for an entire floating and fighting community. Materials from Armada wrecks have been recovered, preserved, and analyzed, with the result that these remains can be used as a basis for inferences that can affect our decisions concerning these historic debates. The conclusions derived from these inferences go beyond mere technology, although technological and materialistic arguments are crucial in each case. In many respects, these analytical arguments from Armada wreck materials can serve as models for shipwreck archaeologists generally, since they represent firm linkages between material residues and the behavior being inferred from the character and associations of those residues. Above all, it is the willingness of these excavators to analyze Armada remains in the light of sixteenth-century European military, economic, and political life that makes this particular literature unusually stimulating.

However, the direction of all these efforts so far has been intensely particularistic, with the emphasis on history rather than on science or social science. The irony is that today, in shipwreck archaeology, we have a field which, on the one hand, employs the latest scientific techniques and high technology associated with those techniques yet which, on the other hand, has thus far addressed only issues of particular historic interest. Even, as in the case of the Armada wrecks, where archaeologists have gone beyond the mere collection of relics or treasure, there is apparent reluctance to venture beyond the bounds of historical particularism.

Much the same can be said, at least in passing, for the general state of aviation archaeology and, in particular, the Battle of Britain wrecks. There are historical debates concerning the Battle of Britain that clearly parallel those of the Armada. As in the case of Medina Sidonia, we are entitled to ask: Was Hermann Goering, German Air Minister and architect of the Luftwaffe's assault on England, incompetent? One can look at the historical records of the Battle of Britain and the wrecks found so far and see that the Luftwaffe's bomber forces were ill equipped for an offensive effort of this magnitude. As Deighton (1980: 31) notes, the Luftwaffe "was designed principally as a short-range tactical air force." Four-engined, long-range bomber prototypes had been designed during the 1930s for the Luftwaffe, but these promising designs had been discarded in favor of dive bombers and twin-engined light-to-medium bombers whose speed, range, and payload were already somewhat marginal by 1940 standards (Bekker 1968: 227–29). Then, too, there was the lack of disposable fuel tanks for the fighter escort, which prevented the fighters (mainly Messerschmitt 109s) from staying over England long enough to provide effective protection for the bombers. Above all, there was the almost incredible failure by the Germans to take the English radar system seriously and neutralize it early in the conflict. Historians have generally blamed these and other deficiencies upon Goering's handling of the assault, and an analytical study of Battle of Britain wrecks might serve to test this position. What, if any, evidence can wreck archaeology provide of the quality of planning involved in preparing for a venture of this kind?

As with the Armada wrecks, it is by analyzing the logistical aspects of the Battle that archaeology can prove most effective. For example, aviation archaeologists can examine the component materials of the engines and airframes used by different combatants for signs of haste in construction or corner cutting with respect to the quality of alloys used. Efforts at such materials analysis are being undertaken (Steve Barrett, Essex Aviation Group, personal communication) and should eventually provide an indicator of the degree to which the requirements of mass production may have overriden considerations of quality control. Similarly, one can ask about the relative merits of different aircraft design and armaments, assessing such variables as the relatively weak defensive firepower of German bombers in relation to the armament of attacking Hurricanes and Spitfires or the failure of Fighter Command to obtain fuel injection for the Rolls Royce Merlin engine, thereby conferring a definite advantage to fuel-injection-equipped Messer-schmitts in combat. These kinds of questions connect the planning carried out by the different combatants under the pressures of war to specific residues like the guns, ammunition, aircraft engines, and other materials found by archaeologists. But in the case of the Battle of Britain wrecks, this prospect is still unrealized, mainly because these kinds of questions are only now beginning to be asked. We do not yet have a body of analyzed evidence for aviation archaeology, as we do for the Armada wrecks, to allow us to match the kind of historical inferences offered by scholars like Martin and Wignall.

BEYOND HISTORY:
WRECKS AS POSSIBLE SIGNATURES
OF DEFENSIVE STRESS

The analysis of Armada wrecks so far provides an excellent example of the effective application of archaeological findings to the process of historical inference, but can such analysis also be used to posit more general propositions about human behavior in time of war? To what extent can we claim that archaeological evidence in any way offers causal explanations of human behavior? Perhaps we should be re-minded of the much-quoted dictum that "there is no such thing as 'historical' explanation, only the explanation of historical events" (Brodbeck 1962: 254; quoted in Binford 1968 and Spaulding 1968). Even the best work done so far on Armada wrecks represents only explanations of historical events, and aviation archaeology applied to the Battle of Britain has not even done that.

Given the wealth of historic documentation available for both the Armada and the Battle of Britain, it should be possible to identify specific relationships between certain kinds of behavior under the stress of war and the characteristic material by-products of that behavior in their final (i.e., archaeological) context of discard. To do this, one must first show how the particular behavior and material residues are related and then specify what it is about that relationship that makes it hold true whenever and wherever the same conditions occur. Ac-cording to Binford (1968) and Schiffer (1976: 1–10), the construction of laws is essential if one is to establish such general explanations. Laws are defined, simply, as "one kind of relational statement, which function (in conjunction with other information) to explain or predict

134

empirical phenomena" (Schiffer 1976: 4). Such relational statements are perceived as aspatial and atemporal but not necessarily immutable or invariable in time and space; such invariability must be established by continuous testing against new bodies of evidence. Unfortunately, "laws" are often regarded as final when, in fact, they derive their main utility from their unfinished quality. We gain new knowledge in research by positing lawlike relationships and specifying how these can be tested—then testing them by acquiring new evidence that is relevant to the questions implied by these postulated relationships. The goal in this effort is not the "law" as such but the acquisition of new knowledge as one is directed by the questions raised through such lawlike formulations.

In other words, one must search for general relationships in order to identify the kinds of evidence that will serve to explain and predict human behavior. By looking at the Armada and Battle of Britain in this way, it should be possible to specify when and under what conditions certain kinds of behavior will occur and to identify the material by-products of that behavior and the way these affect the archaeological record. These are the archaeological "signatures" referred to earlier. It is not easy to posit lawlike relations and the archaeological signatures they will produce when one has not worked directly, at firsthand, with the materials concerned. So any arguments I can offer here must be understood as tentative and subject to further testing. Indeed, I hope one day to attempt such testing with the archaeological materials and original historic documents pertaining to the Armada and the Battle of Britain, but, for now, I can only rely upon secondary sources, published reports, and certain documents that have been reprinted or otherwise made available to scholars.

In both cases, the most characteristic response, although one which has only been noted in passing by historians, is what I shall refer to as "defensive recycling." It consists of urgent salvaging of weapons and/ or strategic materials by the combatant on the defensive for immediate reuse during a period of perceived crisis. True recycling occurs when the component materials of the archaeological discard item are transformed into new products that may not resemble the original item at all (Schiffer 1976: 38). One can, however, also regard reuse as a form of recycling, especially when one can observe the transference of the item from one user to another—termed "lateral recycling" by Schiffer (1976: 39). Both of these kinds of recycling characterize the defensive

135

behavior of the English during and immediately after each of these major military episodes.

As an island nation, England was, to a large extent, under seige-like conditions on both occasions. England's access to raw materials and manufactured goods was most restricted at the time when these materials and goods were most needed. And because they were on the defensive, and the English made extraordinary efforts to husband their military resources as part of their overall preparations for battle. Elizabeth's determination to hold her fleet in readiness in the winter and spring of 1588 and Dowding's equally determined efforts to retain as many Hurricane squadrons in England as possible during the fall of France in 1940 should be viewed, above all, as similar responses to parallel circumstances arising from a perception of England's defensive isolation. In each case, this perception was heightened by battle and events that followed. This is revealed not only by the rhetoric of the leaders at that time but also by organized efforts to obtain and recycle both weapons and strategic raw materials for immediate use.

Following word that numerous Armada ships were being wrecked upon the west coast of Ireland, Lord Deputy Fitzwilliam, acting for Elizabeth, commissioned Sir Thomas Norris, Sir George Boucher, and Sir George Carew on September 22, 1588, to proceed to Ireland and procure the "great store of ordnance, munitions, armours, and other goods of several kinds, which ought to be preserved for and to the use of her Majesty" (Carew Papers 1867: 83). It fell to Carew in particular to pursue this commission, since he was Elizabeth's Minister for Ordnance. Lest anyone doubt the urgency of this commission, it should be noted that the closing line of the commission reads, "Torture may be used in prosecuting this inquiry." Even though, by September, it was clear to Elizabeth and her ministers that the Armada threat of 1588 was finished, it was also apparent that the struggle with Spain would continue with undiminished ferocity. So Carew set forth in the spring of 1589 as soon as it became possible to send divers down to explore the Spanish wrecks, and the Carew Papers contain a stream of correspondence from March 10 to August 24, 1589, referring to Carew's efforts to secure bronze cannons (which were especially in demand) from these wrecks. He was assisted in this by an English ship, *Popinjay*, under the command of one Captain Thornton. Perhaps the most interesting entry appears on June 22, when Carew's diver managed to collect three brass artillery pieces and located additional cannons that were so large and so deep they could not be lifted. Carew's diver nearly drowned in the effort, and Carew bemoaned the fact that he had not been able to obtain the services of the "diver of Dublin" who if "with his instruments were here, I would not doubt to bring good store of artillery from hence."

Despite his extraordinary efforts, it appears that Carew did not find many cannons, largely perhaps because the local inhabitants and/or military leaders had gotten to them first—or, at least, that is the reason he gave (Carew Papers, June 22, July 30, 1589). Carew's efforts were not an isolated case, either, since similar attempts at recovery and salvage of ordnance by the English took place in connection with the *San Salvador* (often referred to as the "Spanish carrack"), a ship which was captured during the fighting and brought into Weymouth (State Papers, Elizabeth: Domestic Series, August 24 and 29, 1588). The inventory of goods taken from this ship included 14 brass guns, 48 iron guns, and 2,246 pieces of shot. Lord Deputy Fitzwilliam also reported on December 31, 1588, that "three fair pieces of brass lie among the rocks of Bunboyes, where Don Alonso was drowned (i.e., the *Girona*) and can be recovered." However, when *Popinjay* got there the guns had already been taken by the MacDonnels to defend their castle at Dunluce against the English (Spotswood Green 1906: 422). Similar efforts are also recorded for Spanish ships wrecked on the Dutch coast, as revealed by a letter from Sir William Russell to Sir Francis Walsingham, Elizabeth's principal secretary of state and spymaster, on August 29, 1588:

Although by the contract her Majesty ought to have half of the artillery recovered from the Spanish ships, yet the States [i.e., the Protestant forces in the Low Countries] seem much to mislike his "staying" a mere eight pieces for the strengthening of the town—Vlisshing [i.e., Flushing] (State Papers, Elizabeth: Foreign Series).

From Carew's activities in Ireland during the summer of 1589 and this remark about the disposition of cannons from Armada wrecks on the Dutch coast we may infer that regular and immediate arrangements were implemented by the crown to recover and reuse cannons from wrecked enemy ships. Indeed, in their haste to obtain such guns, the English sometimes found Spanish sailors still on board drifting or wrecked ships and had to fight with them for possession, as reported by the Earl of Sussex for an Armada ship disabled at Newhaven (State Papers, Elizabeth: Domestic Series, August 30, 1588).

Similar arrangements existed in 1940, although the emphasis in this case was on strategic materials—mainly aluminum—rather than on weapons. Deighton (1978: Fig. 28) states:

Wrecked German aircraft were brought to vast dumps in England. The parts were sorted and salvaged, and the alloy melted down, so that many German aircraft eventually flew again as RAF aircraft.

Crash sites, when known, were recorded by the police and guarded by troops until such salvage could take place. The actual recycling of alloys and other materials was carried out by the Civilian Repair Organisation (CRO), which established an enviable record of repairs to damaged English fighter aircraft. Of the Spitfires, Hurricanes, and other English fighters damaged and grounded during the Battle of Britain, no less than 61 percent were restored to airworthiness and returned to service by the CRO. Of all the English fighter aircraft that fought in the Battle of Britain, 35 percent consisted of restored wrecks supplied by the CRO (Wood and Dempster 1961: 199–201). Many of the materials used by the CRO in this effort came from German wrecks, although the actual extent to which German alloys and parts were reused in English aircraft remains open to debate.

The need for an organization to salvage wrecked aircraft and repair damaged fighters was recognized by the English in 1938, following the Munich crisis. The Air Ministry appointed Lord Nuffield as the director, along with a board of managing directors from Morris Motors. By May, 1940, under the energetic new leadership of Lord Beaverbrook, the CRO pulled together a network of repair centers, training schools, parts depots, and other physical facilities that operated throughout the Battle of Britain. They were organized into Civilian Repair Units (CRUs) whose output rose from 20 repaired aircraft per week in February, 1940, to 160 per week by mid-July. These were kept supplied by the parts depots as well as by eight salvage units:

All crashes were reported to headquarters of the group controlling these units and salvage units' engineer officer decided on the spot the category to which the aircraft were allotted. Salvage units cleared operational airfields of wrecked aircraft, and dealt with crashed German machines after they had been examined by one of the officers from air intelligence at the Air Ministry (Wood and Dempster 1961: 201).

Photographs of three of the collecting dumps to which wrecked German aircraft were brought by the CRO for salvage and recycling appear in Deighton (1978: Fig. 28, 56) and Ramsey (1980: 552).

Attempts at defensive recycling of Armada materials by the English consisted mainly of lateral recycling, primarily of usable cannons, while during the Battle of Britain the emphasis was on true recycling to obtain alloys for remanufacture into aircraft components. In each case, the intensity of this effort at salvage and recycling accurately reflects the sense of urgency felt by the English in their defensive role. Known and accessible wrecks were immediately stripped of usable materials, leaving little, if anything, behind. Wrecks in relatively good condition were usually the first to go, while burned, battered, or deeply buried or submerged wrecks were less attractive to the salvagers and were not recovered. Some wrecks went unnoticed at the time or were poorly documented and were not found until much later. These latter remarks are especially true of the Armada and Battle of Britain wrecks that have been excavated recently. The result, for the archaeologist, is a kind of mirror image of wreck recovery. The best documented and preserved wrecks are those least likely to survive for archaeological study, since these are the ones that will probably have been salvaged and recycled immediately after they were wrecked. As both the Armada and Battle of Britain wrecks demonstrate, extraordinary efforts are required to locate and recover wrecks that contain useful information, precisely because the salvagers made off with the best-preserved and most accessible materials right away. In other words, we are looking at salvage and reuse within a wider context involving the adaptive relationship between this behavior and the circumstances under which the fighting occurred. This is an eco-utilitarian argument that can be tested cross-culturally.

What we have, then, in the Armada and Battle of Britain cases is a proposition which can be stated more generally: *The greater the defensive isolation of a combatant, the greater will be the efforts by that combatant to salvage and recycle items and/or materials of strategic value from any wrecks that fall within its territory.*

Archaeologically, the results of these efforts at defensive recycling will tend to produce a skewed sample of wreck remains, confined mainly to inaccessible locations or poorly documented examples, often with extreme reduction of the wreck due to extensive damage.

While Muckelroy (1978: 160–214) correctly emphasizes the importance of controlling natural processes that affect the deposition and dispersal and/or reduction of shipwreck remains, the parallel cases of the Armada and Battle of Britain wrecks demonstrate the need to examine at least as carefully the behavioral processes that also affect the physical character and deposition of wrecks. While "salvage operations" are considered as a stage in the evolution of a shipwreck (Muckelroy 1978: Fig. 5.1), we still need to incorporate such operations into a behavioral framework that allows us to connect specific kinds of behavior to their effects on wreck remains and related materials. Positive evidence of defensive recycling should be sought in order to test this chain of relationships. For example, the wreck archaeologist should look next for evidence of Spanish Armada guns in use in contemporaneous English ships and land fortifications, or for the use of German alloys or parts in English aircraft from the Battle of Britain. The extent of such recycling, as ascertained by archaeological studies of materials, will reveal the extent of defensive isolation experienced by a combatant. In other words, such tests can tell wreck archaeologists how far they should go in regarding recycling as the archaeological signature of defensive stress.

DEFENSIVE RECYCLING:
GENERAL APPLICATIONS
AND PREDICTIONS

Wreck archaeologists ought eventually to be able to make valid statements about the behavior that produced particular kinds of remains on purely archaeological grounds or based entirely upon archaeological reasoning without necessarily having to rely upon historic documents or other kinds of evidence of a basically nonarchaeological nature. This claim in no way repudiates or belittles historic evidence or the need to understand the particular details of historic events. But it proposes that archaeology, by adopting a circumstantial line of reasoning based upon the analysis of materials and material remains in relation to the logistics of war, can offer general statements about human behavior under the stresses of combat that go beyond the particulars of any specific battle or other historic event. Such an approach offers general statements or propositions that apply equally to the past and present. Given similar circumstances of increased defensive isolation, we should expect to find increased evidence of recycling behavior in any war. And we can extend and test this proposition against the experience of war in particular cases.

One can predict, for example, that the most extreme kinds of defensive isolation would lead to a distinctive kind of behavior that I shall refer to as the "strategy of anticipatory recycling." This consists of procurement of weapons and/or strategic materials from one's anticipated opponent so as to ensure compatability with captured and wrecked material during the conflict. For instance, during the Winter War of 1939–40 and the Continuation War of 1941–44, the Finns learned to appreciate the value of captured Russian weapons, aircraft, ammunition, and so on, which they used against their attackers whenever possible (Luukkanen 1963: 144–49; Bäckström et al. 1976; Keskinen, Stenman, and Niska 1977). The present Finnish policy of purchasing a significant portion of their total military hardware, including tanks, rifles, and aircraft, from the U.S.S.R. reflects treaty obligations but can also be viewed as one way of ensuring a steady supply of captured weapons, parts, ammunition, and materials that will be usable in the event that Finland is ever attacked by the Soviet Union. Indeed, such anticipatory recycling behavior may be the material signature of guerilla warfare generally, which is the most extreme form of defensive isolation there is. Recent news reports (*Aviation Week and Space Technology*, March 2, 1981: 24–25) indicate that guerillas in El Salvador are currently being supplied, by Cuba and other Communist-bloc countries, with American-made weapons obtained from stocks captured in Viet Nam. If true, this would be an extreme case of "anticipatory recycling" behavior in relation to guerilla warfare. One might be tempted to argue further that the idea of "anticipatory" recycling implies intent, but this is not a necessary part of the argument. Like most archaeological hypotheses concerning adaptation, it deals exclusively with observed behavior and the material by-products of that behavior. In this case, those by-products consistently appear prior to the combat situation in which they are needed, hence they "anticipate" the event. Such anticipation may be purposeful or accidental, or it may occur as a secondary result of other kinds of behavior, such as might be the case with the Finnish treaty obligations cited above. In other words, the archaeological evidence by itself cannot tell us whether such adaptive behavior is conscious or unconscious, and this limitation can be seen as part of the larger problem of anticipation and preadaptation in both the biological and behavioral sciences generally (Bennett 1976).

So that same archaeological reasoning that allows us to identify the material signatures of behavior by a combatant under conditions of defensive stress in past engagements like the Spanish Armada of 1588 and the Battle of Britain in 1940 can be applied to identifying and explaining behavior among present-day societies' wartime logistics or preparations for war. Above all, it is this search for general, circumstantial relationships between materials and human behavior as a means of predicting and explaining present as well as past events that should characterize archaeology's anthropological approach to the wreckage of war.

7

History, Smugglers, Change, and Shipwrecks

PETER R. SCHMIDT and
STEPHEN A. MROZOWSKI

*Department of Anthropology,
Brown University*

A THEORETICAL PRELUDE

Why do shipwreck archaeology? Several competing considerations come immediately to mind. Most important, the excavation of any shipwreck site should be significant to the solution of either scientific or historical problems. If our concerns are also anthropological and we want to understand processes of change and the material expression of behavior, then the method and theory of contemporary archaeology should, ideally, provide a set of tools and concepts that would assure anthropological content to shipwreck archaeology. For the New World historical archaeologist the value of shipwreck sites lies in their connection with a system of commercial and informational exchange, the focal point of which was shipping. Most commerce was carried out by merchants who relied almost exclusively upon ships to transport goods to ports throughout the world. However, as parts of a system, these wrecks can only gain significance when examined within the context of the greater system at large, which involved port cities, support facilities, and the like. Furthermore, we believe that the reasoning which the shipwreck archaeologist brings to bear upon the study of

143

wreck sites should remain consistent with that of archaeology in general. For us this means the pursuit of general principles which can be extended beyond the parameters of a specific case study, and which incorporate a concern for important historical problems.

We believe that because the predominant number of shipwrecks in American waters belong to the colonial period, they fall within the domain of historical archaeology which should combine a concern for general principles with the pursuit of important historical questions. But several trends in historical archaeology suggest that we need to rethink our attitudes toward history and how it is used in archaeology. These trends can best be summarized as a denial of anthropological perspectives in preference for scientific, mechanical approaches. This denial arises out of the rejection of the historiographic process (South 1977) and the misrepresentation of history as chronology and chronicle (Binford 1968c, 1977). Any denial of history and historiography also denies systemic cultural context, the very condition required to understand change and behavior.

Bruce Trigger has deplored the antihistorical school of thought in North American archaeology (Trigger 1980: 671–73). One of the consequences, he says, is an insensitive denial of indigenous American history:

Yet, by treating generalizations about human behavior as being the primary or even the only significant goal of archaeological research, archaeologists have chosen to use data concerning the native peoples of North America for ends that have no special relevance to these people. Instead, they are employed in a clinical manner to test hypotheses that intrigue professional anthropologists . . . (Trigger 1980: 671).

We believe that a similar antihistorical perspective negatively affects the historical identity and welfare of Anglo-American history in North America. The detached and alienating perspective advocated by Stanley South (1977) toward history inhibits the solution of significant cultural and historical problems because of its disdain for history:

If in arriving at functional, socioeconomic, status, and other cultural interpretations from archaeological data the archaeologist finds himself leaning on the documents as a crutch, and using archaeological data primarily as padding to the historical record, *then he is bastardizing the archaeological profession.* He should use documentary data, *but the foundation of his interpretation should be archaeological* when his historical-temporal, historical

144

social, historical status, historical-functional explications emerge from the archaeological process (South 1977: 312, italics ours).

South has inverted the process by which history should be employed in archaeology. Documents are not crutches. To the contrary, they provide complex information that allows us to see the connections between behavior and material culture and to perceive important anthropological problems. If an archaeologist ends up padding the historical record with archaeological data, then that process reflects the lack of a problem and can be characterized as redundant or additive chronicle. We see the spontaneous birth of various historical-explicative interpretations from archaeological data as confusion about the role of history in archaeology. If historical documents are available and relevant to the archaeological data, then a set of relationships is available to the archaeologist that can be tested *with* the archaeological data.

South's perspective on historical archaeology stresses the search for replicated artifact patterns as our primary goal. It does not really matter if there are or are not connections between history and archaeology, because "as archaeologists we are dealing primarily with patterned material remains of past behavior" (South 1977: 326).

It is apparent that South prefers to operate in a cultural vacuum that relegates history to an explicative role of regularities that may appear in the archaeological record; the patterns are the critical nexus for South. After creating his Carolina Artifact Pattern, South suggests that the "explanation of *why* the Carolina Pattern exists on British sites is to be found in the examination of hypotheses directed at cultural processes in the British Colonial system" (South 1977: 125). He then goes on to name several historical subjects in which the explanation may be partly discerned: the logistics of the British distributive system, the production system, discouragement or encouragement of colonial manufacturing, and so on. So, South admits that explanation lies in history, but does nothing about integration of historical sources to understand *why* he has a pattern. It is also apparent that South has not considered the importance of Walter Taylor's observation of the value of historiography to cultural studies: "It is superfluous to stress the fact that modern historiography also is primarily interested in context. Full and inclusive context" (Taylor 1967: 32). But South denies the historiographic process when he asserts that "as archaeologists we

145

must depend on our archaeological tools for interpretative statements of archaeological data, and not resort to the easy expedient of superimposing the historical preconceptions onto the archaeological record" (South 1977: 326). In other words, we must stop the practice of historiography, or "the projection, written or spoken, of contemporary thought about past actuality in terms of cultural man and time sequences" (Taylor 1967: 29). Taylor eloquently elaborates on this principle and its importance to anthropology:

Historiography is the discipline characterized by the construction of cultural contexts abstracted from the totality of past actuality. More specifically, it is projected contemporary thought about past actuality, integrated and synthesized into contexts in terms of cultural man and sequential time (Taylor 1967: 33).

We agree with Taylor. The construction of cultural context is the way in which cultural meaning may be added to archaeology and to any patterns that may be deduced from archaeological evidence. Because South and others of like persuasion (Binford 1977) deny historiography and avoid historical research altogether or until excavation of a site has been completed (for example, see South's [1977: 279] chart that positions historical research in the bottom and last slot in a column of survey techniques), they also deny proper study of past behavior thought synthesis of a complex system of different cultural constructs, each derived from a different domain of historical documentation and historical literature.

The significant anthropological advantage inherent in historical archaeology is that it allows access to many more interpretative constructs than are available to prehistorians. Ironically, that advantage is cast aside if, like South, we adopt an antihistorical perspective or if we mistake chronicle or chronology for history.

We want to return to Trigger's concern for an absence of interest in the people whose history and identity are influenced by the archaeology we practice. A quick perusal of the archaeological literature will reveal that we fail to pose important questions in historical archaeology or shipwreck archaeology—questions that are significant to our contemporary view of history. Instead, both aspects of archaeology have operated in a chronicle mode of data collection, where evidence is added to an extant corpus of history. Sometimes gaps in the chronicle are filled, but oftentimes redundancy results. By redundancy we mean the

146

addition of insignificant facts to the historical record, facts that add nothing to our understanding of why and how change occurs.

There is also a reflexive mode of operation in both aspects of archaeology, which occurs when a terrestrial or shipwreck site is encountered, found to be unique (usually without historical research), or found to be threatened and excavated in order to recover the artifacts. Sometimes this occurs as treasure salvage, other times as response to antiquity laws, or possibly because of the aesthetic value of the artifacts. Usually such excavations do not address historical and anthropological problems; instead, at best, they merely add to historical chronicle.

There is another problem inherent in shipwreck archaeology. Lenihan's paper in this volume cautions that there is a critical need for a strong conservation ethic in shipwreck archaeology, given the limited number of wrecks. This being the case we are compelled to excavate only when our excavations help to solve problems that are culturally important to us as a people, or to the people whose cultural heritage is most closely linked to the archaeological evidence.

To meet conditions of anthropological and historical adequacy in shipwreck archaeology, as well as to conserve limited cultural resources, it is important to create problems that are significant and solutions where the archaeology makes important contributions to our ideas about how and why culture changed in the past. Furthermore, we must carefully research different historical documents and the literature of history to derive constructs that can be synthesized to build a complex cultural context for our archaeological excavation, be it a shipwreck, an Iron Age factory site in Tanzania, or a colonial privy in Rhode Island. If we fail to do this, then we overlook cultural contexts that tell us most about behavior.

From various historical documents we may construct variable cultural context, out of which will come our synthesis and the systemic context in which behavior can be attached to the material world. With these concerns in mind, we now want to propose a problem that can be solved by a combination of terrestrial, underwater, and shipwreck archaeology.

GENESIS OF THE PROBLEM

The problem that we will develop here found its genesis in an archaeological anomaly. Excavations in Queen Anne Square of New-

147

port, Rhode Island, revealed three large trash pits, two of which date to the mid-eighteenth century and contained French earthenwares as well as French brandy bottles and Dutch gin bottles (Mrozowski, Gibson, and Thorbahn 1979: 64, 116). Feature one at the Carr House contained 33 percent non-English ceramics, primarily French tinglazed earthenwares. The same feature also held a minimum of two pale blue, square-bodied bottles which Noël-Hume (1974: 70) describes as French, and the partial remains of a large Dutch gin bottle (Noël-Hume 1974: 62).

Excavations on the former Brown property in Newport revealed a second mid-eighteenth-century trash pit that contained two bottles identical to bottles described by Noël-Hume as Dutch gin bottles. This evidence suggests, further, that Dutch gin was illegally imported into Newport before the Revolution.

A third trash deposit partially excavated on Bridge Street during a salvage recovery yielded a French faïence serving-dish cover as well as remains of a Westerwald stoneware mug, combed slipware plate, and a Chinese porcelain tea cup.

These finds do not accord with the claim that the Navigation Acts effectively curtailed the importation of European, including French, painted earthenwares into North American colonial ports until 1775 (Noël-Hume 1974: 140–41). But both history and historical archaeology tell us that the Navigation Acts were notoriously ineffective. They failed to limit the importation of other goods from Europe, especially via Dutch and French colonies in the Caribbean during the eighteenth century. Moreover, the historical reputation of seventeenth- and eighteenth-century Rhode Islanders is that they were " 'a set of lawless, piratical people whose sole business is that of smuggling' " (Williams 1961: 140).

The archaeological evidence and historical evidence suggest that in fact Newporters did acquire, use, and discard French ceramics and Dutch glassware before the Revolution. This observation agrees with Watkins's (1973: 191) emphasis that "ceramics of North America partake of far more than simply English traditions sprinkled with a few other North European ingredients." If we look beyond Newport, we find that French and Dutch ceramics and glassware have been excavated from sites in Philadelphia (Cosans 1974; Liggett 1978), and in Salem, Massachusetts (Moran, Zimmer, and Yentsch 1977)—both centers of shipping and illicit trade. In these colonial cities French or

Dutch artifacts were recovered from what appear to be pre-1776 contexts (Liggett 1978: 33; Moran, Zimmer, and Yentsch 1977: 120–21).

The presence of Dutch gin bottles agrees with a recent study of alcohol use in Newport prior to the Revolution (Pinson 1980). Pinson finds that European wines and liquors were much desired and liberally consumed by Newport's elite in the fifty years before 1776 (Pinson 1980: 35). The more-than-moderate incidence of non-English ceramics in prerevolutionary trash pits suggests that a similar pattern of consumption may have existed for tableware. These two categories represent only a small proportion of the material culture of colonial America, but they are significant of consumer behavior by the elite and artisans in colonial port cities such as Newport. These goods acted as status markers in Newport society, and they also symbolically represented colonial American independence from British authority.

The secondary literature on colonial economic life (e.g., Andrews 1938; Bridenbaugh 1955) affirms that relatively little is known about the details and behavior surrounding the smuggling trade. Furthermore, how do we reconcile the dissonance between the archaeological evidence and the secondary histories on the period? We find that most historians of the illicit trade display considerable bias in their focus on major commercial commodities such as molasses, sugar, rum, and tea. But what of the less-visible and less economically important goods imported by the same ships that carried the primary goods? We realized that the answers to these questions lay in more detailed historical research among the germane primary and secondary sources as well as in shipwreck archaeology.

Primary documents should allow us to see patterns of behavior associated with the smuggling trade into Newport, how and why that trade changed, and what goods were smuggled. But the documentary record is a fragmentary and limited one. Shipwreck archaeology has the power to testify more concretely on how goods were smuggled and why smuggling techniques changed. It also allows us possible understanding of what assemblages of goods were carried in the illicit trade, and how and why smuggling behavior changed through time.

These series of interrelated questions became much more poignant when we were asked to address the question of anthropology in shipwreck archaeology. In harmony with the principles we set out previously, we began to examine the historical record, working primarily in the splendid archives of the Newport Historical Society. We sampled a variety of documentary domains, such as merchants' daybooks and waste books in which the name of the purchaser is entered under the date along with the amount of purchase; payroll or receipt books of merchants in which they entered payment of debts, payment of artisans for work completed, payment of sailors, and so on; bills of lading, on which the goods being shipped are listed along with the vessel's name and master's name; invoices of goods shipped; letters of masters, agents, and factors to ship owners; receipts of shipments to local merchants and farmers; journals; probate inventories; command papers from ship-owners to masters; and many other miscellaneous documents. The secondary historical literature also demanded our attention. This pre-liminary study has provided us with a variety of cultural constructs which are best synthesized for the purposes of anthropology in ship-wreck archaeology around these questions: Why have the noncom-mercial goods smuggled into the colonies been ignored in our cultural view of the past? How did the colonial smugglers conduct their clan-destine affairs? If smuggling behavior changed, then what caused this change and how is the behavioral change manifest in the material record? First, we turn to the secondary literature to discern the major trends in laws, economic life, and political relationships that provide the context for smuggling in colonial Newport and Rhode Island.

HISTORICAL BACKGROUND

Many colonial gentlemen sincerely believed that the clandestine traffic they pursued entailed no stigma of treason or loss of respectability, and a large portion of the citizens agreed with them (Bridenbaugh 1955: 64).

The history of Rhode Island smuggling goes back to the seventeenth century and the regular violation of the Navigation Act by Rhode Islanders. The Act of 1660 required that shipments to the colonies take place in English vessels and listed enumerated products from the colonies that had to be shipped to England; the Staple Act of 1663 prohibited importation of goods not loaded in England; the 1673 Plan-tation Duties Act closed a loophole, requiring that goods shipped from colony to colony could not be reexported to Europe; and the 1696 Act set up new enforcement machinery (Bigelow 1930; Andrews 1938: IV). These laws had little effect on commerce in the colonies, and violation of their provisions was commonplace. In that respect, virtually every-one involved in international trade was, technically, a smuggler.

150

By the beginning of the eighteenth century a customs service similar to that of England had been established. Significantly, Rhode Island was the last colony to enter the system (Williams 1961: 140). By this time Rhode Island merchants had already gained a reputation as aggressively resistant to any exercise of authority over their free trade, especially with the foreign islands of the Caribbean. Rhode Island participation in trade with the foreign islands increased rapidly between 1714 and 1724. In 1714, 50 percent of the incoming vessels from the West Indies came from Barbados and only one from a foreign possession; by 1724, 40 percent of the vessels returning from the West Indies came from foreign ports (Bigelow 1930: I, IV, 4–6). Protests from the British planters in the Caribbean finally resulted in the passage of the Molasses Act of 1733, which laid prohibitive duties upon the importation of foreign rum, molasses, and sugar into the colonies (McClellan 1912: 34; Andrews 1938, IV: 242).

The levy of 6d. per gallon of molasses from the French islands, if enforced, would have had disastrous economic consequences for Newport. While Boston merchants felt the effects of enforcement in 1740 (Andrews 1934, IV: 242–44), the Newport trade in these illegal commodities continued uninterrupted. The distilleries of Newport consumed foreign molasses with no apparent difficulties from customs officials. Furthermore, during the 1740s French goods were brought in legally by privateers who operated successfully out of Newport during King George's War, 1744–48.

It is clear, however, that the local merchants were aware of the law and that they realized that their active trade with the French islands was illegal; hence, there was some concern that their off-loading of goods not be observed by customs officials. For example, James Brown of Providence wrote to one of his captains in 1736 to warn him

not to be too bold when you come home, Enter in the West Indias [west inlet between the mainland and Conanicut Island, avoiding Newport] if you can, and if you cannot bring too, down the River and send your Cargo. Some to Road Island, and some up here in boats, so as not to bring but a few hhds [hogsheads] up to my Wharff . . . (quoted in Bigelow 1930, I, V: 8).

This letter indicates that Rhode Island merchants were clearly involved in what was then and is now considered smuggling. Furthermore, the duties collected by customs officers could not have paid for their salaries in that self-sufficient system. They lived in a style much beyond their means. The total customs duties in all of North America between 1733 and 1750 averaged only £ 350 sterling each year; the Molasses Act and Navigation Acts had been neutralized by successful evasion of the law (Bigelow 1930, II, III: 11). To be sure, smuggling and bribery were widely practiced, but smuggling was carried out without fear of reprisals.

Newporters continued to trade with the French islands with impunity into the 1750s. With the advent of the Seven Years War in 1756, trading with the French increased under Flags of Truce issued by the Rhode Island governor.

A major source of conflict between the British and the colonies developed from the widespread commerce that the colonies carried on with the enemy (Bigelow 1930: II; Sachs and Hoogenboom 1965: 146). New Englanders ran the Caribbean blockades at great risk but for significant profit. Newporters actively participated in this trade, simply continuing their open intercourse with the French which prevailed in the early fifties, when French traders could be found in Newport recruiting trade to Cape Breton and Cape Francois (Bridenbaugh 1955: 66). Much of this trade apparently had the open sanction of colonial officials, as customs officer Robert Robinson complained that Deputy Governor Ellery refused to assist customs and openly allowed Newport merchants to unload their ships on the west side of Conanicut Island (Bridenbaugh 1955: 66).

British efforts to suppress trade with the enemy increased in 1758 and 1759. By 1760–61 the British blockade was a complete success. Up until this time Newporters had carried out their trade without fear. Detection of smuggling in Narragansett Bay was difficult. The many islands, coves, and rivers of the bay were easily accessible to Newport, situated at the head of the bay (see Fig. 7.1). Once goods were offloaded on Conanicut Island or onto small boats west of the island, goods were transported by boat to Rhode Island (Aquidneck Island), where they would be transported by wagons to the wharves and warehouses along Newport's waterfront.

All this changed in 1763. As the expenses of the war increased and British debt grew, the treasury realized that the North American deficits had to be covered and revenues increased (e.g., Andrews 1938, IV: 217). In 1764 the treasury recommended harsh new measures to bring smuggling under control in the colonies. This was a critical turning point in resolve to suppress the trade that Newporters and other Rhode Islanders thrived upon.

Figure 7.1. Southeastern New England and the surrounding islands.

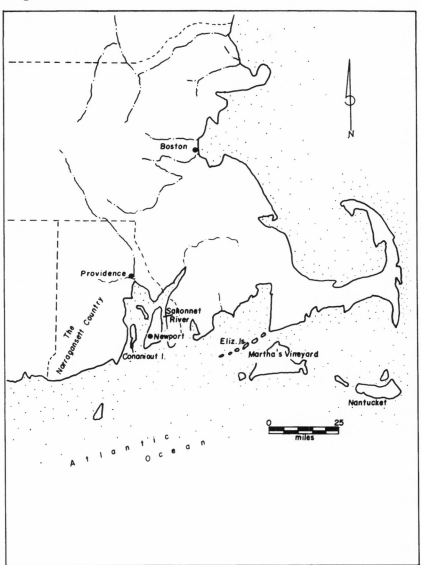

British irritation over Newport's central role in smuggling led to the posting of H.M.S. *Squirrel* to Narragansett Bay in the winter of 1763–64 "for the enforcement of fair trade and the prevention of smuggling" (Bridenbaugh 1955: 259). The presence of a British warship in Narrangansett Bay created an unprecedented stressful situation for smuggling. This and other related enforcement measures created an altogether different climate. The British resolve resulted in the Trade Acts of 1764, 1765, and 1766, the second Townshend Act that established the American Board of Customs Commissioners, and the Townshend Duties of 1767.

Pressure mounted in 1763 with the circulation of a letter to all governors reminding them of their responsibilities to enforce trade laws (Barck and Lefler 1958: 511). At the end of 1763 and early in 1764 the colonies prepared various memorials against the renewal of the Molasses Act. The Rhode Island petition admitted that 82 percent of its molasses came from foreign sources (Jensen 1968: 79–80), and that the Dutch colonies of Surinam and St. Eustatius also supplied bills of exchange and some molasses. Nevertheless, the Revenue or Sugar Act of 1764 soon followed. Particularly obnoxious to Rhode Island were the new enforcement policies of the customs service and the new court of vice-admiralty to be located in Halifax. If enforced, the legislation meant dire consequences for the Rhode Island merchant-smugglers. Prosperous merchants such as Aaron Lopez, a Portuguese Jew who eventually grew to be Newport's most illustrious merchant prince, stood to lose their fortunes.

The Sugar Act reduced the molasses duty from 6d. to 3d.—still enough to make smuggling a profitable enterprise until 1766, when the duty was lowered to 1d. But foreign rum was prohibited. Certain wines, especially French wines, were subject to higher duties, as well as new duties of £ 7 per ton on wines of Madeira and the Azores (Sachs and Hoogenboom 1965: 159). In 1767 new duties followed upon glass, painters' colors, pasteboards, strawboards, milkboards, painted paper, tea, and various stationery papers (Atton and Holland 1908: 285). These were modified in 1770, so that such goods manufactured in Great Britain were exempted (Atton and Holland 1980: 290). Silks and other fine textiles from France and the Orient were also heavily dutied in the 1764 Act. Particularly critical for the Newport merchants was the extension of the Hovering Act of George I into the colonies (Barck and Lefler 1958: 512); the act stipulated that any ship within two leagues of the coast had to carry a list of goods. Failure to produce a list of verified goods meant possible confiscation of unlisted items.

The response of Newport merchants to legislative pressure and the presence of British warships was to increase their trade. The British sent men-of-war to Narragansett Bay to patrol, particularly after 1768. Tensions grew between the Newport smugglers and the British between 1763 and 1776, reaching their peak with the burning of H.M.S. *Gaspee* on June 10, 1772, in Narrangansett Bay. The *Gaspee*, significantly, had been harassing the smugglers of Narragansett Bay; the group that burned her included prominent merchants.

THE PROBLEM REVISED

Smuggling was an integral and popularly accepted part of the Rhode Island economy during the early and mid-eighteenth century. Before 1763 smuggling had been conducted with caution but free of intimidation. The only evidence we see for particular tactics is the off-loading procedures in the passage west of Conanicut Island and on the west side of the island. There is little reason to believe that complex techniques of concealment were used prior to 1763 or that elaborate strategies or tactics were necessary.

The enforcement of British law in Narragansett Bay after 1763 abruptly changed conditions under which smuggling was conducted. We suggest that the stress caused by British attempts to suppress smuggling by the Newport and Providence merchants caused significant change in the way goods were concealed in ships, behavior that left distinct material signatures that should be discernible in shipwrecks from this period. These principles should have cross-cultural applicability for the archaeological recognition of stress related to competition between commercial shipping interests and political authority. We also propose that careful analysis and synthesis of various documentary sources will show that adaptation in response to stress caused change in the locales used for smuggling and in the strategies and tactics used to avoid British officials.

PRE-1763 SMUGGLING

The smuggling trade in tea and wine appears to have been active for the four decades after the Molasses Act was passed in 1733. In a

155

letter from Mayne Burn of Mayne Co. in Lisbon to Johannes Roderick in April, 1757, we learn that the Lisbon agents want "to acquaint you that there is plenty of Bohea Tea to be had at about 2/ to 2/6 / pound on board" (NHS 1). (To avoid cumbersome citations, all Newport Historical Society Archives have been numbered for reference in the bibliography.) Agents regularly provided price lists to merchants such as Lopez, Champlin, and the Vernons. Mayne also commented widely on the condition of grain crops in Spain and Portugal, and provided comments on other items such as wines and fruits while soliciting business.

John Banister, one of the prominent merchants of Newport, concluded a scheme with a Dutch trading house in Amsterdam during 1743; Banister's plan was to carry on a direct trade between Newport and Amsterdam (Bigelow 1930, II, III: 5). Inspection of his bills of lading for the subsequent period may reveal whether or not Banister traded directly with Holland, or whether he obtained Dutch and other European goods through Surinam, St. Eustatius, Curaçao, the French Islands, or the Mole on Hispanola (on the northwestern section of today's Haiti). Banister's daybooks provide glimpses of what was being sold, at least openly, across the counter.

The daybooks of Aaron Lopez from the 1750s show that he carried on numerous transactions in tea, most of it Bohea tea obtained from the Dutch in the Caribbean (NHS 2). We have found that on November 23, 1756 Lopez sold in his retail outlet one chest of tea (NHS 3). This suggests that the original packing in chests still prevailed and that the origin of the goods was not concealed—either from customs or the public. Merchants during the 1750s traded without fear of enforcement on the Newport end. The Caribbean was a different matter, as the British presence during 1759 and 1760 in the Caribbean meant the virtual cessation of northern trade there by 1761 and 1762 (Bigelow 1930, I, VII: 65). This trend is hard to discern in the account books, however, for we see a surge of exotic goods in Lopez's daybook in 1758; mohair buttons, shalloon, and silk romals were sold along with silk alamodes in 1759 (NHS 4). It is difficult to establish if these goods were shipped via Great Britain, but the extra freight, port charges, and some loss in drawbacks would have been adequate motivation for the profit-minded Newporter to circumvent those costs by smuggling. The early 1760s again experienced increased sales in mohair buttons after their ban, as well as in Barcelona silk handkerchiefs, coutreaux (*sic*), and even "rich black Persian silk"—undoubtedly a non-English import (NHS 5). However, Lopez was not directly involved in the Caribbean trade at this time. He sent few ships before the four he sent in 1766 (Bigelow 1930, I, VII: 19). These goods, then, Lopez obtained in trade with other merchants more active in the Caribbean, or he was having his whaling ships return with the goods. Lopez continued to deal in tea throughout the sixties, as well as in China bowls and dishes (NHS 6).

We see very little evidence of evasion in the historical documents prior to 1763–64, when the British escalated their enforcement of trade laws to eliminate smuggling. Bigelow (1930, II, III: 6) says that the usual method of smuggling from Surinam and St. Eustatius before 1763 was for a merchant "to load a few chests of tea and a few bolts of duck between his hogsheads of molasses. This plan appears to have been very general." Bridenbaugh echoes this, but claims that the tea and cloth were hidden among wine pipes (Bridenbaugh 1955: 66); he also suggests that Lopez stopped doing this after 1763, but we know that only Lopez's whaling vessels touched St. Eustatius or Surinam.

STRATEGIES AND TACTICS

There is clear behavioral change in smuggling after 1763–64. The stress caused by the presence of men-of-war and the fear of being seized and condemned compelled merchants to develop more clandestine techniques in their smuggling. These behavioral changes were expressed in the material culture of the time, particularly the means by which foreign goods were smuggled into the colonies. Furthermore, we can also see a distinct shift in local attitudes toward the smuggling trade. Suppression of smuggling became a politically volatile issue; it reinforced, at an ideological level, the determination of local merchants to continue to prosper at the expense of the crown. One consequence of this was greater caution in avoidance of official authority. We see great caution in owners' orders for this period. There are separate letters to factors in Surinam and St. Eustatius (that could be thrown overboard if necessary) and detailed instructions about how to smuggle successfully, without risk. Instructions about smuggling techniques, absent from official orders, appeared with increasing regularity after 1763. Adaptation to British enforcement can also be seen in the

157

shift in geographical locales for smuggling in Narragansett Bay and the use of off-loading facilities outside the bay.

Aaron Lopez made explicit his plan to evade detection in tea smuggling when he wrote during 1764 to his agent in Holland:

I have reason to think that the proceeds of such a Loading with the addition of some bills of Excg. being invested in Linseed Oyle & Bohea Tea, put up in Casks made English fashion to contain from 30 to 40 Gallons & shipped directly to St. Eustatia to the address of your Correspondent there . . . (Bigelow 1930, II,III: 6; NHS 7).

Lopez admitted that his reason for packing illegal commodities in special casks was to avoid risk (ibid.). The size of the cask suggests that a tierce (of approximately forty-two gallons) was the vessel used. However, letters from Lopez to his Amsterdam agents in the latter 1760s indicate that hogsheads of sixty-three gallons capacity or larger were employed by Lopez to transport illegal goods.

Lopez was not alone in his evasive tactics. The Browns of Providence began to employ similar devices in 1764 when the brig *George* was sent to Surinam, but cleared for Barbados. If Captain Whipple failed to purchase molasses at a reasonable price, then he was to buy Russian duck, "which you will pack into Dry melasses Hogsheads or other proper Package, and secret in ye most Effectual manner possible and proceed home" (Bigelow 1930, II, III: 7; Hedges 1968: 44–45).

Prior to 1763 the Narragansett Bay smugglers landed most of their illicit goods on Conanicut Island (Fig. 7.2) west of Aquidneck Island, where Newport is located. Taylor's Wharf was a favorite off-loading spot, used by the privateers during the wars and by smugglers. We have not yet found Taylor's Wharf, but it is perhaps located near Taylor's Point, on the east side of the island. Small boats would subsequently carry the goods across the bay where they would be collected by wagon for final transport into the warehouses of Newport. Taylor's Wharf and Conanicut Island were ideal locations as long as the customs officials remained without assistance on water. But British men-of-war in Narragansett Bay changed this pattern of smuggling. It became too dangerous to off-load on Conanicut Island because the smugglers risked detection and possible seizure. Newporters adapted to this stress by altering their tactics. Captain Whipple, in the employ of the Browns,

Figure 7.2. Narragansett Bay and the surrounding communities.

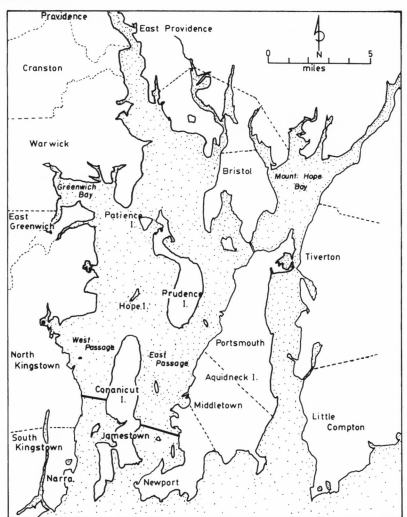

received careful instructions from the Browns in 1765 about how to return from Surinam:

As times are now we think if we can once Get the Brigg buy Conamicutt [Conanicut] without their knowing, in Newport, of her arivel Unload and send her Cargo pritty safely without much danger of being Seized, but how the severity of the Officers may be by the time of your arrival we Cant Say, . . . we Desire you'l Either Com in to the west end of the lite House (which is now in Very Good order in the Ninte [night] or in the Secunnit way and proceed up as fast [to Providence] as you Can with the Vessill in Case the Wind is so as Can Come along as a man Can buy [by] Land, or other wise Lett your mate Mr. Hopkins on Shore to proceed to us as fast as possible, not stopping for Nite nor foul weither nor telling no person from wenth he Come and we will meet the Brig in Schows and as many hands as needful to unload (JCB, vol. 64 SF; Nicholas Brown & Co. to Capt. Abraham Whipple, Jan. 13, 1765; Bigelow 1930, II, III: 16–17; Hedges 1968: 45).

The plan as set out by the Browns was that Whipple should pass to the west of Conanicut Island or pass by Sakonnet Point up the Sakonnet passage east of Rhode Island (now Aquidneck Island). Failure to make Providence would mean off-loading at night into small boats in either of these passages.

The reduction of the molasses duty to one penny per gallon in 1766 obviated any need to smuggle that commodity. But duties continued on other commodities and rum from the West Indies was prohibited, thus encouraging smuggling. The Newport merchants continued their clandestine activities. By 1768 enforcement had escalated further, even though customs officers at Newport felt helpless. The Champlins were involved in the prohibited rum trade, as most merchants were, and took precautions to avoid British officials. George Champlin wrote to his brother in Newport from the West Indies in 1768:

. . . shall take 18 or 20 thousand good sug. [sugar] and the Remainder of the Cargoes in Rum. If I get home by the 20th May as it appears here I shall go in the Secunnit way and desire you will leave me a letter at Clarks on Situwist [Sachuest] Point how to Conduct if no danger can come in the Harbour say as usual otherwise at my Arrival there will acquaint you of it and you can send a small Vessel and take the Rum out Run up the River with it take some Wood on deck and Cary it to Town and I can come a round in the Harbour way with the Sug. which will be a Set of Ballast (NHS 8; Bigelow 1930, II, III: 22).

160

OTHER TACTICS

The desire for French goods continued to run high after 1763. Some commodities such as sugar remained attractive because they were cheaper and higher quality than what the British islands produced. French manufactured goods remained attractive to the elite because of their limited supply and distinctiveness. There is no indication that there was any abatement of illegal French goods into Newport in the years following 1763. In fact, merchants such as Aaron Lopez went out of their way to devise clandestine plans that would lead to the successful purchase and transportation of French goods back to the willing markets of Newport. The effort which Lopez invested in the formulation of schemes that might gain him access to French goods is illustrated in his detailed orders to Captain Heffernan, master of his sloop, *Lovely Lass*, on October 24, 1770 in Newport. The bill of lading openly consigns goods to Martinique. After first directing Captain Heffernan to proceed to Martinique, Lopez provided a set of instructions that is brilliant testimony to the behavior required to gain entry to the French port.

If there is any probability of trading your cargo to advantage without running the risk of a seizure, to prevent which, I am to recommend *you'll (before your arrival) stove most of your water casks, so as you may enter under pretences of distress.* Soon as you come with your Boat into the Harbour first apply to the Commandant to whom you are to present your request in want of Water. The Consequence of which will most probably be that he will direct you under the care of a Soldier to the Governor, to whom you are to repeat the same distressed situation as you did to the Commandant & I am no way doubtful that the Governor will grant you a permission to refit: when you have obtained that Liberty, you are then to apply to some of the principal merchants & acquaint them with what you have to sell: If they are want of it they will in course intercede with the Governor to grant you a permission to dispose of such Goods as they are in need of, which will once give you a sure change of a [illegible] trade; but if there should be a glut of such articles as you have, the merchants will neither intercede for you nor do I see any advantage in stopping any longer at that Port to run the risk of a seizure (NHS 9).

It seems improbable that a master would risk the possibility that the ruse might fail. Were Lopez's ships and those of other merchants outfitted with extra water casks? This is a question that cannot be answered at present from the historical documents, but it is an observation that may help to explain possible anomalies observed in the archaeology of shipwrecks belonging to this period.

Noteworthy in Lopez's discourse on commercial duplicity is the absence of any mention of goods that may have been purchased from the French at Martinique. This is undoubtedly purposeful, for an itemization of illegal goods to be purchased in his captain's orders would have been an unnecessary and obvious risk. Such orders were usually communicated orally from owner to master. In the instance of the *Lovely Lass*'s call at Martinique, the sale of goods to Martinique merchants, if successful, probably was not conducted in hard currency or bills of exchange. The transaction was very likely conducted as barter, with Heffernan trading goods mentioned in his bill of lading for French goods—perhaps wine, cloth, and ceramics of equal value.

We do not know if Heffernan succeeded in his Martinique ruse, but if the outcome left him with surplus goods, then he was instructed to sail on to St. Lucia where he was to obtain rum, molasses, coffee, cocoa, and sugar at the cheapest price that would assure the best profits. If he failed to procure sufficient illicit goods at St. Lucia, then he was to go on to other islands until he found the best market.

However, we know that less than one month after his departure from Newport Captain Heffernan was in St. Eustatius, the Dutch entrepôt in the Windward Islands. The chance preservation of an account kept by Samson Mears, Lopez's agent in St. Eustatius, suggests that St. Eustatius was the primary port of destination for the *Lovely Lass* (NHS 9). In the last section of his orders, which are partly destroyed, Lopez told Heffernan to go on to St. Eustatia where he was to deliver "the annexed letter to Mr. Samson Mears . . . [who] may have some effects of mine to ship. . . ." Lopez further said to pay Mears whatever charges he incurred for storage of "such effects as he delivers you" (NHS 9).

It is difficult to discern what goods made up the "effects," but we see from other documents that this linguistic term was a euphemistic reference to illicit goods. Mears's account from St. Eustatius indicates that Heffernan disposed of all 19 hogsheads of codfish, all 15 tierces of rice, 3,400 staves (400 more than listed on the bill of lading), 40 barrels of fish (probably the Monhaygden), the parcel of Danish money, 1,600 or 3,000 bunches of onions, and one of 22 cheeses. In return

Mears supplied 29 hogsheads of rum and a new mainsail, likely made with foreign duck (NHS 9). We do not know if the rum was the "effects" or if other goods were handled under separate account with Heffernan and Mears. The annexed letter to Mears from Lopez undoubtedly refers to contraband goods. The mainsail purchase was planned in Newport for St. Eustatius because of the higher quality of illegal, foreign duck. It is a virtual certainty that the contraband goods conveyed to Newport by the *Lovely Lass* compelled Lopez to instruct his ship's master, "if possible enter into this Harbour early in the Evening that we may have time to do the Needful with your Cargo" (NHS 9).

Lopez's explicit instruction to enter Narragansett Bay in early evening, rather than during the day, admits a concern to avoid detection by British men-of-war or customs officials. The early evening arrival would allow sufficient time to unload and transport illicit goods during the night. The next day the *Lovely Lass* would have put into port with her legitimate goods, if any.

It is apparent that by 1768 the coves and beaches of the Sakonnet passage were the preferred off-loading points, with small boats bringing products to shore. Customs records from the time indicate that this was not the only change that had taken place. Frustration by customs officers over the lack of government support and unified opposition by the local populace ran high in 1768. In a letter to the Commissioners of Trade, April 22, 1768, a customs collector in Newport lamented:

from want of support from the government here, and from the spirit that has prevailed so much of late throughout the colonies there are so many discouragements and embarrasments in an officer's doing his duty as to almost put it out of his power to behave with that fidelity . . . that the service of revenue requires (NHS 10).

Even when the customs officers successfully discovered and seized goods, the items were sometimes robbed out of the customs warehouse (NHS 11), as happened with molasses seized from the brig *Betsy* in 1768.

As stress mounted in the smuggling business, the Newport merchants began to develop dumping areas further afield, out of the immediate territory of the men-of-war and customs officials, as well as improved methods of concealment. Martha's Vineyard and Nantucket apparently became popular entrepôts for illicit goods, though we know this only through the testimony of the customs officers. Ships sailing from the

West Indies or Europe with illicit goods or commodities subject to duty would unload their cargoes at one of the two islands. Then the goods were loaded onto small fishing boats which sailed into Newport unmolested. As Newport customs officers became aware of this tactic, they obtained an order issued by the commissioners "to make seizure of all vessels and their cargoes that shall arrive from the said island of Nantucket without proper documents" (NHS 12). The local customs officers informed the commissioners that neither Martha's Vineyard nor Nantucket had the capacity to produce the mass of goods coming in on nondeclaring ships from the two islands (NHS 12, October 22, 1768).

DISCUSSION OF CHANGES

It is clear, then, that the Rhode Island merchants-smugglers adapted their behavior during the 1763–68 period to accommodate for the increased efforts to suppress their trade. They began to secrete goods such as tea in casks that resembled those of English manufacture, so that when they returned from the Caribbean with false papers obtained at St. Eustatius or at some British port their cargo appeared to be uniformly English in character. The use of molasses hogsheads (fixed at 100 gallons during George II's reign) for textiles similarly shows attempts to secret goods more successfully in the holds of ships. The first documented instance we have of English-style hogsheads used for contraband goods is their use to convey French molasses from Hispaniola during the English embargo during the Seven Years War. This innovation arose out of the stress created by English attempts to suppress the colonial trade with the enemy (Bigelow 1930, I, IV: 57). These changes should be possible to document in the archaeology of shipwrecks from the period. Similar patterning in shipwrecks from other historical and cultural contexts should mark similar adaptations to economic stress caused by political regulation. The documents alert us to the possibility that there may be great subtlety in the cargo holds of wrecked ships. The necessity for careful analysis of the contents and form of all casks, hogsheads, tierces, and barrels is apparent. For pre-1763 vessels involved in the Caribbean the evidence suggests that random goods such as textiles may have been scattered among the larger cargo or buried beneath the ballast.

164

TECHNIQUES FOR WINES, SPIRITS, CLOTH, AND TEA

We know from bills of lading that the Newport merchants sometimes transported European spirits directly to North America. The brig *Royal Charlotte* with William Pinneger as master sailed from Amsterdam during August 1769 to Bona Vista, Newfoundland with a cargo that included twenty-four cases of spirits such as gin and brandy (NHS 13). These spirits likely made their way to Newport with a cargo of fish loaded in Newfoundland. Given the times, it is reasonable to suggest that these goods were probably repacked into hogsheads or other casks, possibly with fish. Only six months early Pinneger had received elaborate orders, both false and genuine, from the Vernons. His genuine orders reflect the increased caution exercised by the Newport merchant-smugglers after 1763:

it's best to Fill your lower hold with Rum take a few cask of Very good Sugars . . . in your hatchway and Proceed here go in the Back side of the Island at Either End and Give us Intelligence these of as soon as Privately Possible, if you Meet with any Men-of-War or Cutter, as there is two In this Port at Present, you must say you Put in Distress for want of Provisions, Water or something Absolutely Necessary . . . concealing Every Paper that may give the Least Intimation of your stopping here (NHS 14; Bigelow 1930, II, III: 20–21).

The archaeological evidence from Newport's Queen Anne Square supports the interpretation that Dutch gin was a regular illegal import in the years before the Revolution. It is clear, furthermore, that the elite of Newport liked to drink foreign wines, other than the Madeira that entered without duty until the mid-1760s.

The pre-1763 illegal wine trade into Newport is difficult to document. The open operation of smuggling may have allowed the importation of French and nonexempted Portuguese wines in their original casks. But after the 1764 Revenue Act wines were subjected to heavier duties.

It appears that wine was illegally imported by shipping it in English-style pipes (126 gallons) so the origins would be camouflaged. In 1759 Mayne in Lisbon supplied Johannes Roderick with 40,000 gallons (about 317 pipes) of white wine in English-style pipes, presumably to avoid duties on non-Madeira wine. In 1767 Aaron Lopez received an order from Mayne in Lisbon for 10,000 pipe staves, with their length stipulated at 4 feet 10 inches, the English measure (NHS 15). During November of 1768 we find that Lopez ordered four thousand double-length red oak staves from a local farmer (NHS 16). We may surmise that these pipe staves were destined for the illegal importation of foreign wines. Ships of the period often carried coopers to make up hogsheads to receive West Indian rum and molasses, and many coopers worked in St. Eustatius, where foreign wines could easily be transferred to the "English" pipes. We see this as another important material by-product of adjustments in smuggling behavior to stress caused by increased enforcement.

Aaron Lopez actively pursued his illegal trade in wine, although not always in pipes. In the late summer of 1772 after the burning of the *Gaspee*, the pressure of British enforcement may have fallen off sufficiently to lull Lopez into incautiousness. Ezra Stiles (Dexter 1901, I: 270) comments in his journal entry of August 25:

The Man o'War yesterday seized his [Lopez's] vessel and wines by Accident and Folly of the people who in 5 row Boats were endeavoring the night before to run 91 Quarter Casks of Wine. The Vessel and Wines will be condemned— but it is said that they will be set up at a Trifle and Lopez will bid them off at far less than Duties so that he can make his voyage good.

Stiles in the same entry commented extensively on the corruption of the local collector, Charles Dudly (Dexter 1901: 270–71); his commentary shows, however, that the outright bribery that prevailed in earlier times had grown more subtle, more circumspect. Lopez's captains, for example, were exempted from swearing at the customhouse and made their entries without oath. The merchant-prince's refusal to support the non-Importation Agreement meant certain advantages with customs, and his largesse with Dudly was known to those who saw wines and fruits delivered to the collector's house (Dexter 1901, I: 270).

The clandestine trade in tea was actively pursued throughout the period of heightened tension after 1763. Accounts of daily sales show a fairly constant activity in teas, most of which were never taxed. Along with tea came textiles from the Far East and Europe, as well as other goods such as Barcelona silk handkerchiefs, which were plentifully represented in the retail sales of Newport merchants until 1775. The correspondence between Aaron Lopez and his Amsterdam agents from

1767 to 1774 shows how the trade in Russian duck, tea, and other goods was conducted. As we have seen, Lopez initiated the suggestion that the tea be shipped in casks during 1764. In early 1767 he responded to an inquiry from Charles Crommelin about the sales of his "two chests of fine tea" (NHS 17). His use of the term *chest* may mean that the repacking of tea into casks had not yet been effected, but it is more likely in direct response to an inquiry that used the term. In July of 1767 Lopez acknowledged the receipt of six bales of Russian duck free of damage from Daniel Crommelin & Sons. On the 19th of July, 1770, Crommelin & Sons wrote Lopez to advise him that they had shipped him " Eight Casks Tea Repacked in 12 Barrels . . . bound to St. Eustatia . . ." (NHS 18). During October, six months later, Lopez wrote them requesting other goods, including Russian duck. On the 26th of November, 1770, his agents in Holland replied:

We duly noted the further contents of your letter; & as we are no less inclined to cultivate your correspondence we have now shipped on your account . . . the sundry articles you requested us to send you via Surinam.

You'll observe that we've omitted the China Cups and Saucers as the price is high & could not find any of wch the fashion would suit your market and taste. Of the Ravens Duck we've only sent you 16%: as there was no more remaining of that parcel (NHS 19).

Three weeks later, on December 16, Crommelin & Sons again wrote Lopez to inform him that they had shipped seven barrels containing five chests of tea to Surinam consigned to Captain Hathaway, but that they had to hurry to get the barrels in one day, having to take what they could get (NHS 20).

Three months later, in February 1771, Lopez instructed Captain Hathaway of his sloop *Mary* to proceed to St. Eustatius, contact Samson Mears, sell his cargo, and invest the proceeds in molasses, Bohea tea, Russian duck, and coffee (NHS 21). Another port of call was undoubtedly Surinam, where Hathaway would have collected the tea and other consumer goods shipped from Holland. While details are not available, we suggest that the dry goods and other items were likely disguised in a manner similar to that used to conceal the tea.

Some hint of how dry goods were smuggled in Lopez's ships may possibly be seen in other Lopez orders. His orders to Captain Brotherton Daggett dated November 20, 1771, told Daggett to obtain the best-proof rum and molasses in the islands near Antigua until he came

167

to St. Eustatius. There he was to use money obtained in prior sales and "Pay it OUT in the few Articles I have told you if to be had reasonable" (NHS 22). Lopez's use of the generic "articles" is similar to "effects," but in this letter we obtain a hint that Lopez may have referred to illegal dry goods: "Should Mr. Mears or any other Gent[n] there incline to ship any effects . . . you may Receive them on board *taking care to have them stowed in a Dry place in the Vessell*" (NHS 22; italics ours). It is likely that goods sensitive to wet conditions were also packed in hogsheads in a manner similar to that used for the illegal Bohea tea imported by Lopez. However, there is also the possibility that a "Dry place" may have referred to special, false bulkheads constructed to accommodate smuggled goods.

There is a standard against which North American smuggling can be measured. English smuggling reached its height during the mid-eighteenth century (Atton and Holland 1908; Chatterton 1912; Hoon 1938). It was not uncommon during the 1740s for armed gangs of hundreds of men to accompany smuggled goods as they left the coast and were transported inland. Tea and French brandy were among the more common items smuggled. But the English smugglers worked under far more stress than their American counterparts. The customs service was much larger, more complex, and better equipped. In Newport in 1769 the collector begged for a boat to police one of the most active North American ports, whereas in the second half of the eighteenth century the English added boat after boat. Between 1763 and 1783 the number of armed cutters nearly doubled from twenty-two to forty-two, and the tonnage, number of men, and number of guns increased by 300 percent (Hoon 1938: 178). When the commissioners added large boats, the smugglers resorted to light craft—useful in the shallows where the large boats couldn't run. Brandy runners used lug sails while the customs boats with ordinary sails often stood by, unable to follow.

The English smugglers developed a repertoire of techniques that resemble those of North America. The use of forged papers was common, as well as bribery of officials—especially the tide-waiters who stayed on a vessel until it was cleared (Hoon 1938: 255). Because the English customs service was more active and operated over a much smaller coastline, smugglers there were more likely to be apprehended than were the smugglers of New England. The English smuggler developed a variety of techniques to avoid detection, especially in the

1820s. Some of these techniques included structural modification of ships to accommodate illegal loads. The construction of false bulkheads to create special compartments was employed and became so widespread that special officials were charged with measuring the ship inside and outside to detect such hiding places. We have no record of this type of compartment in the ships carrying goods from the Caribbean to North America. Nor is there evidence for false bottoms, false bows, false keelsons, or hollow planks (Chatterton 1912: 196 passim). Shipwrecks of this period may, in fact, hold material information of this sort. If the colonial smuggler turned to false hogsheads, secreting under ballast, packing goods inside flour, and mislabeling goods, then it is possible that structural alteration of ships was also practiced.

The details of the illicit trade in consumer goods are, very clearly, elusive and imprecise. But there is sufficient evidence that we cannot conclude, as does Bigelow (1930, II, III: 4), that such goods were scarce. For the elite of Newport, they are a critical part of the public display of status. The 1764 prohibition on hair buttons, for example, does not affect the continued trade in that commodity and the sale of mohair bottons in Newport (e.g., Lopez daybooks 1764–72). Nor do prohibitive duties on spirits and wine inhibit elite consumption. To the contrary, the regulations stimulated ingenious innovations to avoid detection. Many of the changes in smuggling behavior that resulted from stress—fear of seizure and loss of income—have left material signatures that we should be able to discern in the archaeological record.

A PROGRAM OF RESEARCH

The historical context that we have provided shows that smuggling in the two decades before the Revolutionary War is a complex behavioral phenomenon that is subject to change through time. It is a subject that has been reduced to simplicity in our historical literature, and it is an activity that leaves only a very fragmentary record because of its highly secretive nature. We have chosen to concentrate on those behaviors that most readily leave signatures in the material record. However, the use of false papers and the corruption of officials are equally important and deserve much closer attention as part of a larger attempt to establish a more complex cultural context for smuggling in Rhode Island.

The political and ideological ramifications of smuggling activity, though, are perhaps most important to our historical identity. Smuggling and the conflicts that arose out of it were a significant contribution to the formation of an ideology of resistance to arbitrary political authority. The innovations that led to more successful techniques are material manifestations of the successful opposition to British authority; this success was an important prelude to the Revolution.

While we know that exotic goods such as French ceramics and Barcelona silk handkerchiefs entered through smuggling, we lack sound evidence for the full range of goods, how their volume varied through time, and how they were smuggled. Did the technology developed to conduct clandestine operations involve alterations in ship construction as well as accompanying changes in the paraphernalia of the shipping industry, that is, false bottoms in wine pipes and so on? Much of this technology remains a mystery that can only be investigated through the excavation of shipwrecks.

The art of smuggling is an old one. It has been conducted in a variety of historical and geographical contexts. As anthropologists our reasoning leads us to search for general principles which can be extended beyond the realm of our specific case studies. Surely, parallels can be drawn between the adaptive behavior we have witnessed in eighteenth-century Rhode Island and that of other groups of smugglers throughout history. The excavation of shipwrecks can provide us with knowledge about the adaptive measures employed by American colonial smugglers. The clandestine measures visible in the use of false compartments, camouflaged containers, and other techniques provides the archaeologist with a set of comparative constructs in the study of the changing technology of seaborne smuggling. Once the congruence between behavior and the material record is established, these principles can be applied to other eras and areas to enable us to understand better the behavioral significance of similar patterns in the material record of shipwrecks.

We have looked at history with the view that it provides us glimpses of cultural process, of behavioral change that we need to understand better because it impinges directly upon our ideas about who we are and how and why certain aspects of our culture have developed over time. We have found that each domain of historical documentation provides a distinctive, partial, and biased account from which we may derive a cultural construct. Daybooks and store blotters, for example, provide selective but detailed merchandising evidence for some categories of illicit goods and their volume through time; letters from shipowners to agents provide a different perspective, one that is more consumed with strategy and tactics of the smuggling trade. Synthesis of these data allows us to develop a systemic context, wherein behavior and material culture are integrated. Once we have that systemic context derived from history and archaeology, then we may proceed to ask questions of anthropological value that shipwreck archaeology can help to solve.

8
Land and Water, Urban Life, and Boats:

Underwater Reconnaissance
in the Patuxent River
on Chesapeake Bay[1]

MARK P. LEONE

Department of Anthropology,
University of Maryland, College Park

The Patuxent River flows east into Chesapeake Bay between Washington, D.C. on the south and Baltimore, Maryland on the north. The river is 110 miles long, drains 25 percent of the state of Maryland, and has been a settled area since the early seventeenth century. The Patuxent River is among the first to be subject to a survey of drowned archaeological resources, and the survey is among the first to be guided by a systematic sampling strategy carried out in a turbid, black-water

1. Donald Shomette shared all his data, reports, and ideas generously for this paper, and I am grateful for his cooperation over the course of the year it took to do this essay. He has granted permission for use of his material and has read this paper sympathetically and carefully. I assume responsibility for errors and interpretation.

Of the two volumes of the 1981 Shomette citation, Ralph E. Eshelman prepared the section on the geomorphology of the Patuxent drainage basin. The rest of the work was prepared by Shomette.

Wayne Clark, Administrator for Archaeology at the Maryland Historical Trust, made copies of Shomette's reports available to me on generous loans.

Dr. Ann Palkovich brought Fernand Braudel to my attention.

riverine environment. The survey is presented here in order to demonstrate the potential of the underwater archaeology of rivers and of an anthropological treatment of the results. The paper is a summary of the survey and also presents a hypothesis to explain some of its findings.

The Patuxent is one of the Chesapeake's chief rivers, and its history and archaeology show a close and changing relationship between underwater remains like boats and wharf supports and aboveground remains like abandoned towns and changing crops in the fields along the river's banks. The survey revealed that a dynamic, evolving relationship existed between features like boat form, length of boat life, and the condition of the land along the river. It showed that boat form changed as the shape of the river changed, and that the river's evolution was shaped by the economy of the land. The hypothesis built on the data established by the survey is that the relationship among land use, river conditions, towns, and boat life is a function of capitalism, as a particular kind of economic system, and is not just a function of ecological change or industrial development.

First, the survey of submerged cultural resources should be described. All the following material is drawn from Shomette (1979) and Shomette and Eshelman (1981). The Patuxent River is 110 miles long, and its width varies from a few feet in the upper reaches to over 2 miles near the entrance into Chesapeake Bay. Only 50 miles of it were navigable by ocean going vessels during the colonial era. Less than 3 miles of it are today navigable by ocean-going-sized craft, though small vessels occasionally penetrate higher. The use of the river, important to Europeans since the 1580s, became intensive in the seventeenth century. Plantations and small towns along the river were settled in the seventeenth century and remained agricultural into the eighteenth. Tobacco was the chief crop until the area began cultivating grains in the mid-eighteenth century, and it went back to tobacco in the nineteenth century. The river also played a role in the Revolution, and during the War of 1812 it provided the launching place for the successful British effort to burn Washington.

Before the archaeological survey, it was well known that the river contained a number of wrecks; although the documentation had not been fully studied, the potential richness for underwater research was clear. This survey was designed, conducted, and extensively reported by Donald Shomette. It was sponsored by both the Calvert Maritime

174

Museum and the Maryland Historical Trust, two agencies deeply con-cerned with the scientific recovery of archaeological resources.

Shomette chose four geologically and historically representative tran-sects of the Patuxent to survey (Fig. 8.1) and covered each completely, including adjoining riverbanks. He interviewed local people for oral history about both wrecks in and uses of the river. Since the river is muddy now, and shallow in many places, sophisticated remote-sensing instrumentation was used to aid in discovery, and specialized high-resolution low-light underwater video units were employed to assist in hands-on survey and evaluations.

Within each of the four sample areas all indications of human activity were recorded. Most of the remains were boats, with the most impressive being the flotilla built during the War of 1812 to protect the Chesapeake shores from British raids. The United States Chesa-peake Flotilla of 18 vessels constructed in Baltimore and St. Michaels, Maryland and commanded by Commodore Barney, had to be scuttled in the Patuxent in 1814 to avoid capture by the British who were on their way to Washington. Shomette (1981) discovered the location of the sunken flotilla and recovered the contents of one of the largely intact but buried boats archaeologically.

Shomette's survey produced extensive maps of the archaeological resources of the varied sections of the river. From these he will draw a model to project the density, date, and the significance of the rest of the river and like riverine systems throughout the Maryland–Virginia Tidewater. This is a well-known method in cultural-resource man-agement and is important on a river like the Patuxent, which slices across the rapidly expanding area between Washington and Baltimore. New projects along the river have daily impact, disturbing its banks and bottom and thus the wealth of archaeological material buried there. Bridges, roads, sewers, subdivisions, and dredging crews all affect the the condition of the river, and one of the aims of the underwater survey was to build a holistic predictive model of the resource base for the whole river so that sensible preservation of its archaeology could be planned.

The survey and its results nonetheless serve other purposes and answer other questions. One of these is whether the results of under-water archaeology, which involve expensive, difficult, and time-con-suming procedures, yield information available no other way. Shomette's work has given an affirmative answer. The underwater survey found

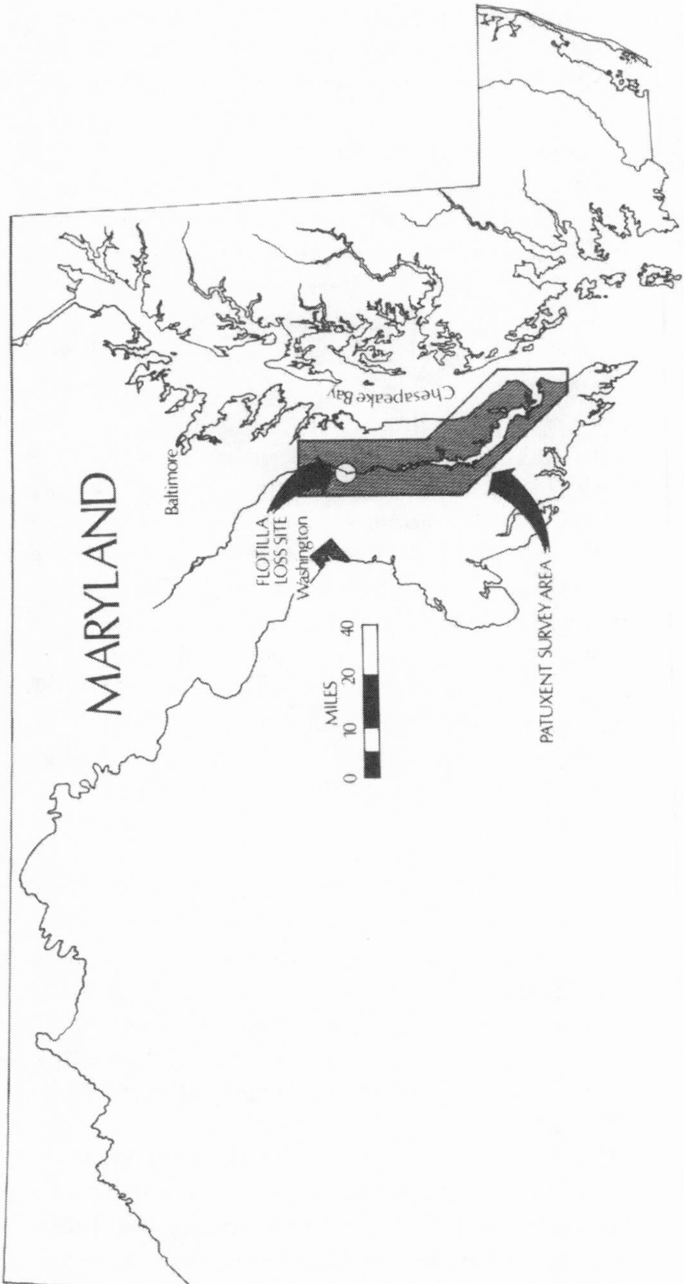

Figure 8.1. Patuxent submerged cultural resource survey area.

and recorded examples of all the boat forms used on the river from the earliest colonial times up through the present. Everyone knew that the Patuxent was gradually silting up and had been since the eighteenth century. The source of silt was unclear, and in the late seventeenth century the colonial government passed ordinances against dumping ballast in the river to prevent blockage. But even with our own extensive knowledge of erosion, which is the cause of the blockage, we did not know that boat bottoms became shallower through time as a way of adapting to changing requirements. It is usually presumed in the history of navigation that techniques come first and are then applied to seafaring. Thus, we do not normally presume that changes in the water environment cause changes in vessels, as Shomette's survey showed.

Vessel form, vessel life, landings, and wharves all record the ecological degradation of the Patuxent River, whose history is microcosmic for the other rivers of the bay and for the bay itself. The Patuxent survey revealed that vessel bottoms flattened, decks appeared on boats of certain sizes, oyster tongs evolved, wharves became longer and more complex with the advent of steam and later the internal combustion engine, and river towns died and disappeared. The changing river bottom and the adjustment of the river traffic along it reflect the progression of commerce and capital up the river in the seventeenth and eighteenth centuries, and then the flight back down the river, reaching a peak with the War of 1812. The materials from the river show its gradual silting up, which is reflected in the places boats are abandoned. The survey provides the latest dates boats of specific depth and size were built and used. It provides the dates for the sinking of useless craft and shows the decline in water traffic, the development of wharves, the rate of bank erosion, and the growth and decline of towns. All this focuses attention on the river itself, not on the land, and it shows the unique material provided by archaeology and unavailable from documentary sources.

Shomette surveyed 100 percent of the four areas he designated for survey. He documented 142 sites specifically, 120 in the river directly, of which 10 percent were located and investigated. He presents a complete list of vessel losses in the river by date, which he compiled from documents and which was one means for locating vessels. Lists of partially inundated or abandoned river port towns and landings were also compiled, along with figures on siltation and erosion rates. These provide the context for understanding drowned resources, as do the

177

dates and data on naval battles from the American Revolution and War of 1812.

Shomette's historical survey, which accompanies the archaeology, shows the economic transitions occurring on the land along the river since the seventeenth century. Tobacco plantations of between 1,000 and 10,000 acres were the first form of settlement along the Patuxent. Although the Maryland proprietary government insisted on settled towns from the early 1630s, none emerged until well into the seventeenth century. Economically, by the mid-eighteenth century grain replaced tobacco, and it required more land and more intensive cultivation methods. Town life, never truly substantial, beginning to grow in the late seventeenth century, reached a peak during the eighteenth, and all but died by the early nineteenth century. The British ruined the Patuxent economy during the War of 1812 by capturing boats, looting and burning plantations, and devastating towns. Destructive raids launched from the British squadron wrecked the agricultural economy of the Tidewater. The only goal that eluded them was Baltimore, the celebration of whose escape in "The Star Spangled Banner" takes on greater meaning when one understands that between 1812 and 1814 the economy of the bay collapsed and many towns, including Washington, were burned. Baltimore, Annapolis, Norfolk, and Richmond were the only big towns to escape.

By the end of the War of 1812 Baltimore and Annapolis, both near but not on the Patuxent, had attracted the area's population, commerce, and capital. Even though ferries which carried goods and passengers up and down the Patuxent continued to run throughout the nineteenth and twentieth centuries, the river's productive days were over. Even shellfishing, which developed after the mid-nineteenth century, formed an important local industry for less than a century. In 1900, 50 percent of the income of Calvert County, at the Patuxent mouth, was derived from oyster fishing, with grounds and beds up as far as Benedict, Maryland. The industry involved 400 boats, and is now completely dead. Between the world wars the armed services, particularly the navy, bought large tracts around Chesapeake Bay, including some along the Patuxent, used some of the lands and waters for testing arms, and decimated the shellfish beds. Now the Patuxent is ecologically dead; in many areas it is a sewer. In places, 70–100 percent of its flow is effluvium; in 1965, the Patuxent carried 285 tons of silt annually per square mile. Erosion was first noted in 1707 at

Anne Arundel Manor, and extrapolating backward from the present into the eighteenth century, geologists calculate that the area along the Patuxent has been losing .01 percent of its land annually through erosion.

From the underwater archaeology and the archival research came the conclusion that the originally clear and provident Patuxent had been degraded by the very people who lived off it. The silt filled the river's bottom, created shoals, blocked channels, and filled whole branches beyond use by even the most shallow boats. Plowing and consequent erosion from the tobacco and grain fields along its shores, and intensive gravel mining, carried large volumes of soil into the river, keeping it continually muddy. The mud settled out and, once deposited, changed the river's shape. Shomette argues convincingly that the agricultural practices of over three centuries of farming along the river's banks and upper reaches ruined the chief corridor needed to get the farm produce to market. He concludes that farming practices clogged the river with silt, closed its smaller branches, caused boat form to change, wharves to be altered, and towns to be abandoned. This argument, so often used to describe the impact of European commercial practices, states that environmental degradation, technological readjustment, the quality of town life, and ultimately productivity itself were all a dynamic cycle. A river and its lands made possible the creation of considerable wealth, which, once created, was transferred beyond the area that created it. Care was not taken of the source of wealth in nature, and ultimately a resiliant environment, unable to regenerate itself fast enough, ceased producing because the cycles protecting it were not considered worth observing. Thus, the argument goes, commercialism and capitalism destroy their own environment. In this form the argument is familiar, accurate, and depressingly complete.

The argument that economic development and ecological degradation are tied draws its force from descriptions of the environment before pollution. The early Patuxent was clear, full of fish, and navigable into its upper reaches. It is understood that this primeval condition was not altered by American Indian use, which, if not the acme of wisdom it is purported to be, was at least conservative in most senses. The question is, What did the Europeans do to ruin the land and water that the Indians did not do? The answer is, at least in the case of Shomette's work on the Patuxent, they farmed in a new and destructive way. They plowed widely, deeply, and often the wrong way; failed to see the connection between erosion of land and deposition of that land as silt; and, once they realized the connection, either could or would do nothing about it. The dynamic of wealth creation and wealth destruction is thus the product of a commercial farming technique.

In the context of underwater archaeology this is a powerful conclusion. It has been derived from submerged materials interpreted through surviving documents. Certainly the conclusion is not unique, nor is that claim made. The finding probably could have been reached without underwater work. Using only documents, however, the conclusion would only have been inferential and qualitative. The conclusion would not have focused on the river and probably would have missed the force of the destructive dynamic. Land-based research would likely have underestimated the ties between the river's early condition, the extent of its degradation, the evolution of its vehicular traffic, the cost of merchandise transported, and the close tie among ecological change, economic ruin, and the rapid emergence of new boat forms for new conditions.

Given the reasonableness of Shomette's conclusion and the clarity of its link to surveying underwater resources, the remaining problem is to situate essentially historical conclusions within an anthropological framework so that an extension beyond the Patuxent might be possible. A move toward anthropology would involve taking parts of the Patuxent pattern and generalizing from them to build a model applicable to similar settings. Once a general model had been built, the original Patuxent material might be readjusted so that odd or miscellaneous pieces from the survey might make more sense and create an even more satisfying conclusion.

A whole model cannot be built within the scope of this paper, given limited knowledge of the needed historical details, but a move to a general theory can be made in order to create a suggestion of generality, which in turn might clarify some of Shomette's data.

I would like to turn to Fernand Braudel's *The Structures of Everyday Life* (1981), in which the conventions, organizations, institutions, and conditions of capitalism are described as they existed in Europe and associated areas from the fifteenth to the eighteenth centuries, the beginning of the Industrial Revolution. In turning to Braudel I am turning explicitly to capitalism, to materialism, and to a scholar directly tied to both the Marxist and the anthropological traditions. Braudel is

180

celebrated for both the comprehensiveness of his historical knowledge and the power of his analyses, a power derived not only from his command of detail but also from his understanding of capitalism as a worldwide phenomenon and of the major theoretical tradition for analyzing it.

Braudel is particularly insightful on town life, and that understanding will illuminate conditions along the Patuxent. He observes that "capitalism and towns were basically the same thing in the West" (1981: 514). Towns grew up in Europe in the Middle Ages and Renaissance and were free of princes and state governments. The towns belonged to merchants, and towns which were both free from territorial governments and supportive of mercantile needs produced the roots of modern life.

In the financial sphere, the towns organized taxation, finances, public credit, customs, and excise. They invented public loans . . . one after another, they reinvented gold money, following Genoa which may have minted the "geno-vino" as early as the late twelfth century. They organized industry and the guilds; they invented long-distance trade, bills of exchange, the first forms of trading companies and accountancy. They also quickly became the scene of class struggles. For if the towns were "communities" as has been said, they were also "societies" in the modern sense of the word, with their tensions and civil struggles: nobles against bourgeois; poor against rich. . . . The struggles in Florence were already more deeply akin to those of the industrial early nineteenth century than to the faction fights of ancient Rome . . . (Braudel 1981: 512).

Manners of thinking about time, space, movement, change, and other dimensions of reality which are necessary for taxation, credit, customs, loans, bills of exchange, accountancy, and long-distance trade formed "a new state of mind . . . a collection of rules, possibilities, calculations [for] getting rich and of living" (1981: 513). Such habits of mind accompanied town life and the capitalism found within it. This new state of mind is not incidental, epiphenomenal, or psychological. The mercantile and urban frame of mind "included gambling and risk: the key words of commercial language. . . . No question now of . . . letting the future take care of itself. The merchant was economical with his money, calculated his expenditure according to his returns, his investments according to their yield. He would also be economical with his time . . . as 'time is money' " (1981: 513–14). Further, "the cities were the West's first focus for patriotism—and the patriotism they inspired was long to be more coherent and much more conscious than the territorial kind, which emerged only slowly in the first states" (1981: 512). These concrete ideas identify the urban and capitalist frame of mind for Braudel.

Switching back to the Patuxent on Chesapeake Bay, there are three isolated and seemingly unimportant pieces of data Shomette mentions in his survey which may have more significance than at first appears and which, understood in the context of Braudel, may strengthen Shomette's interpretation of Patuxent history. The first is that after the founding of Maryland, throughout much of the seventeenth and eighteenth centuries, the colonial government attempted to found towns along the Patuxent, an effort that largely failed. Second, although the Patuxent was only moderately damaged during the American Revolution, it suffered very heavily during the War of 1812, but neither its population nor the Maryland legislature cared to defend the area when it was most heavily attacked. Maryland called on the new national government for defense because the local Maryland militia frequently ran away from fighting. Third, the Patuxent area's towns and farms never developed a long-term program of systematic dredging to reopen the river's channels. Dredging was tried sporadically even in the eighteenth century but was only episodic and was never geared to erosion and siltation rates to form an effective counterbalance to blockage of the river. Consequently, the river's death was inevitable and deliberate; it was accepted despite knowledge of what would keep it open and alive.

Taken together, these three events or sets of repeated events over three hundred years of Patuxent life may create a different perspective. Shomette's conclusion is right: the Patuxent, as a viable river, was killed by those who owned the plantations and farms along it. But it was also killed by the absence of town life which could have created the capital needed to pay for continually keeping it clear. It was also killed because the fighting spirit, or patriotic commitment, required to keep it alive after it had silted up would have come from town life. Moreover, the patriotism created by town life would have defended the river during the wars when its lands suffered ruinous attack.

In contrast, both capital and commitment existed at the mouth of the Susquehanna in the city of Baltimore. There has been intensive dredging for as long as it has been needed to keep that city's harbor open and to deepen it. Silt removal has gone on continually. Baltimore possesses the intensely political urban identity needed to create the large, single-minded voting blocks required to marshal the sums for such work. Even slender urban development could create the spirit and capital needed for the dredging required to maintain the economy. "In 1759 the Western Branch of the Patuxent, the only approach to Upper Marlboro, the river's most successful port town, became so choked up with rubbish, dead trees, and sediment that the town of Upper Marlboro was practically cut off from its access to the main river." The merchants used a lottery successfully to raise money for clearing it (Shomette 1979: 81). So, my addition to Shomette's accurate insight is that the initially nonexistent and finally slow development of urban life along the Patuxent is as responsible as exploitative farming for the Patuxent's death. Towns would have created the capital, loans, credit, public debt, and internal sense of citizenship that could have counteracted the ecological degradation that killed the river and caused the flight of capital to other areas.

Some sense of the strength of this hypothesis comes from the century-long effort made by the Lords Baltimore and the colonial government to found towns along the river. The colonial administration understood that urban life created income, and the administration, especially the proprietary government, may even have understood that town life could create a source of money and independence beyond that achieved through taxation. A strong town life in the colony might have provided enough wealth to lessen the influence of London politics on the colony.

During the final third of the seventeenth century the government of Maryland began to experiment with the development of an urban basis upon which to expand and exploit the commercial and maritime resources of the colony and to facilitate the collection of revenues and taxes. On June 5, 1668, Governor Charles Calvert, acting under instruction of Lord Baltimore [in London], issued a proclamation designating eleven sites in the colony as "Sea Ports Harbours creeks and places for the discharging and unlaiding for goods and merchandizes out of shippes and boates and other vessells" (Shomette 1979: 38 [Archives of Maryland, V, 31]).

Rudimentary town life existed in the 1670s in three places on the Patuxent. In 1669 " 'an Ordinance of the . . . Lord Proprietary' specifically ordered all exports and imports to be routed through twelve designated ports of entry. . . . In many parts of the colony this ordinance was met with stout opposition by the planters who would be obliged to divert transportation of their neighbor's private wharves and shipping . . ." (Shomette 1979: 40). The number of planned towns was enlarged to fifteen in 1671.

In 1676 St. Mary's City was a rudimentary town even though it was the colonial capital. At " 'other places wee have none that are called or cann be called townes. The people are not affecting to build nere each other but soe as to hae their houses nere Watters for conveniencye of trade . . .' " (Shomette 1979: 41 [Archives of Maryland, V, 265, 266]). Town growth was slow even though "all rents due the Lord Proprietor and all public levies payable in tobacco were to be sent to one of the towns" (Shomette 1979: 43). In the 1690s and in 1706, 1707, and 1708, the Maryland Assembly passed new town legislation including the building of " 'warehouses, and for the setting out of and appointing of wharves and keys exclusive of any other places for the lading and unlading of ships' " (Shomette 1979: 60 [Larabee 1935:II: 539–40]). None of the new towns matured until the second decade of the eighteenth century, and town life was frail even a century after settlement. Worse, substantial damage was done in the 1770s and 1780s during the American Revolution. British and Loyalist crews raided up and down the bay freeing slaves and burning plantations, boats, and towns. Shipping and commerce slowed substantially for years.

In addition to the absence of substantial town life, a second problem was the frailty of self-defense, a problem which appeared during the War of 1812. The Patuxent area faced "the same problem encountered throughout the state—a lack of willing man-power. . . ." Even with the governor's prodding, the state legislature "lethargically responded to the enemy attack" (Shomette 1979: 101–2). Between 1812 and 1815 the British burned everything they could touch in and around Chesapeake Bay; only Annapolis, Baltimore, Richmond, and Norfolk, of the large Tidewater towns, escaped. The shipping, plantations, and towns of the Patuxent suffered badly. But neither would the Maryland militia fight nor would its members defend their own property. The British could not get local Marylanders to fight, but saw them repeatedly flee into the woods. During a crucial naval battle in the Patuxent between the American flotilla of Commodore Barney and the British, the militia, important as land batteries, failed. Barney, the American naval commander hosted a strong repugnance for the militia, and, in particular, the Calvert County Militia (along the Patuxent). They were, he noted, "to be seen everywhere but just where they were wanted—whenever the enemy appeared they disappeared: and their commander was never able to bring them into action. . . . They rendered no assistance whatever to the flotilla, nor did they even attempt to defend their own houses and plantations from pillage and conflagration. . . . The men had neither discipline nor subordination, and receiving no check from their commanding officer in their irregularities, gave themselves up to disgraceful inaction . . ." (Shomette 1979: 149–50 [Stein 1960: 152]).

By the end of the War of 1812 the Patuxent, as well as other areas around Chesapeake Bay, had been so wrecked they never recovered. Even Annapolis, never invaded, was laid low economically. The war was the immediate, but multifaceted, cause since British pillage met with little or no local, organized, armed resistance on the Patuxent. The area cooperated to kill itself.

The continued frailty of town life along the Patuxent and absence of a willingness to defend the area against an enemy, or, in Braudel's terms, the absence of patriotism, help account for the decline of the river and its lands. Towns generate capital and popular cohesion, and both probably would have made a difference in conserving the river as a resource through the money needed to dredge on the one hand and the resistance needed to repel an enemy on the other. By contrast, of course, Baltimore defended itself with singular success. When requested by the governor, the Baltimore mercantile community provided ships, guns, and armed soldiers in the War of 1812 (Shomette 1979: 101–2). It is marvelously American that the poem that became the national anthem celebrated a victory made possible in good part by the merchants, their willingness to put profits to defense and to dredging: in other words, by urban patriotism.

The plantation economy of the Patuxent and of the greater Chesapeake had a number of internal flaws which limited its life. These flaws are best seen through the evolution of the river, in which case underwater archaeology has been crucial in establishing patterns of boat evolution, wharf building, town siting, traffic, tonnage, and siltation. Shomette has done all this and thus has reconstructed an entire local economy.

For two centuries the Patuxent produced only weak urban life, which in turn suggests, if Braudel is right, that capital was not abundant.

185

Thus there was little local money to protect the river. Since town life often produces a strong sense of citizens vs. outsiders, and thus spirited defense under attack, the weak defense of the Patuxent can also be linked to the frail urban development along its banks. The contrast which may strengthen the hypothesis is the behavior of nearby Baltimore under identical circumstances.

The cycle of ecological change and boat evolution that describes the Patuxent was influenced by a second process which needs to be acknowledged—the relationship between hinterland and urban center. It is already clear that, in not having a strong urban life, the Patuxent's development was limited in the capital it could generate, which would in turn enhance its own growth and well-being. But the slow growth of town life on the Patuxent also meant that other cities like London and Baltimore could dominate its economy more easily and completely. The Patuxent was the hinterland of those cities, and the exploitation and drain of capital from the river to London and then later to Baltimore forms the larger process of capitalist development into which the process of the Patuxent's degradation fits.

Lois Green Carr has seen this larger process as tied to the slender urban development of southern Maryland in the seventeenth century. The mouth of the Patuxent is in southern Maryland; the river's goods passed through the area and its wealth passed well beyond. In the seventeenth and eighteenth centuries,

given the organization of trade, the English merchants called the tunes. They controlled the shipping and they extended credit, not only to merchant planters but through the factors [middlemen] to small planters as well. Probably no merchant in the seventeenth century Chesapeake had capital sufficient to compete, and there was no need for the English merchant to share profits with a middleman in Maryland or Virginia in any major way. The whole Chesapeake was the hinterland of English urban centers, especially London (Carr 1974: 40).

The provincial government may have wanted towns in the colony to counterbalance the economic stranglehold of London, but it is doubtful that London did. Further, the absence of towns along the river meant that when Baltimore replaced London as a key urban center after independence, the Patuxent was no better off; it was still a hinterland, and its water life reacted accordingly. In the first decade of the nineteenth century Baltimore, near the Patuxent but in a dif-

186

ferent drainage, "swallowed up in its surprising growth the trade of all the towns in Maryland, and [took] to itself the mercantile importance of the state' " (Shomette 1979: 107 [Calendar of Maryland State Papers, 4: 204, item 1300]).

Shomette's work makes it clear that the context for shipwreck archaeology is economic development. Shipwrecks may be used to create a link between boats, technology, urbanism, and the social conditions surrounding the creation and use of money. The link is best stated by Braudel: "Nine times out of ten the patents of invention, serious or not, recorded on the pages of registers and dossiers in the Venetian Senate correspond to the particular problems of the city. . . . Social considerations were uppermost . . . the successful inventor had to have society on his side" (1981: 433–34). As the Patuxent shows, it is a mistake to look at technology and see technological progress and development; the Patuxent may demonstrate the reverse. When looking at technology—that is, boats—"The matter of greatest interest to the capitalist [is] the question of costs" (Braudel 1981: 434). Inventions and innovations are always possible but they may create unemployment, be too costly, be perceived as unneeded, increase the tempo of demand too much, interfere with inherited structures, or encounter inflation or high credit. So, for the underwater archaeologist, who is frequently concerned with how a boat was built or how it was operated, the context for these questions is that of costs. This is particularly true for those underwater archaeologists working where documents are available, which is to say within the context of historical archaeology.

Beyond the mistake of seeing boats and ships as markers of progressive technology, wrecks are seen frequently as time capsules, thought to represent their society in microcosm. It is frequently said that finding one amounts to finding all the events and parts of society going into a vessel's creation, use, and destruction. It may be possible to understand shipwrecks as microcosms, but understanding ships as part of land-based economic processes, particularly those of capitalism, allows for creation of a larger context. Certainly all the ships and boats off North America, indeed in the whole nonaboriginal New World, are tied to one stage or another in the emergence of capitalism.

The dialectic of money and towns released the enormous energies of capitalism, . . . as Europe sought to "devour, to digest the world. . . ." Europe, and capitalism, mastered "maritime organization," owning the oceans, particularly the Atlantic [in order to monopolize] the markets (Leonard 1982: C21).

This relationship is significant for creating a larger understanding of the Chesapeake. We can see that the Patuxent lost its autonomy first to London and then to Baltimore. Maritime plantation life lost to maritime urban industrialism. Plantation economy without towns and sufficient capital lost to cities which generated money. The victory was nationally significant and may even be recorded in poem and song, and the victory, understood within the context of capitalism and the rules governing it, takes the death of the Patuxent and foretells the later relationship between the capital-generating cities to the north and the lands to the south of the Chesapeake.

188

9
Answering Our Questions with Experiments

CHERYL CLAASSEN

University of Cincinnati

An experiment is one of several ways to answer archaeological questions. The purpose of this paper is to summarize and critique the history of experiments in nautical archaeology. Several suggestions are made for improvements in the conception and implementation of experiments as well as of topics for future investigation.

REPLICAS AND CRITIQUES

Experimentation in nautical archaeology has been almost exclusively vessel replication. The concern has been primarily with the success of a certain design and the accomplishment of a certain voyage or distance.

According to Johnstone (1974: 68) the earliest known boat replica was that of a trireme built for Napoleon III in 1861. A tradition of making replicas, however, did not begin until 1893, when Captain Magnus Anderson of Norway built and sailed a replica of a Viking longship across the Atlantic from Norway to New York. Since then there have been numerous replicas built by several North Sea groups and individuals, notably: Heyerdahl's *Kon Tiki* of 1946, the Hugin Gokstad replica of 1949, the Ladby replica of 1963, *Ra I* in 1969 and *Ra II* in 1970, the Hortspring replica of 1971, the Kalnes Bronze Age skin boat of 1971, the Gokstad faering replica of 1971, the Graveney boat replica begun in 1974, the Brendan project begun in 1976, the *Tigris* of 1976, and the *Hokule'a* of 1975.

Replica building has also been undertaken in North America (Baker, in McGrail 1977: 268): a Mayflower lifeboat, a seventeenth-century logboat, a 1725 Potomac River plantation boat, a whaling boat of the 1770s, an English longboat of the same period, and a late-nineteenth-century small fishing boat, among many others.

Coles has devised tools to measure the success of an experiment. His numerous publications on the topic (1966, 1973, 1977, 1979) have established his procedures for the experimental work being done in Europe and frequently in the United States. He requires original materials and methods, an assessment of any scaled work, and repetition and recording of the experiment (Coles 1979: 46). Consequently, a replication project can be (and several, such as the Kalnes and *Hokule'a*, have been) faulted for failure to adhere to the principles of original materials and methods, and of similar environment and use. But, according to Coles, the most serious fault of all the replicas is the lack of repetition.

McGrail (1975: 4) says that few, if any, of the replicas built before the Kalnes skin boat could be called successful archaeological experiments because their motivation was not scientific. Along with other members of the British National Maritime Museum, he undertook the building of a replica of the Gokstad faering "in an attempt to put boat replica building on to a firm academic basis" (McGrail 1975: 4). One review of this project called it the "best well-documented piece of experimental boat archaeology carried out," while criticizing the accuracy of the replication of the original (Christensen and Morrison 1976: 275).

The experimenters and critics seem to agree that the goal of experimentation, and even the relevance of the technique, is the successful imitation or replication of an object from the past.

THE SCIENTIFIC EXPERIMENT

Coles concluded in 1977 that "there are few hard rules in experimental archaeology except those of honesty, self criticism, and determination. Yet with all this, there still remains the problem of how to assess the results of the experiments, how much reliance to place upon the answers that emerge" (1977: 241). Coles's question about reliability can be answered by referring to the logic of experimental design as it is understood in other physical and social sciences. While holding one variable constant (the dependent variable), the experimenter carefully and consciously manipulates several independent variables to isolate their effect on the dependent variable. Several significant procedural features can be scrutinized in assessing results—the hypothesis, the controls, and the measurements. Measurements will not be discussed in this paper.

Perhaps it is best at this point to contrast an ideal experiment with those listed at the beginning of this discussion. They differ in three significant ways: in conception, in implementation, and in results. Most of this discussion will be directed to the conception of experiments since it is here that the most significant errors can be made and here that the previous theoretical work can prove misleading and inadequate.

Conception of Experiments

At issue are three points in the conception of any experiment: the suitability of subject matter for experimental manipulation, the nature of hypothesis testing, and the use of controls. Each of these will be discussed in turn.

It is my belief that there are no questions or problems in archaeology that cannot be better understood through the use of an experiment. If experimentation is to develop into an important analytical tool for archaeologists, several assumptions about its appropriateness must be eliminated and the scope of its utility widened. For instance, Coles (1977) identifies several levels of inquiry, object display, object production, and object function, but these are essentially one kind of experiment, the replicative experiment or in Ascher's (1961b) words, the imitative experiment. Tringham (1978: 182) takes experimental conception one step further, delineating the behavioral experiment as well as the behavioral by-product experiment or replicative experiment. A good example of the behavioral experiment is Baker's (1981) study which illustrates how the behavior and decisions of college students can inform archaeologists about prehistoric decision making. In addition, I have argued elsewhere (Claassen 1981), in obvious contradiction to the thinking of Coles and Ascher, that modern materials can and should play a leading role in archaeological experiments.

191

Rather than being limited to replication of old objects, the subject matter of experiments can be profitably expanded to include behaviors and modern materials. Coles himself concedes that comparative tests could assess the influence of modern tools and techniques but assumes this sort of testing is so expensive as to be prohibitive (Coles 1977: 238). It is not.

The logical approach to hypothesis testing is to attempt to disprove the hypothesis. The rationale in this case is that although one positive demonstration of the hypothesis does not prove its validity, one demonstration of its being wrong proves it invalid. Although one failure and one success are no different in a statistical sense, the primary assumption (or the null hypothesis) is that the hypothesized treatment or situation is not true. Coles (1973, 1979) and other archaeological experimenters emphasize forming a positive inference and then testing it.

In her discussion of experimentation, Tringham (1978: 179) reminds experimenters that hypothesis testing is done in an effort to refute the hypothesis. Muckelroy (1978: 236) concurs. Marstrander's hypothesis (1976) that the Scandinavian rock carvings illustrated skin boats, rather than plank boats as is commonly assumed, was tested with the Kalnes skin boat. A plank boat was not built and tested. No control was used to assess the conclusions of the skin boat trials. Consequently, the situation has not changed: the drawings may still be interpreted as plank boats, and one may still wonder if they could be skin boats.

Coles's experimental principles are not controls, as he may think, but rather a hypothesis. The hypothesis is that if I build a boat using the same techniques and materials available in year X, I will know whether or not those people could have produced a seaworthy craft. Procedural checks or controls are virtually eliminated in this hypothesis. The only check on the procedure is the result—does it or does it not float, sail, row, and so on. If the answer is no, the conclusion, as constrained by the hypothesis, is that it could not float, sail, or row then either.

The selection of controls and variables has been the most neglected element in discussions of the experimental procedure for archaeologists. Although the word *control* occurs rarely in theoretical discussions by Coles, Ascher, or McGrail, controls can be identified. For Coles, these have already been listed—to duplicate the methods of the time, the materials, and the environment. He calls these "principles" rather than controls and introduces a control at the completion of the project—repetition of results. The principles, however, operate as procedural controls. The experimenter is warned to hold constant the methods, materials, and environment, leaving the assembly of the vessel or artifact variable and uncontrolled. McGrail reiterates these principles and also offers procedural controls for the assembly variable.

I believe that these variants [in assembly] should be thoroughly investigated in a variety of ways *before* a decision is taken which version the replica builder is to use in his practical experiment. Thus, by small scale model building, by naval architectural calculations and the plotting of hydrostatic curves, by computer simulation, and by tank tests, these theoretical alternatives can be evaluated for practicability of building, for stability and load carrying effectiveness, and for performance with different methods of propulsion under a range of operational and environmental conditions. These are experiments which can be repeated using many different values of the parameters, and they can be repeated by others (McGrail 1977: 255).

Nearly all of the replicas mentioned in this review have adhered to Coles's principles, which may or may not be relevant. Until the kind of variable testing has been done that McGrail is suggesting (see also Coates 1977 and Claassen 1981), these principles are merely hypotheses.

Using materials and methods similar to the original has produced some ridiculous statements and situations. For instance, it has been said that in building a boat replica the effects of the twentieth-century environment must be neutralized as far as possible. Since ninth-century boatbuilders would not have used a boathouse, the building of ninth-century replicas should occur on an open riverbank (McGrail 1975).

An example of the problems that arise from a belief that only original methods should be employed is illustrated in Marstrander's (1976) description of the building of the Bronze Age skin boat. Ethnographically hides were prepared by Eskimo women who first soaked them in salt water, cleaned and worked them with a sharp tool to soften them, and finally rubbed fat into them. "As none of our wives were willing to assist us in the same way as the Eskimo women, we could not follow this very involved method" (Marstrander 1976: 21). In this case the control was irrelevant. He could have prepared the hides himself utilizing other male help with no ill effects on the experiment. Instead the hides were purchased commercially and utilized with the hair still adhering to them, a feature that was later said to interfere with water absorption during the sea trials.

In the case of nearly every replica discussed in this paper, the research question has been, Is that kind of craft seaworthy? For this question the procedural controls or principles of Coles are relevant on a general level. The controls used, however, have to be selected with reference to the research question and hypothesis. Positing and accepting these principles prior to the development of a research program limits the scope and range of the questions that can be answered with this technique.

Controls are an essential element of every experiment. They can take many different forms and will vary from experiment to experiment. Several examples will serve to demonstrate their role in anthropological and archaeological research.

Eggan described controlled comparisons in his presidential address (1954) to the American Anthropological Association. He pointed out that Boas issued the requirement that only those phenomena can be compared that are derived psychologically or historically from common causes. Failing to question the restrictiveness of the principles, most of his students avoided the comparative method.

Eggan stated (1954: 747) his own preference was to utilize the comparative method on a small scale with as much control over the frame of comparison as possible. The controls he suggested were to compare regions of relatively homogeneous culture or to work within social or cultural types. He also called for the control of ecological and historical factors as much as possible. Using Radcliffe-Brown's work among the moieties of Australia as an example, Eggan illustrated his own approach by suggesting a comparison of Australian moieties with moieties from southern California and further with Northwest Coast moieties. Each additional step serves as a check or control on the conclusions of the previous steps.

In their study of the fishermen of Galilee, Rhode Island, Poggie and Gersuny (1974) compare the social life of the fishermen to that of the region's millworkers. "Our interest here is to make a controlled comparison of fishermen with millworkers in order to find which characteristics of fishermen are strikingly different from those of a comparable landbound occupational group" (1974: 51).

Deetz's (1965) study of the Arikara was an exercise in determining unknown residence rules from artifacts. His assumption that objects made by women would cluster in a particular way spatially was based

194

on the study of pottery clustering and use in a society for which the residence rule was known. The known group served as a control for the unknown group.

A study of the effects of inundation on archaeological sites and objects used as a control group artifacts removed from submerged caves and sinkholes (Lenihan et al. 1977: 13). Many such sites have yielded objects thousands of years old, giving the project a perspective on the effects of long-term submersion. A comparison between objects removed from recently flooded and long-flooded contexts helped the researchers identify the various factors that operate to preserve archaeological remains.

In each of the four examples just given, cross-cultural comparison or the isolation of a specific variable served as a control both during the project and in assessing the results. Several kinds of controls will be illustrated at this point: variables, cross-cultural comparison, models, repetition, and ethnoarchaeology. As mentioned earlier, the controls employed in a project depend on the research question.

An excellent example of the use of variables is available in the Brendan project. Extensive experimentation was performed on the ethnographically suggested oak-bark leather to determine its suitability for the hull membrane of a boat. Samples were both wet and dry, treated with different dressings, and placed in dynamic and static conditions. "The laboratories checked tensile strength, weight, extension, and impermeability as well as the suitability of various fatty dressings such as cod oil, tallow, butter, and the wool grease from sheep" (Severin 1977: 260). The variables were moisture content, dressings, tensile strength, weight, extension, and impermeability. Similar tests were conducted on sail leathers and lashing materials.

The whole process of identifying variables controls and guides the conclusions drawn. The fewer the variables identified and examined, the less repeatable the experiment and informative the conclusions.

Cross-cultural comparison includes both temporal and spatial variation. It can operate as a control during the experiment to give direction to later work, and can also be used to assess the geographical and temporal suitability of the conclusions. The studies by Eggan and Deetz just cited illustrate the use of cross-cultural comparisons.

Models and other forms of simulation are among the most frequently used controls of the more recent boat replication projects. McGrail, whose comments on the use of models as controls have already been quoted, utilized models during the building of the Gokstad faering and Graveny boats. Models also play a significant part in the work of the Institute of Nautical Archaeology (Steffy 1976). For the Kyrenia ship a research model at 1:5 scale using comparable materials and techniques helped confirm the accuracy of the ship lines as drawn. A fiberglass model was made for sea trials, and a model of the aft section was made and destroyed under controlled conditions to understand the collapse on the seabed (Katzev 1980).

One of the most sophisticated experiments undertaken to date was Haasum's (1974) work on the sailing abilities of Viking ships. Using scaled models she performed wind-tunnel tests of Viking sail shapes and tank tests of hull drag. Several critiques are available (Crumlin-Pedersen 1975; Kay 1977).

Repetition of experiments is perhaps the easiest way to authenticate results, but it is probably the least feasible method in boat replication because of the expense. Repetition of the replication is not, however, always necessary. Poor procedures as well as inadequate recording would, in most of the replicas mentioned, make it impossible to produce a duplicate design. Repetition in sea trials is more feasible and informative. Here the aim is to duplicate the controls in an attempt to replicate the results. Ethnoarchaeology is also a control for both experiments and excavations. In its earliest use, it served as the "cautionary tale," informing us just how erroneous some of our interpretations were.

The use of ethnology and ethnographic analogy in boat replication, and in nautical archaeology in general, has been just as prevalent as in the other subfields of archaeology. Ethnoarchaeology requires that an individual be familiar with the archaeological record while observing the interaction of human behavior and material objects in a living society. When considering information gathered on boats currently in use as well as on rowing and paddling styles, it becomes very difficult to distinguish ethnoarchaeology from ethnology. If, however, the scope of interest in nautical studies is broadened to include maritime societies, not just their boats, the distinction is clearer. There are very few examples of ethnoarchaeological research in maritime societies.

Kirch and Dye (1979) point out that although the ethnographical tradition in Oceania is replete with detailed descriptions of hooks, traps, nets, and so on, it is sadly lacking in information that could answer questions about how the items were used, what labor groups used them, and in what specific microenvironments the items were effective. Kirch and Dye studied Polynesian fishing strategies, observing the use of specific marine-related environmental zones. This control data was then applied to the archaeological record of the area to facilitate interpretation of the material.

What may well be the first ethnoarchaeological study of a full-time maritime society, the Chaw Lay Sea Gypsies of Phuket Island, Thailand, is in its final stages (Engelhardt, personal communication). Interviews and observations of present-day inhabitants were collected, with an emphasis on discerning the amount of energy and resources individuals devote to pursuing marine-related activities in proportion to their other activities. Other topics of interest include: patterns of consumption and refuse disposal, especially as they concern marine products; the networks of commodities and people transported by boat; the social components and oral traditions associated with fishing as a means of subsistence; patterns of curate behavior, especially with articles from the sea or used in conjunction with maritime activities; the location and mobility of maritime settlements; and the artifactual and ecofactual assemblages of fishing societies.

In addition to the questionnaires and observation of the systemic record, prehistoric burial caves and terrestrial sites, recently abandoned villages, and submerged sites are also being investigated.

Muckelroy (1978: 219) claimed that no discussion of the potential for research into fishing vessels and their economic role was possible since no such remains had been discovered in an archaeological context. I hope this brief description of the Phuket Project will illustrate that such research is possible.

Before concluding this discussion of controls and the conception of archaeological experiments, I should point out that ethnoarchaeology is actually a behavioral experiment. Inasmuch as the investigator determines the question, selects and/or creates the behavioral situation, uses controls, and records observations of specific behaviors and results of those behaviors, the exercise is conducted within the procedural framework of an experiment, similar to some experiments in psychology.

Implementation of Experimental Designs

Coles believes that the materials and methods used in an experiment should be relevant to the culture under study. Coles's objection to the use of modern materials and behaviors is overcome when the experiment investigates dependent and independent variables. In order to understand the properties of oak-bark leather used in the Brendan hull, it was necessary to compare it in tests with modern leathers.

To test the hypothesis that the Spanish Armada cannonballs shattered upon impact with the hulls of English ships one would need to examine, for example, the variables of velocity and hardness of the target material. A range of velocities and hardnesses should be tested. The use of many different propulsive machines, including totally modern ones, would be appropriate, as would any other way of achieving different velocities. Any quantifiable hardness is appropriate, including wood, concrete, iron, and fiberglass. This author has supported the use of modern materials in archaeological experiments elsewhere (Claassen 1981).

Several boat replications have, in fact, used modern materials and passed Coles's (1979) written inspection. Most notable among these is the replica of a double-hull Polynesian canoe, the *Hokule'a*. This vessel, built in 1975 in Hawaii, sailed around the islands and, for the Bicentennial year, made the round-trip voyage between Hawaii and Tahiti, demonstrating that the Hawaiian Islands could have been populated by Tahitian seafarers (Finney 1979).

The hulls were made of a plywood skeleton overlain by three rows of laminated plywood, all covered with a protective layer of fiberglass. Coles (1979: 68–69) remarked that the use of modern materials in this case eliminated the collection of data on the strength and use-life of this vessel, but since the canoe was basically of native design in hulls, rigging, and sail plan and was probably comparable in its displacement, native materials would have been sufficiently well chosen to yield a native craft capable of making the same voyage.

Results

The differences in results between the ideal and the typical experiment should be apparent by now. When testing variables, the investigator concludes that hull design X of materials Y and Z performs in an observed way for variables A, B, and C. The more variables tested, the more useful the experiment. An entire boat could be described in this manner.

Perhaps the most significant outcome of these replica projects has

198

been to expose our arrogance in assuming that only modern Western minds are technically adept and innovative and that prehistoric minds were not only inept but incapable of accurate or meaningful artistry. The typical conclusion of the boat "experiments" performed to date is that the resources and the technological standards of the time in question would have enabled the boatbuilders then to construct a serviceable boat. I have criticized these positive testing programs elsewhere in this paper. I predict that any tool kit that contains adzes and axes could be used experimentally to produce a serviceable boat; thus "experiments" offering this conclusion have not enlarged our knowledge at all.

The accumulation of data useful from experimenter to experimenter has been minimal, if any. McGrail (1977) remarked that the expense of replicas could be better justified if the use-life of the vessel was extended past its trials. The expense could also be justified if the use-life of the vessel was extended past its own creator. This would involve quantifying the design as much as possible and offering alternative designs.

SUGGESTIONS FOR WORK

Boat design and seaworthiness have attracted a great deal of experimental attention, while answers to other questions in nautical archaeology are sought elsewhere. This situation reflects the belief that experimentation is for the achievement of replication. Boats and their accessories are the only distinctive objects to replicate in this subfield of archaeology. However, as stated earlier, it is my belief that there are no archaeological problems—whether the concern is with natural or cultural processes—that cannot be better understood by a well-designed and well-executed experiment.

In addition to the historical application of experimental procedures to questions of design success and seaworthiness, future experimental work should be directed toward the process of a shipwreck, the natural processes affecting the formation of the archaeological record underwater, and the cultural processes operating on the underwater record as well as on boats and ships in systemic context. Some illustrations follow.

199

The Process of a Shipwreck

"The shipwreck is the event by which a highly organised and dynamic assemblage of artefacts are transformed into a static and disorganised state with long-term stability" (Muckelroy 1978: 157). The process of wrecking has been dealt with to some extent by Muckelroy (1978: 169–73) and several types of wrecks tentatively identified. His definition of shipwreck is a broad one, including the continued breakup of the wreckage on the seabed as well as the stages by which it got there.

Loss and displacement of objects through floating is one of the processes during wrecking that Muckelroy explores. Experimental work could yield information on the floating and displacement of various kinds of materials in both freshwater and saltwater. Carol Spears (personal communication) has observed the nature of artifact accumulation in rapidly flowing streams in Arkansas. Guiney and Vitelli (no date) performed a flume test of transport and settling of ceramic pieces. Not only are there hundreds of questions to address at this level of inquiry, but tests and observations need to be repeated. Besides the process of wrecking, the disintegration of perishables and seabed movement can and should be investigated using experimental techniques.

An excellent example of experimentation in this area is a project undertaken by the Institute of Nautical Archaeology. A model of the aft section of the Kyrenia ship was built and destroyed under controlled conditions. An explanation for the artifact clustering and distribution observed on the seabed was the result of this experiment (Katzev 1980).

Natural Processes

The natural processes that shape the archaeological record underwater are poorly understood but probably are very different from those affecting the terrestrial record. Muckelroy (1978: 175) draws particular attention to the need to understand the behavior of mobile sediments on rocky and irregular seabeds. He suggests (1978: 181) that one could place an artificial scatter of objects presenting a range of materials on an excavated site area underwater and map, at regular intervals, both the horizontal and vertical evolution of the artifact distribution. One would then need to identify and quantify the variables assumed to create this distribution—for example, sediment particle size and density, current strength, maximum fetch, depth, density of an object, its

200

sphericity, and so on. Muckelroy also mentions a phenomenon observed underwater at the Kennemerland site (and other sites as well) of objects clustering around the larger rocks and boulders (1978: 178). Spears noted the same phenomenon in freshwater streams.

The inundation study of the National Park Service is a monumental effort along these lines. This project has examined the effects of submersion on characteristic raw materials such as shell, bone, clay, cloth, and iron; on items such as pollen, charcoal, and seeds; and on archaeological features and profiles. The published results form an invaluable record of natural formation processes for the underwater archaeologist (Lenihan et al. 1977).

Cultural Processes

Many of the cultural processes affecting boats while they are in systemic context are known, but several others are not and have bearing on interpretations of wrecks. For instance, archaeologists know little about abandonment behavior and the factors that influence decision making. I suspect that knowledge of destination (location, and distance in time and space) and the length of the preparatory period are the two most important factors governing which objects are moved or left, and in what spatial arrangement they are left. While not every land site is uniformly or instantaneously abandoned (as opposed to differentially abandoned), the vast majority of shipwrecks are. We need modern observations of abandonment that examine numerous variables and their combinations so that interpretations of underwater wreck inventories can benefit from an understanding of who takes what, when.

Muckelroy (1978: 240) asserts that boat travel uniformly necessitated a rigid hierarchy on board. Such an assumption places all water craft in essentially one social structure. Perhaps the smaller the number of people the less hierarchical the structure on both land and water. Perhaps familiarity with the job on the part of crew members influenced the extent of the hierarchy, or the nature of the mission. An erroneous application of this assumption could lead to misinterpretations of mission and personnel.

The assertion that the ship's or boat's passengers and crew were all male could also lend to misinterpretation. Female-related artifacts may indicate a trading inventory, or may have belonged to actual women

201

passengers. We simply have no quantified data on the amount of time women spend aboard ships and boats in the numerous societies we study, nor do we know what activities they perform while aboard. An anthropological study of fishermen's wives is one small step toward such an understanding (Danowski 1980).

Muckelroy makes a third assumption that requires further investigation—that "many of the objects used in seafaring are rarely brought ashore" (Muckelroy 1978: 6). He goes on to say "any artifact collection made [on shore] will represent very poorly the seafaring community itself." There has simply been no study to date that provides us with the data necessary to accept or refute this statement. Perhaps the assumption is true for trade cargoes but false for deep-sea fishing paraphernalia. This is, in fact, one of the research questions of the Phuket Project mentioned earlier.

Several factors are important in creating a need for specialized activity areas for seafaring equipment and products. Size and smell are no doubt two such factors. For instance, the larger the vessel is, the more likely there will be a specific area for harbor and equipment transfer and storage. The probability of finding a specialized area during archaeological fieldwork varies from site to site.

In addition to special manufacturing and storage areas, there may be special areas for discard of these objects. On Amchitka Island, in the Aleutian Islands, part of the fishing kit from a prehistoric community was found on a bluff with the remains of the fish, while the rest of the kit was found on the beach (Desautels et al. 1970: 345). Thus, the poor representation of seafaring objects may frequently be due to the archaeological work rather than to past human practices.

Adaptation to the water, salty or fresh, can be found in great variety ranging from subsistence fishing to specialized merchants to floating villages. Each group leaves archaeological evidence of its interaction with the water. The study of a number of these various communities would extraordinarily enhance our understanding of ships and boats in modern context as well as strengthen our understanding of them in archaeological context.

The cultural processes affecting underwater wreck sites are most assuredly the same ones as those that affect terrestrial sites. Scavenging of objects by people from the same cultural system will happen much less frequently underwater, particularly as time after the incident increases.

202

Treasure is more likely to be lost at sea than abandoned or lost in a cache on land. The knowledge or suspicion of treasure would attract both ancient and modern peoples to the wreck site, and with scuba gear, such sites are more accessible to present-day looters. Even though the collection of sites by the untrained or amateur may happen less frequently underwater than on land, the effects of such activity are no less serious. Private collections from underwater sites need to be examined and attributes quantified so that correlates of collector behavior may be drawn up and applied to authorized and systematic collections from these sites. I suspect that the classes of artifacts and the physical condition of those objects collected will reflect the same decision criteria employed by terrestrial collectors (Claassen 1975).

The archaeologist's activities and physiology also affect the archaeological record. Studies need to be made on the physiological and psychological effects of depth, weightlessness, fluidity, and so on. Problems created by the underwater environment in areas such as communication, dexterity, and memory will affect data recovery and interpretation in ways that must be understood and factored out of interpretation.

The techniques used to excavate also need examination. For instance, Muckelroy (1978: 50) mentions that the suction of sediments from objects can be likened to wet screening in its improvement of recovery but that more tests need to be done.

While artifact replication has been the work of archaeologists, testing natural and cultural processes is assumed to lie outside our domain (Muckelroy 1978: 167). It should be recognized that modern engineering, chemistry, physics, and biology are concerned primarily with questions of current economic relevance and seek very specific data. The attitude that archaeologists must wait for the other disciplines to turn to questions of interest to us is both naive and unproductive.

CONCLUSIONS

Boat replica building has a long and glamorous history in archaeology. McGrail (1977) says, however, that few of these projects can be considered experiments. The procedure used and the results of these exercises certainly underscore McGrail's assessment. Repeatedly the problem addressed is whether a certain boat design can travel a certain distance in water without sinking or capsizing. Unlike the builders of the *Wasa*, the builders of the replicas do not assume their craft will be seaworthy. This element of doubt has historically (in archaeology) made the situation an experimental one. It is not the element of doubt that creates an experiment but rather the formation of a hypothesis, the identification of variables, the use of controls, and measuring and recording observations, all conducted with the attitude of disproving the hypothesis.

The variables and controls in experimentation should facilitate understanding of the phenomenon being explored. The principles offered by Coles (duplicating materials and methods) instead prevent understanding and restrict the kinds of questions that can be asked. The impact of these principles is to relegate the utility of experimentation in archaeology to replication. The assumption that replication equals understanding can be undermined with a number of examples to the contrary. Historically, then, the use of experimental techniques in nautical archaeology has been crude. Hypotheses, when dated, were tested for affirmation without the use of controls, measurements, or records. The goal was a floating boat and a successful voyage.

When problems other than replication are considered, some archaeologists expect that we must wait for solutions to come from a more relevant discipline. Muckelroy considers even ethnology and ethnoarchaeology to be disciplines distinct from maritime archaeology (1978: 7). Any fudging of the boundary between the two will only lead to both bad ethnology and bad archaeology.

This paper takes a radically different stand on the issue of the marriage of archaeology and ethnology. Ethnoarchaeology, like excavation, ethnology, historic-record consultation, experimentation, infra-red photography, and so on, is a data-gathering *technique*, not a discipline. Our discipline is archaeology, distinct from all others because of our data base—objects—and our questions about how objects reflect human behavior, not because of our techniques.

Beyond being a data-gathering technique, ethnoarchaeology is a distinct type of experiment, and behavioral by-product experiments are useful as controls for information derived from other experiments and other data-gathering techniques, particularly excavation both on land and underwater. Interpretations of archaeological data everywhere are suffering from our lack of a detailed understanding of material culture in contemporary societies. Several suggestions for ethnoarchaeological research problems have been provided in this paper. Added

to this concern is Poggie and Gersuny's (1974: 6) warning to archaeologists that relatively little is known about the full range of technological, sociocultural, and economic factors involved in the human
adaptation to the ocean.

It is tempting to designate two schools of experimentation in archaeology, the replica school and the variable school, but to do so
would be to weaken a valuable technique. There are no problems
peculiar to nautical archaeology or archaeology in general that cannot
be better understood with a well-designed experiment, including the
replication of a boat and the accomplishment of a voyage. This paper
has compared an ideal experiment, which is markedly different in
conception, implementation, and results, to some replica projects.
The results of an ideal experiment are quantifiable and useful as building blocks for future work.

10
A Trial Classificatory Model
for the Analysis
of Shipwrecks

WILBURN A. COCKRELL

State Underwater Archaeologist,
Tallahassee, Florida

In discussions of the archaeology of shipwrecks, semantic confusion sometimes arises regarding the nature of such sites. One discussant will consider the archaeological data to be the principal aspect of the wreck, another will have the vessel structure as a referent, and yet another will focus on the materials contained within the wreck. In order to facilitate communication in such situations, it has proven helpful to devise a three-part model to illustrate the distinction among the three categories of remains (Cockrell 1981: 216). This model, shown in Figure 10.1, is particularly helpful to culture-resource managers in dealing with people who frequently confuse the archaeologist's concern for data acquisition with fantasies of "treasure" acquisition. It is also useful in separating the anthropologist's concern with data from the naval historian's interest in vessel structure. Throughout this paper, I will deal exclusively with the site as data; these data, of course, in my own conception, include the structure and the objects contained therein.

The bulk of the literature about the archaeology of shipwrecks has concerned itself with studies of method and technique. On a lesser scale in the past, but now on the increase, are studies that transcend

Figure 10.1. Aspects of the archaeological site.

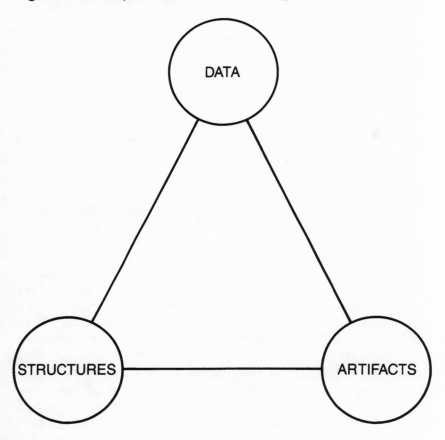

mechanical aspects and direct attention to description of both vessel structure and artifacts, in historical context. This latter approach has produced some excellent descriptive studies which view the archaeological site in its relationship to the external world; outstanding examples of this type of work are George Bass's Cape Gelidonya study (Bass 1967), and Barto Arnold's work on the 1554 Padre Island fleet (Arnold and Weddle 1978). A third topic for attention, principally within the past decade, has been the problem of preservation of shipwreck sites from the ravages of development, decomposition, and looting; several archaeologists have consistently addressed this problem, among them George Fischer (1973), Dan Lenihan (1974), George Bass (1980), and myself (Cockrell 1980).

While attention to these aspects of shipwreck archaeology is essential, they are nevertheless mechanistic topics; it is obviously necessary to conserve wreck sites if they are to be available for study. It is essential that the fieldwork follow the same high standards as traditional archaeology, and that subsequent site reports be of superior quality. An approach designed to transcend simple description and explication and address processual topics with scientific explanation, however, has been rare or nonexistent. General laws that make predictive statements possible are the ultimate goal.

Apparently the paucity of attention directed to processual shipwreck studies is due to a feeling that such studies are either not justified or too complicated, or perhaps even impossible. Archaeologists attempting explanatory studies have traditionally confined their analyses to social groups that are assumed to be less culturally "complex," in the hope that data from these "simpler" societies will prove manageable. Given the vast amounts of available and potential data, it is understandable that studying human variation in segments and factoring out behavioral data for examination is usually attempted on less complicated societal units. In the case of shipwrecks, however, most under study are representative of relatively complex societies. Watercraft from less complex, older groups will eventually be found, but given the approaches in present use, they would produce only descriptive statements. Although I have not attempted a quantitative analysis of the literature, my impression is that most papers generally addressing the archaeology of shipwrecks have as the ideal or normative type wrecks of Western origin, from the seventeenth to the nineteenth centuries.

On the assumption that more sophisticated analysis is possible and justified, I suggest, then, that our reluctance stems largely from an unarticulated sense that scientific analysis is too complicated. If we are to transcend the practice of studying less complex archaeological manifestations and attempt to direct more sophisticated anthropological approaches to shipwrecks, it will be helpful to examine formally the unique nature of ships as loci of a specific type of human interaction. Primary to this uniqueness is the feature that distinguishes shipwrecks from most archaeological sites: as Keith Muckelroy, among others, has noted, the ship is a closed community (Muckelroy 1980: 221). For reasons to be discussed later in this chapter, I would like to be more specific. If one views a ship on a voyage as a temporarily closed community, open at either end of the voyage, it is a nonexistent community before and after the voyage. It is isolated from the external world (in the era prior to the development of wireless radio at the end of the nineteenth century); in this respect, a shipwreck differs from other types of sites. The community exists as a temporarily closed social unit; individuals in a voyage necessarily alter their terrestrial social interaction network from an expanding-option network to a limited-option network. This feature alone holds fascinating potential for shipwreck studies. Shipboard behavior is necessarily altered, and therefore is potentially distinguishable analytically from behavior in an open terrestrial community. A study comparing group behavior in the closed community with behavior in an open community contains the potential for controlling variables in experiments.

In addition to being closed communities, the wrecks may be seen as "time capsules," and "microcosms of the culture at large" (Lenihan 1974: 32), because, unlike most other types of sites, wrecks contain the record of an entire microcosmic social group, arrested suddenly at a point in time, rather than the cast-off debris or abandoned ruins of a group. These factors give the shipwreck enormous potential for anthropological studies, both as data repositories not typically available to the archaeologist, and as discrete cultural units abstracted from larger cultural units. In discussing the ship as a microcosm, however, Lenihan states that "the ship . . . can reflect in its own internal makeup, the structure of the parent culture" (Lenihan 1974: 33). If the "parent culture" is perceived as a specific influential culture, although not necessarily the generative culture, modification of this concept will be useful, for in a number of situations there is not one "parent culture" but several. For example, an eighteenth-century Spanish Plate Fleet

210

ship could conceivably be closely related to, and interacting with, several parent cultures: Spain, New Spain, Arab slave-traders, Cuba, Tierra Firma, and perhaps more. This complexity will, of course, complicate analysis, but if an adequate conceptual framework is utilized, it should be possible to isolate the various interaction networks that provide the ship, as a closed community, with its initial basic character.

As a proposed first step in the direction of analyzing shipwrecks as anthropological phenomena, ordering the data through the use of various classificatory conceptual devices is a valid approach. My goal in this chapter is to provide valid yet nonexclusive conceptual devices designed to order certain classes of shipwreck data, in hopes of offering a differing perspective on shipwrecks.

At this point, in the interests of clarity, I would like to propose a functional classification of vessel types. Keith Muckelroy (1978: 215–23), in discussing "the archaeology of ships," considers "three aspects of a ship involved in its normal activities": the ship as a machine, the ship as an element in a military or economic system, and the ship as a closed community, as discussed above. While this concise functional classification is certainly useful, I would propose another functional classificatory system, to be used solely as a heuristic device, which seems to subsume all uses in a more specific fashion. In this system, the ship is:

a family-subsistence conveyance;

an exploratory conveyance;

a military conveyance;

a commercial conveyance;

a pleasure conveyance; and

a ceremonial conveyance.

Of course, in actuality, many vessels will have plural functions; for a functional analysis, however, the use to which the vessel was put at the point of focus of our analysis is central.

The ship as a family-subsistence conveyance would perhaps be the earliest type, and would include personal subsistence as well. Vessels of this type potentially represent a less complex structural type, as well as one of the earliest social organizations; of course these craft would tend to be smaller and contain less evidence of material culture than larger long-range vessels serving larger groups.

The ship as an exploratory conveyance would range from the time

211

of the earliest log or skin boats to the twentieth century. As a pioneering entity, it would tend to have more extensive interaction networks with parent cultures at its points of beginning and termination than with cultures it encountered during exploration. The *Pinta* and *Niña* on Columbus's first voyage to the New World are good examples.

The ship as a military conveyance is here seen as any vessel utilized by a group exercising, or attempting to exercise, dominance for purposes of conquest, tribute, obeisance, or looting. Pirates and privateers would be included in this category.

The ship as a commercial conveyance, unlike the ship as an exploratory conveyance, will have extensive interaction networks at one or more places, and is probably the most complex in terms of analytic potential. To locate commercial vessels from Minoan Crete, for example, would allow an unparalleled analytic view of that early thalassocracy.

The ship primarily as pleasure craft is necessarily a signifier of groups sufficiently complex to allow economic surplus and personal leisure, if only for the privileged classes, but has potential for considering anthropologically significant behavior from a unique viewpoint.

The ship as ceremonial craft, such as the Sutton Hoo ship, possesses vast potential for elucidating not only behavior directly related to its principal use, but other social systems, such as kinship, exchange, and the like.

A classificatory approach with significant potential for analyzing four-dimensional variations of shipwrecks and related terrestrial cultural groups, and thereby allowing specific consideration and manipulation of their various components, is essential in scientific explanation. J. O. Brew, in his classic exposition in taxonomy (1971: 77), stated in 1946 that "we advocate not less but *more* classification of a given series of objects, specifically more than one classification. The classifications, however, are personal to the student and his problem and are conditioned by the nature of the information he seeks to extract from his series." The conceptual devices presented in this chapter are formulated in this spirit, and are viewed as devices for manipulation of complex data, to be used or discarded as necessary. Again, as Brew states (1971: 105–6), "We must recognize that any given system in its entirety will probably be applicable only to the given set of problems it was designed to meet. The main value of a published description of a given system is that it may then be adapted by another student to his problems, not that he should force his material into it."

Following, then, is a classificatory scheme designed to encompass and order various relationships, ranging from the intrasite or intraship study of a single vessel (of any of the six types discussed above) to the combination of comparative interfleet and related terrestrial cultures. It becomes apparent, when the examination is so structured, that intraship study is common; interfleet/related terrestrial culture study is virtually nonexistent. This concept seems to demonstrate a point made earlier in this chapter, that this latter type of study, particularly when it involves commercial vessels and complex related terrestrial cultural groups, is so complex that it has been avoided. I hope my classificatory scheme will assist in isolating discrete behavioral elements for analysis, a basic procedure when dealing with complex cultural phenomena.

A discussion of the scheme, utilizing known shipwrecks as examples, follows. It must be emphasized that most of these types of study have not been attempted, so I am unable to describe actual studies. This failing on the part of archaeologists stems from several factors. Primary, I believe, is the pervasive bias in our profession that shipwrecks are not worthy of serious studies, and may be treated as treasure troves, with "finders keepers" being the appropriate attitude. A secondary, yet central, factor is that, while many of the known wrecks have been "excavated," the data were not addressed professionally, and the artifacts were destined for private collections and ultimate decomposition as a result of improper conservation and curation practices. Of course, those sites destroyed as a result of these attitudes and activities are forever removed from the limited universe of shipwreck sites.

Intraship study is, as noted earlier, the most common type of shipwreck study done to date, and parallels closely the traditional archaeological site report. Done properly, as by Bass on the Cape Gelidonya Bronze Age merchantman, it represents a paradigm of description and historical integration. Such a pioneering study, published in 1967, becomes even more significant when compared to the intraship study of the 8Mo141 or S-8, an early seventeenth-century shipwreck in the Florida Keys, destroyed by treasure hunters. (Stockholders in the corporation that sells the artifacts and investment contracts claim this is the wreck of the 1622 *Nuestra Señora de Atocha*, but an examination of the archaeological evidence offered to date does not readily support this contention.)

Intership (as opposed to intrafleet) study is far less common, but has exciting potential and is readily amenable to cross-cultural comparisons, or to comparisons of vessels originating from the same terrestrial culture but at differing temporal levels. An example would be the comparison of the early seventeenth-century Spanish wreck mentioned above with another wrecksite destroyed by the treasure hunters in the Florida Keys, designated 8Mo130, known by the finders as the "British Pirate" or "New Ground" wreck, although insufficient archaeological evidence existed for such precise national identification. Nevertheless, the Spanish wreck, representing a terrestrial culture that maintained some of its peasant worldview characteristics even to the present, is characterized by a plethora of religious articles, ceramic (as opposed to metallic) containers, a paucity of tobacco-related products, and clumsy matchlock firearms. (George Orwell, as a wartime journalist-soldier in the Spanish Civil War, noted in *Homage to Catalonia* [1952: 80] that, despite the Industrial Revolution, Spanish peasants continued to use wooden beam barrows with flint spikes to curry soil for planting.) The other wreck, from a nearby shoal (New Ground), while not necessarily British, as some have claimed, contrasts clearly, even though it is also a (late) seventeenth-century wreck; this wreck has a paucity of religious objects, a plethora of metallic containers, and has the characteristics of a northwestern European origin and crew. This combination, in an intership study, would allow for comparison of the cultural dynamics governing a Mediterranean-based vessel from a culture with a peasant worldview and a northwestern European vessel from a region characterized by ready acceptance of change, just prior to the appearance of capitalism and the Industrial Revolution.

An example of an intership study of vessels from the same cultural background, but from different time periods, would be the comparative study of the ca. 1618 Spanish wreck off the Florida East Coast, 8IR 22, the "Green Cabin" wreck, and the 1715 Spanish Plate Fleet wreck some sixty kilometers to the south, 8SL 17, known as "Douglas Beach" (Cockrell and Murphy 1978). This diachronic study, if not biased by improper collection and conservation techniques (these sites, too, are being "worked" by treasure hunters), could be of significant value, particularly to studies of economic and related systems, as the War of the Spanish Succession (1701–14) greatly altered Spain's role in the affairs of both Eastern and Western hemispheres.

Utilizing a Florida example again, the wreck in 1565 of the French Huguenot fleet of Jean Ribault possesses exciting potential as an intrafleet study. This fleet, destroyed by a hurricane, has yet to be located and looted. Although there were several hundred survivors (before Pedro Menendez had most of them massacred), no contemporary salvage by Europeans is recorded. The fleet, on a military mission against the Spanish based at St. Augustine, was peopled by French Protestants from virtually every class, from nobles to servants, and was composed of vessels of varying sizes and types. A fleet wreck of this size could produce marvelous data; one envisions the potential for attempting class-caste studies, among others.

An interfleet study could be directed at parallel or cross-cultural fleet studies. An example of the former would be the comparison of the 1554 New Spain Fleet reported by Arnold and Weddle (1978) and the two ships of the Panfilo de Narvaez wrecked off Cuba during a hurricane in 1527 (Cabeza de Vaca 1961: 27–29). An example of a cross-cultural interfleet study would be the comparison of the aforementioned 1565 Ribault fleet and the 1554 Padre Island fleet. This would prove to be most interesting; the former was French Protestant in origin, the latter, Spanish Catholic. To my knowledge, no one has attempted such a comparative study, but it would provide virtually limitless analytic approaches.

An intraship/related terrestrial culture study adds the dimension of a terrestrial society. It is necessary, of course, that anthropological data on the target parent culture be of the same high quality as the anthropological data derived from the shipwreck, which obviously presents problems, as many parent cultures of earlier times are poorly described, if at all, in an anthropological framework. Otherwise-cautious scholars might attempt to compare anthropologically derived shipwreck data with data on the parent culture derived from historical approaches; I contend that, unless the historical data are viewed through refined ethnohistorical frameworks, one risks comparing incompatible data sets.

A fascinating study which could satisfactorily meet this criterion, with added study of the parent culture, is Robert Grenier's yet unpublished work presented orally at the Tenth Annual Conference on Underwater Archaeology in 1979, entitled "Underwater Survey on Two Mid-Sixteenth Century Basque Sites with Discovery of a Galleon on the Coast of Labrador." Grenier compared his excellent data on the Basque ships with the parent Basque culture; while the data presented on the parent culture are not of the caliber of the shipwreck data, this is the kind of project that could most readily exemplify this type, given adequate anthropological data on the parent group.

A further refinement would be the study of an additional interaction network with a secondary terrestrial culture. Here again, Grenier has approached this variant type, by considering the Basque colonies on the northeastern coast of North America, to which the Basques emigrated from their homeland in northern Spain.

Intership/related terrestrial cultures can be clearly understood by utilizing the same two shipwrecks discussed under intership studies, and comparing each with the respective parent cultures. As noted, while the 8Mo141 early seventeenth-century wreck is Spanish, the national origin of the "New Ground," or 8Mo130, wreck is not known, although cursory examination alone demonstrates its northwestern European origin. I do not equate shifting national political entities with identifiable cultural entities, so I feel that these two sites meet the criteria for this type of study.

The intrafleet/related terrestrial culture type of comparative study, the comparison of intership anthropological data from within a fleet as well as with the parent culture, while complex, allows a multifaceted analytic approach. One would necessarily be in control of the intraship and intership data, as well as parallel anthropological data from the parent culture. A comparison of the 1715 Plate Fleet wrecked off the east coast of Florida and its Spanish parent culture would be the ideal subject for this type of analysis, had not the bulk of the shipwreck data been destroyed by treasure hunters. In addition, as this fleet was interacting with New Spain, the Native Americans, and other distinctive cultural entities, this analysis could potentially consider the relationships with plural parent cultures.

An interfleet/related terrestrial culture study, as in the case of interfleet studies, may attend to parallel or cross-cultural fleet studies, with the addition of their relationships to one or more terrestrial societies. This is the most complex of all situations constructed here, and to my knowledge, has not been undertaken. In the case of parallel (cultural) fleets, the comparative studies of the 1715 and 1733 Plate Fleets on Florida's Atlantic coast, and their interaction with their parent culture, Spain, exemplify a study of this type. An excellent cross-cultural example would be the fleets discussed as interfleet studies—

the 1565 Ribault Fleet and the 1554 Padre Island Fleet, and their parent cultures, France and Spain, respectively.

It is hoped that making these conceptual devices explicit will assist in clarifying complex sets of data, in order that they may be more creatively manipulated. Additionally, given the ship as a temporarily closed community, both spatially and temporally, the ship (or fleet) possesses vast potential as a control for examining the terrestrial parent culture. In isolation one may address various cultural systems and study their adherence to, or variance with, the open terrestrial cultures with which the ship community interacts prior to and after its closed status. In a fascinating letter written in 1573, Eugenio de Salazar, a Spanish judge and poet, describes vividly a voyage from the Canaries to Hispaniola (Parry 1968: 348–64). Careful reading of this compelling document indicates that social systems on board were at variance with their terrestrial counterparts, most particularly interaction networks and linguistics.

The isolation of the ship community creates a rare human situation, a limited-option network. We are provided with a singular laboratory situation, which, if comprehensible, will enable us to transcend description in an approach to that elusive and perhaps unattainable goal of scientific archaeology, explanation—and consequent prediction.

Even in the absence of this ultimate goal, the study of postmedieval shipwrecks has the potential to elucidate and clarify processes not so easily derived from studies of less complex societies. These wrecks are the near antecedents of contemporary Western society.

I trust that anthropologists will soon recognize shipwrecks as phenomena deserving legitimate scientific attention, and join the losing battle for their preservation; unless both moral and legal restraints are adopted, discussion of the potential for study of shipwrecks as anthropological phenomena will be academic, as none will remain to be studied. In the three decades since the advent of technological advances, the rapists have decimated these once-plentiful windows to the past.

11
The Mystery
of the Prehistoric
"Chinese Anchors":
Toward Research Designs
for Underwater Archaeology

E. GARY STICKEL

Environmental Research Archaeologists:
A Scientific Consortium
Los Angeles, California

INTRODUCTION

Underwater archaeology (including its subfield of shipwreck archaeology) is undergoing an identity crisis. All who attended the School of American Research seminar were well aware of it. That is why we were here. This identity crisis is justified, in my opinion, because underwater archaeology (like Western civilization in general) has technologically advanced beyond its ideological ability to cope with the advancement. As several other papers in this seminar have nicely surveyed (e.g., Lenihan, Watson), underwater archaeology is an outgrowth of early interests in wreck salvaging, treasure hunting, or relic hunting. Even after underwater archaeology was established (particularly with the work of George Bass, which resulted in the publication of his book *Archaeology Under Water* in 1966), the data base was still being referred to as a "Blue Museum" (Ceram and Lyon 1958); a sort

219

of "Poseidon's cornucopia" for statues, gold coins, and other art objects that could be wrenched from the sea floor without regard for their contextual cultural meaning. So all of the hydrosphere became a happy hunting ground for adventurers in search of gold or glory. A dramatic example, which has no doubt whetted the appetites of many fortune seekers, was the J. Paul Getty Museum's acquisition of a beautiful late fourth-century B.C. Greek bronze of a standing athlete, presumably by Lysippus, the court sculptor to Alexander the Great. This statue was taken from an underwater site off Italy, in less-than-clear circumstances, and was sold to the Getty Museum for between three and six million dollars (Getty Museum 1981, personal communication). It is easy to see why the "sea hunt" goes on despite our attempts to promote scientific and fully professional underwater archaeology and to stop illicit collecting and the international traffic in antiquities.

The scuba revolution, which occurred during and especially after World War II, made the submarine part of the planet accessible. No longer did the cumbersome hard-hat suits, which greatly restricted movement, have to be worn. Scuba equipment gave the diver freedom and relative ease of aquatic movement which, in turn, greatly increased public interest in diving. Thus the 1950s saw a rapid development of scuba gear. It is almost inconceivable in view of the wide range of gear available today that our colleagues got their first wet suits by lying down on a sheet of rubber and having friends trace their outlines with sharp knives!

Underwater archaeology, to distinguish itself from less-legitimate pursuits, next went into a phase emphasizing high technology, which characterized most of the field during the 1960s and 1970s. A result was the use of a glamorous and dazzling array of new types of air tanks, diving suits, diver accessories, both dry and wet submarines, and remote-sensing equipment such as side-scan sonar and marine magnetometers (Holmquist and Wheeler 1964; Du Plat Taylor 1966; UNESCO 1972; Blackman 1973). In uninitiated terrestrial archaeologists, a bias against underwater archaeologists started to develop: they considered them "gadgeteers" and "macho adventurers" rather than true scientists concerned with studying and finding answers to important questions of culture history, culture process, and the evolution of cultural systems.

Most of underwater archaeology was, and is, devoted to wreck sites, with little or no attention being given to research design development and implementation. The methodology that was employed was devoted to cultural historical questions of nautics and where a given vessel would fit into nautical history. Most of the advances in subaquatic archaeology were in methods, not methodology (I define methodology as the relation of theory to data for purposes of interpretation, and methods I restrict to those uses of techniques, tools, equipments, or instruments for data acquisition and analysis). Thus, for example, new and useful developments were made in sea-floor-site grid frames and in underwater photography (Rebikoff 1972).

The most notable exception to the lack of methodology primarily involved underwater prehistoric archaeology, not shipwreck archaeology. In fact the first use of underwater archaeology per se (not for goals of salvage or collecting) was conducted on prehistoric subaquatic sites in Switzerland in 1854 (Martin 1979). During the late 1960s, but continuing to the present, the Swiss spearheaded a highly systematic and technical cultural historical approach to underwater archaeology (Ruoff 1972, 1981; Stickel 1974). My own work in Switzerland emphasized methodology, and discussions of underwater archaeology methods were deliberately kept to a minimum (Stickel 1974). Instead I placed an emphasis on a computerized approach to locational analysis, and ecological and chronometric analyses, that is, a newer but mainstream research orientation. I had few precedents in developing a research design for that study (e.g., Goggin 1960; Gluckman 1976; see also Lenihan, this volume, for other references to method and theory at that time).

Underwater archaeological research designs are essential if the field is to take its productive place in archaeological science. This is especially critical today as the data base is rapidly disappearing. Archaeologists must be concerned with research designs, not because they sound fashionable or are a nonessential "frosting on the cake" that make a project appear to be scientific and worthwhile, but because they are essential for the conduct of efficient, productive science. They are essential because they ensure the most efficient collection of field data; an example is the sampling theory, which to my knowledge has not been applied to underwater archaeology because, unfortunately, entire wrecks are usually excavated, or as much as possible are retrieved from an inundated prehistoric site. Research designs also yield the most rewarding and accurate information because they provide for explicit relational studies of data to theory which, in turn, serve as the

221

basis for valid interpretations of culture history, internal cultural system dynamics, and those cultural processes that shaped long-term cultural developments worldwide. An issue that will have to be resolved is whether we can afford to have researchers excavate (which destroys a site and precludes future analysis unless sampling theory is utilized) to investigate only cultural and historical questions. An ideal situation, it seems to me, is to have well-organized interdisciplinary excavations and analyses of shipwrecks (and any other subaquatic site) address all three sets of research questions—those of culture history, internal cultural system dynamics, and cultural process and change over time. The result would be a more complete knowledge of the data, which ultimately is more meaningful and useful to us. I see this book as a real landmark in the history of underwater archaeology. No longer will it be accurate to say the field lacks a concern for theory, methodology, and research designs.

Here I will attempt to provide a research design for an unusual and challenging "shipwreck site." In fact, it is not even certain that the site in question is a shipwreck. The site is located in the Pacific Ocean off Palos Verdes, California. It consists of more than thirty large stones, each of which has been perforated and/or shaped, obviously by humans. The basic question is, Who made these stones? What culture are they a product of? Why and how did they come to be located in fifteen to twenty-five feet of water? This site has already been interpreted as a "prehistoric Chinese wreck site" predating Columbus (Pierson and Moriarty 1980; Zhongpu 1980). Zhongpu based his recent article, in part, on James Moriarty's suggestion, made to the Chinese paleo-archaeologist Jia Lanpo, that the stone artifacts off Redondo Beach were "stone anchors," "were 3,000 years old and were Asian in origin" (Zhongpu 1980: 66). Moreover, a former wreck salvor-diver and student of Moriarty's has stated on the questionable television program "In Search Of" that the site is "definite proof," for the first time in history, of a prehistoric New World Chinese wreck. It would appear that this site has already been scientifically evaluated.

Stylistic comparisons with historical, archaeological, and ethnological data indicate great antiquity for the *anchors*. Geologic studies show that the stone from which they were made is not of California origin. Circumstances, such as the covering layer of manganese and the physical conditions point to great antiquity for both sites [a Patton Escarpment site and the Palos Verdes site].

It seems clear to us that Asiatic vessels reached the New World in Pre-Columbian times (Pierson and Moriarty 1980: 22).

Consequently much has been made of this site in news media exposure, on national and local television, and in magazine articles. During the seminar session in which this paper was discussed, Richard Gould pointed out that the site represents one of a number of "paranormal" archaeological sites (such as the "Bimini Wall" or the Kensington Stone) which have enthralled the general public and have advanced the incomes of their nonprofessional author-publicizers. Generally, professional archaeologists have avoided the study of such sites.

Archaeological evidence in the past has been scanty, and sometimes impossible to track down. This may well result from the fact that early investigators were reluctant to report on intrusive evidence, fearing academic ridicule. Such timidity is very much in evidence, even now (Pierson and Moriarty 1980: 19).

It is unfortunate that academics have avoided such sites, for there is no need to fear criticism if interpretations are taken out of the realm of wild speculation (referred to as the "Von Däniken syndrome") and based on adequate scientific research design. As will be seen below, unfortunately, the Palos Verdes site has not been so scientifically investigated. Adequate research into this archaeological site may well indicate that it is only a trivial one adding virtually nothing to our knowledge of the past. Alternatively, if the site is indeed what it has been prematurely interpreted to be, then it is highly significant and should be studied in terms of interesting anthropological questions about early human movement.

Regardless of the actual import of the site, to evaluate adequately and implement the proposed research design would be a worthwhile exercise in itself in terms of demonstrating how a scientifically oriented anthropological-archaeological program can deal with such paranormal sites. Research on the sites, presented as "detective stories" involving the scientific testing that leads to interpretation, might stimulate public interest.

I would like to present a preliminary research design for this site, with the goal being a scientific identification and study of the human behavior associated with the origin and use of the stone artifacts. I can do so with little bias, for I am not convinced that the stones are old, are Chinese (or "Asian"), or are foreign to the Americas.

A PROPOSED PRELIMINARY RESEARCH DESIGN FOR THE PALOS VERDES MARINE SITE

Any research design must have an implicit or explicit organizing format. I prefer an explicit one based on a deductive-inductive testing process (Stickel and Chartkoff 1973; see Fig. 11.1). This format is rather detailed in order to facilitate an explicit relation of problem formation, data acquisition, testing, and interpretation. Some examples of the types of research questions noted above will be posited here and the stage set for their testing and objective evaluation. It is important to note that these propositions have not been tested as yet; the outcomes are still unknown. This testing format, which will be used as the organizing framework for this research design, will be referred to step by step from A_1, the data to be studied, through A_9, the interpretation.

THE ARCHAEOLOGICAL PHENOMENA AND THE HYPOTHESES TO BE INVESTIGATED

The archaeological phenomena of the real world to be investigated (A_1) in this case instance are the stone artifacts (see Fig. 11.2) located at the Redondo Beach site as well as a sample of other artifacts or ecofacts which may be present at the site.

Simply, the research problem (A_2) in this case is to identify the cultural origin, age, function, and reason for the location of the subject data; to ascertain the cultural dynamics of the human behavior associated with the data; and to ascertain some of the cultural processes responsible for the presence of the data. These will be discussed below.

With regard to A_3, the conceptual and theoretical framework for research, most underwater archaeology has been conducted in a theoretical vacuum. Muckelroy (1978) is a notable exception, for he advocated a sort of systems-theory application in his book *Maritime Archaeology*. The use of systems theory for addressing cultural processes

224

Figure 11.1. Hypotheses testing format.

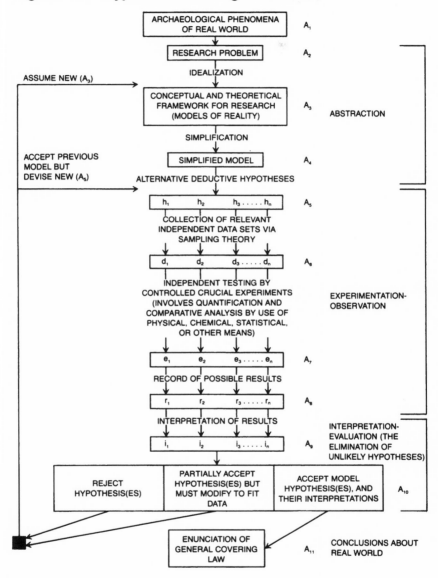

Source: Stickel and Chartkoff 1973

Figure 11.2. Types of stone artifacts from the Redondo Beach underwater site (after Pierson and Moriarty 1980:20).

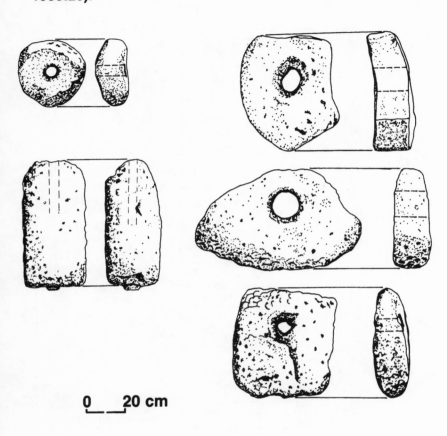

0   20 cm

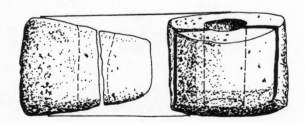

utilizing underwater data has also been advocated elsewhere (Stickel 1974). Muckelroy devised and proposed a

three-dimensional matrix . . . which represents a present-day view of a past society, broken up into a number of compartments [including] . . . various aspects of social life, placed under five arbitrary headings (economic, political, religious, social and technical), and analogous to the sub-systems within a society discussed by Dr. Clarke in *Analytical Archaeology* (Clarke 1968: 101–23; Muckelroy 1978: 227–28, also see his Fig. 7.1).

He went on to list five "subcultures" (including a "maritime" one) and five research disciplines with archaeology as part of his maritime studies. I admire his advocating systems theory even though I find his version of it inadequate. A more germane systems model, entitled *A General Human Systems Model for Archaeological Analysis*, has been formulated (Stickel 1982). This model has been contrasted with Binford's "cultural systems" model (1962, 1968a), with his three technological, sociological, and ideological subsystems, and with David Clarke's (1968) "sociocultural systems" model including five components—economy, social pattern, material culture, religious pattern, and psychology (see Fig. 11.3). The Binford and Clarke models (and Muckelroy's by extension, being based on Clarke's) fail to recognize, or provide for, essential system variability. Foremost of these is the critical subsystem which I term the "biological" component of a human system. This component includes all the human beings, and all their genetic variability, that operate or actuate and, in turn, are dependent upon a given human system. Members of the biological component, for example, of a distinct human system are sometimes directly represented in a shipwreck as the skeletons of the drowned victims.

Beyond the critical biological component—and there is no system without the biological operators of the system—are six others, including the material, technoeconomical, sociological, ideological, psychological, and communicational. These components are interrelated by complex feedback mechanisms (see Fig. 11.4). These feedback mechanisms are so developed that it is possible to analyze one component and from it reconstruct aspects, or monitor variability, of all other components in a given system. This salient tenet of the model will be used for the analytical strategy (A_3) advocated here, that is, a portion of the material component of the human system responsible for the Palos Verdes site artifacts will be analyzed. Thus this strategy will

227

Figure 11.3. The cultural system models of Binford (1962, 1968a) and Clarke (1968).

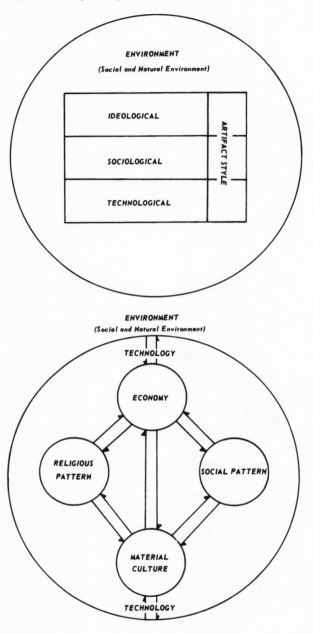

Figure 11.4. Proposed model of the composition and organization of a human system.

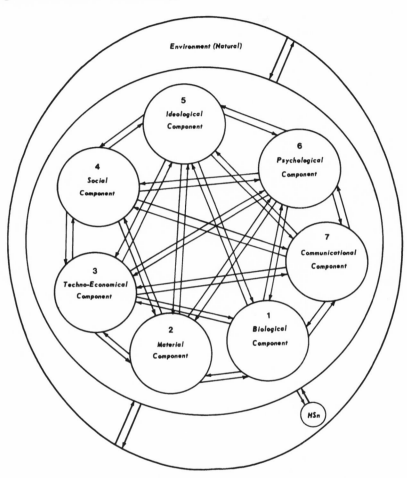

KEY

Human System: Biological, Material Cultural and Non Material Cultural Variables.

Biological Variables – Component 1   Material cultural variables – Component 2

Non Material Variables – Components 3–7

Human System : (HSn)

Environment: 1) HSn : Social Environment (all other HS which interact with a given Human System)

2) Natural Environment : Climate, Geology, Flora, Fauna, etc.

229

enable analysis to proceed in order to ascertain the specific human system involved, how the material cultural elements functioned in that system, and how the material cultural elements reflect other componential aspects of that system, and then to study those cultural processes responsible for the deposition of the subject data at the site. These goals will become clearer as the hypotheses are presented and discussed below.

In short, the conceptual and theoretical framework for research is based on a systems-theory approach which I feel will be most productive if systematically adopted for shipwreck and other types of subaquatic archaeology because this model provides for the analysis of both cultural and human biological variables in a given human system.

The underlying goal, however, is not just to deal with this particular site, no matter how potentially exciting or mundane it may be, but to test hypotheses using a methodological and theoretical framework that will enable those tested hypotheses to be related to cultural scientific generalizations. As Muckelroy correctly maintained:

Without a corresponding level of generalization, maritime archaeology would be mere antiquarianism, a fascinating and relatively harmless leisure activity, but not a serious and rewarding academic discipline, demanding of considerable expertise, sophisticated equipment, and support from public funds (Muckelroy 1978: 226).

Since the General Human Systems Model (A_3) asserts that all elements of a system are interrelated, the simplified model to be used in this research (A_4) asserts that the site's artifacts, and other relevant data, will reflect the parent system of which they were functioning elements. These specific material items should have functions that can be ascertained or reconstructed through appropriate analyses. And some of the ways they represent the parent system should be reconstructable. In short, only a portion of that system's material component will be investigated—the stones and other associated relevant data—to determine how and why they functioned and how and why they came to be placed in their site context, that is, what cultural processes were involved. Specific models must be clearly formulated in order to facilitate the generation of objective, logical, relevant hypotheses that can be definitively tested. For instance, the following specific model was previously presented relative to the Palos Verdes site.

230

To achieve this level of absolute proof, one should: 1) ascertain whether the artifact is, or is not, intrusive at the site; 2) subject the artifact to chemical (lithological) examination to see if the material matches with that in the supposed area of origin; 3) demonstrate that the artifact has a positive cultural connection with the assumed culture of origin and is not a legitimate material element of the culture in which it is found (Pierson and Moriarty 1980: 17).

The authors went on to state that since the work of Joseph Needham (1954, 1969) showed that the Chinese and Japanese did have ships capable of making transoceanic voyages, "clearly, then, the first condition of proof has been fulfilled" (Pierson and Moriarty 1980: 18). Similarly they state that since

the Chinese were indeed in proximity to the Japanese current in the pre-Christian era, and the Japanese in the early period following Christ. Moreover, that major flow of water would have provided the avenue by which rafting or early shipping could have reached America from Eastern Asia. The Spanish, even in 1565 were still using it to advantage, when sailing from the Philippines to America. Thus, the second element of proof has been fulfilled (Pierson and Moriarty 1980: 18).

Then they went on to state that the only "missing link in the third element of proof" was actual archaeological data of an early Asian shipwreck, which they believe is in evidence at the Palos Verdes marine site.

The first two asserted aspects are not "proofs." For knowing that the ancient Oriental populations had seacraft capable of making a transoceanic voyage to California cannot be considered evidence that they indeed made such trips. Secondly, the proximity of the Chinese and Japanese to the Japanese current also does not, in itself, provide evidence that such ancient voyages were made. Obviously, it should be remembered that California became well known to the Old World through its discovery by the Spanish who were not able to take advantage of the Japanese current. Thus the purported "elements of proof" do not constitute proof at all but are only necessary conditions for their hypothesis. They are certainly not sufficient conditions to establish their hypothesis. One may, for example, have the necessary conditions of air, fuel, and a heat source, but (as any beginner Boy Scout knows) those variables do not necessarily make a fire. The following alternative hypotheses were formulated with an eye toward establishing, once they are all tested, both necessary and sufficient

231

conditions for adequately interpreting the archaeological data. And as will be seen in the discussions below, the "evidence," as presented by Pierson and Moriarty (1980), is not there to support a transoceanic voyage by the prehistoric Chinese, or by any other group for that matter.

ALTERNATIVE DEDUCTIVE HYPOTHESES, DATA REQUIREMENTS, MEANS OF EXPERIMENTATION ANALYSIS, THE RECORDING OF THE DATA, AND THE INTERPRETATIONAL PROCEDURE

Hypothesis h_1

A number of basic hypotheses testing (step A_5) need to be addressed in order to gain relevant information about the site. The first step is to determine the natural origin of the stone artifacts. Pierson and Moriarty (1980) maintain that the stones are from China, that is, not from a local California context but from a distant foreign one. The following hypothesis, h_1, can be proposed to test a local, vs. exotic, origin for the stone materials:

If the stones in question are from a foreign source, then the geological (petrographic) material of the stones should be totally foreign to the natural geologic formations of California and relatable via objective methods with their place of natural origin.

The place of origin, whether in the eastern or western hemisphere, can be objectively identified if the geologic material of the site's stones and quarry sources can be matched.

Thus the data set d_1 (step A_6) for this hypothesis would be geological thin sections from the subject stones and comparable ones from possible quarry sources.

The experimental e_1 stage (A_7) of the research design, to test this hypothesis, would involve geologic and petrographic inspection and analysis of samples both from the site stones and from possible source lithologies. Once the geologic material has been identified, it can be compared to the geology of the Palos Verdes area first; then if a match cannot be found, one would proceed in ever wider "circles" of possibility throughout California and then to foreign contexts until the sources have been identified. Pierson and Moriarty (1980) believe that the stones are made of material ("dolostone") that came from China. However, it has been reported to me that the University of California at Santa Barbara Geology Department has identified the material as "typical" of the local California Monterey formation (Love, personal communication). This identification, as well as a number of historical accounts, was used by a UCSB History Department professor, Frank Frost (1980), in a paper that rejected Pierson and Moriarty's interpretation, asserting that the stones were associated with recent historical behavior in the area.

During the seminar, Cheryl Claassen pointed out that samples of lithic material from the "anchor stones" and control samples from the natural geologic formations at the site should both be taken and analyzed in order to determine adequately the similarities or differences of the lithic materials. Thus adequate testing remains to be done to determine the sources of the lithic material.

Relative to this research design, two geologists, Dr. Alan Crawford (of Union Oil Research Facility, Brea, California) and Cathy Crawford (of Woodward Clyde Consultants), will kindly provide (e_1) analytical help to test this hypothesis. They have already taken thin sections of the five stones that the discoverers of the site (Wayne Baldwin and Robert Meistrel) raised from it. (Baldwin and Meistrel have assured me they will take no further data from the site until a formal research design can be implemented.) The thin sections are currently undergoing petrographic analyses at the geologic laboratory of the Union Oil Research Facility in California. Similar analysis should be conducted of the site's natural geologic samples for comparative study.

It so happens that the stone artifacts in question also have some relevant environmental variables associated with them, for they have embedded within their natural geologic matrix at least two types of fossiliferous data. Research paleontologist Robert Arends (also of the Union Oil Research Facility) has kindly agreed to identify these fossils and to ascertain the natural, original habitat of the fossils as another means to test for the source of the stone material. The adjunct hypothesis here is, if the stones are from a foreign source, then the fossil data within them should not be from local fossil species but from organisms whose original habitat can be specified.

The data recording stage (A_8), in the testing, r_1, would be represented

233

by the petrograph thin sections, the photographs of them, and written descriptions of that material, all of which will be produced at the research laboratory.

The important hypothesis interpretation i_1 stage (A_9) would depend on the outcome of the geologic and paleontologic analyses. Obviously if a matching of the stone and fossiliferous material with local California sources is definitely made, then the foreign-origin hypothesis can be objectively and safely rejected. If not, then the various possible foreign sources can be studied until a clear relation can be established. Involved in the final interpretation should be the consideration that if the stones were brought to the site by a vessel, then the possibility that they were acquired en route, and not from the vessel's homeland, must be taken into account (see Renfrew 1975). Also, I am not suggesting that if the stones are foreign an Asian locus is necessarily indicated. Other Old World and New World sources must also be considered.

Hypothesis h_2

It has been argued that the stones in question were nautical artifacts, mainly anchors (Pierson and Moriarty 1980; Zhongpu 1980). This assignation of function to form remains to be established. Zhongpu (1980) emphasizes the columnar form and cites an ethnographic example of early Chinese use of such stones as "anchors":

Such stones are known to have been used for thousands of years as anchors [in China]. In the Eastern Jin dynasty (317–420) a ship carrying the monk Faxian returning to China from India was hit by a gale east of Sri Lanka. Faxian wrote in his book *Records of Buddhist Countries:* "The sea was so deep that we could find no place to drop our stone pillar." A pillar is cylindrical, so "to drop a stone pillar" can be understood as casting a stone anchor (Zhongpu 1980: 66).

He then relates this columnar form to the Palos Verdes examples, but the stones at the site do exhibit variability of size and form. There are at least five different types ranging from "columnar" to "barrel-shaped" to "trianguloid" types (see Fig. 11.2). Most of the forms either are perforated or show an attempt at perforation, and they all seem to be made of the same lithic material. The variance of size causes them, of course, to vary considerably in weight. Meistrel raised five of the stones using a 2,000-pound winch on his own vessel. The largest of the stones he raised (larger ones remain on the site) is columnar in shape and is drilled with a bore hole of over a meter completely through its longitudinal center. This stone cleaved in two lengthwise. Meistrel weighed this stone at about 1,030 pounds (467.2 kilograms) and estimates that five or six men would be needed on a vessel to raise and lower the stone by hand using some form of a primitive capstan or block and tackle (Meistrel, personal communication). The cleaved specimen clearly shows the regular channel of the bore hole on each of its split halves (h_2).

If the subject stones functioned as anchors of a given culture, then their size, shape, exterior finish, and type of bore holes should correspond with documented ethnographic historic counterparts of that culture.

The data sets (d_2) required for testing this hypothesis would consist of metrical data of the stones, resulting typological data, and information from informants or literature.

Experimentation (e_2) of this hypothesis would involve either establishing or rejecting a functional ethnographic analogy. Such an ethnographic analogy, however, must be established in a very careful, rigorous fashion (see Ascher 1961a; Binford 1968b for the pitfalls in making false ethnographic analogies). Hence experimentation for this hypothesis would determine whether valid ethnographic analogies could be made or not.

The record of possible results (r_2) would simply be the written descriptions of the ethnographic "goodness of fit" or lack thereof.

Interpreting (i_2) the outcome of this hypothesis would depend on e_2 above; the anchor hypothesis could be rejected outright, totally accepted, or only partially accepted. In partial rejection, for example, some of the stone types may indeed have been anchors, but others may not have been. For instance, Pierson and Moriarty (1980: 20) suggest that the smaller stones may have been "messenger stones: used to assist in removing caught anchors on a sea floor." They interpret other larger stones, without citing specific relevant evidence, as line weights, boom-hoist counterweights, ballast for compound anchors, and a rolling millstone.

One cannot assume a priori that any of the stones are anchors, nor that they are other nautical artifacts, for that matter. Test expectations for functional "use-wear" variables should be devised; if the stones functioned as working anchors an independent test of hypothesis h_2 could also be devised (see Frost 1973 for a discussion of such anchor variables).

I concur with other California-based archaeologists such as Clement Meighan and William Clewlow that some, though not all, of these longitudinally perforated specimens and the technology that produced them are beyond the capability of native California Indian tribes (see Heizer 1978 for the latest general description of the stone-working technology of Native Californians). Hence a nonnative technology may be indicated. But an ancient Asian technology cannot be simply asserted for the stones; it must have valid supportive evidence. Shape alone may be sufficient but not necessary to prove function and cultural origin. As an extreme, literally far afield, observation, I have seen a stone anchor, similar in type to the trianguloid Palos Verdes specimen (see Fig. 11.2), not in an Asian context but from an early Greek vessel on display in Athens. This illustrates the well-known anthropological view that similar artifact forms can be found in widely separate cultural contexts both in terms of space and time (see Muckelroy 1978: 146–49, who illustrates a similar form from Lebanon, Fig. 4.11; and George Bass [1981] showed me a similar specimen from his Cape Gelidonya Bronze Age wreck off Turkey).

Hypothesis h_3

It has been argued that these stones are 3,000 years old. A simple hypothesis (h_3) could be tested to verify that age date.

If the stones are 3,000 years old, then chronometric dating should result in a corresponding age-date.

The data (d_3) required to test this hypothesis would be dateable material, of course, that would determine the time of the manufacture and/or use of the artifact, not the geologic age of the stone.

Some possible bone material was found wedged into the hole of one of the stones. A piece of this material was submitted to Rainer Berger at the UCLA Isotope Laboratory for (e_3) radiocarbon analysis. The results (r_3) in this instance would consist of the printed ^{14}C counts of the sample and its calculated age. The radiocarbon results are not available as yet; hence, the interpretation (i_3) of the valid age of the artifacts remains to be made.

236

Another aspect of interpretation is that even if the stones themselves are old, that in itself would not establish that the site is old. For example, if the stones were indeed transported on an Asian vessel, it is altogether possible that they could be "curated" ancient stones used as ballast and that the transporting vessel in question could date to very recent times, such as the Gold Rush era, when numerous Chinese junks sailed the California coastal waters transporting goods (Marshall 1978: 55–58; Frost 1981). Only if other dated artifactual or ecofactual material consistently corroborated the dating of the stones could the site be unequivocably assigned a valid date. Thorough chronometric dating of the site could "burst the bubble" of excitement over the site, or it could corroborate the early age, making it a historic, highly significant site (if the foreign connection is also established). Furthermore, the style of these artifacts cannot be taken as an absolute indication of their locus or date of manufacture and last use (Bass 1981).

Hypothesis h_4

Once the origin and function of the stone artifacts have been determined, and their cultural affiliation and age identified, then the type of site and the processes of the site's formation (see Muckelroy 1978: 157–214) would remain to be established. Questions relevant to these topics would include the following: Is the site a shipwreck site, as Pierson and Moriarty (1980) maintain? If it represents a single wreck, why are there so many "anchor" stones present (over 30) and why are they so widely dispersed (see Fig. 11.5)? Wouldn't one or a few suffice for a vessel? If it is a wreck site, then why are the stones located in 15 to 25 feet (up to about 9 meters) of water and not closer to the present shore, as presumably the vessel would have been driven toward shore into shallower surf? If the stones were not connected with a shipwreck, but were deliberately jettisoned from a vessel, why would they have been jettisoned off Palos Verdes in an unprotected and exposed shore with incoming waves when close by are safe anchorages. Each of these questions can be formulated as an hypothesis and tested. As an example (h_4):

If the site were a shipwreck of a certain culture, then one would expect to find at the site (depending on the cultural origin and age of the vessel) other stone artifacts and/or possible metal artifacts, ceramics (e.g., possibly porcelain if it were an Asian vessel), and so on which would preserve through time in

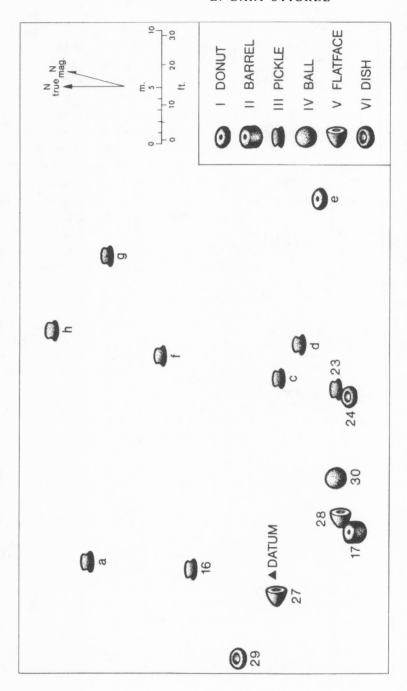

Figure 11.5. Stone artifact distribution at the Palos Verdes marine site.

the near-shore marine environment and include within that assemblage nautical artifacts in such a distribution indicating that the assemblage had in fact been part of a shipwreck identifiable with a certain culture.

As one investigator of this site pointed out to me (Love, personal communication), the site's pattern should be compared with patterns of anchorages or ballast stones from known wrecks. The distribution of the artifacts would certainly have been affected by a number of factors such as their preservability and how they were involved in the way the ship went under, how the shipwreck was salvaged (if at all), and the natural environmental processes affecting the presence and distribution of data on a shipwreck site such as the material that floated away, the material that disintegrated, the data-scrambling devices—how natural forces deposited and/or broke up the vessel underwater—and then any postsinking seabed movements (Muckelroy 1978, Chapter 5). So far only the stone artifacts have been observed at the Palos Verdes marine. But if it were a true shipwreck, given the factors above, other nonperishable indicative artifacts should also be present.

The relevant data sets in this instance (d_4) would be those other material cultural items, if present. It is recommended that a formal sampling program be implemented at the site involving some sea-floor excavation within the distribution of the known stones (see Muckelroy 1975 for a systematic approach to a scattered wreck site). A formal sampling approach would be the best way to explore the site for additional data as well as to estimate, with a mathematical measure of reliability, the total number of the known "anchor stones" and to determine their frequencies by morphological type (see Mueller 1975). Dwight Read of UCLA will be consulted about this unique sampling problem at the site.

The experimentation step (e_4) here would involve typological analysis, cultural affiliation analysis, and functional analysis (including their relation to nautics if any) of the collected sample of data.

Recording those results (r_4) would entail the compilation of any literature-searched material, formal written descriptions, and possibly a review of the statistical analysis by cluster analysis in order, if appropriate, to make typological-statistical patterns to facilitate interpretation (see Muckelroy 1978: 196–214).

The interpretation (i_4) of those results would, of course, depend on the presence of any data (or lack thereof) and the findings of the testing program of the experimentation. Simply, if the data conclusively indicated a shipwreck, then that site type would stand. If not, other hypotheses identifying the type of site would have to be formulated and tested.

Hypothesis h_5

Once basic hypotheses are tested concerning the cultural historical questions posed above, depending on the availability of data, hypotheses relative to each component of the human system which generated the site could be formulated and tested, thereby yielding useful information on the internal dynamics of the operation of that system. The following hypothesis (h_5) is offered as an example of conducting analysis from the perspective of the model:

If this "wreck" was an Asian shipwreck which took some of its crew as victims, then those human remains at the site (the preserved skeletal material) should be identifiable as coming exclusively from an oriental population and should exhibit variability indicative of the shipboard life-support system (e.g., diet) utilized on long voyages.

Thus this hypothesis would entail the study of the human remains from the biological component of the given human system in order to identify that human system and other aspects of its internal dynamic variability such as genetic variability (represented by stature, dentition, etc.) and physiological-health parameters (e.g., the "normal" vs. "abnormal" health status of the crew based on their diet as reconstructable from their remains at the site).

The data for this hypothesis (d_5) would also be collected through a formal sampling program at the site and would, of necessity, consist of human skeletal material. It should be noted here that there are no indications that such human remains are present at the site, or that they may have been lost through a lack of preservation, although the possibility of their presence remains. This hypothesis is offered only to exemplify how the model could be used to advantage given the presence of relevant data.

Experimentation (e_5) would involve a physical anthropological analysis using pertinent human osteological techniques. Particularly indicative may be the dentition of the remains from which the ethnic origin may, in some cases, be deduced (Jurmain, personal commu-

240

nication). The osteological analysis in general may result in important statements about the physical stature, diet, health status, and so on of the crew that manned the vessel (see Lenihan, this volume, where he mentions shipboard health aspects, hygiene, and diseases such as scurvy).

Records (r_5) of the analysis would consist of the tabulations, measurements, and other statistical-metrical data compiled in the human osteological laboratory and their formal descriptions.

The interpretation (i_5) of the results would be predicated on the assertion that different human systems have different biological components including and caused by distinctive genetic variations. It is realized that different cultures do not have totally distinct gene pools and that different populations certainly did and do intermate, causing gene flow from one population to the other. But it is maintained here that the total "polythetic set" of genetic variability is greater between two human systems than within any given one. Such genetic differences would have been perhaps greater in the past when less human movement occurred between systems than today. Therefore distance would have been an important factor, especially if we are considering an Asian gene pool vs. a Native Californian or American one. Thus the local or foreign origin of the crew of the vessel could be established.

Internal dynamics of the system that produced the stone artifacts in question could be ascertained by testing hypotheses relative to each of the human system components. For example, aspects of the system's material component can be learned by identifying the material variability of artifacts and any ecofacts at the site (such as the lithic materials selected for artifact manufacture). Aspects of the type of technoeconomic component of the system could be determined by reconstructing the drilling technology that was involved in piercing the stones. As previously mentioned, it was probably beyond the capability of Native Californians. Other technoeconomic factors could be ascertained, such as the power-energy requirements for transporting, lifting, and using the stones; the number of men required; what type of machine, if any, or type of capstan or counterweights, block and tackle were employed; and the energy expended. The sociological component could be addressed as well and tested if the site is found to exhibit spatial integrity in the distribution of required data, and hypotheses relative to differential access by the ship members to goods, services, and/or vessel space-use could be determined (see Lenihan, this volume). Ideological component variation could be partially determined by testing the variability of the information represented by the extant data at the site, such as the diversity of the technological information required to make, transport, and use the stone artifacts.

Important information about the site and its creators could be obtained from analysis of the stylistic variation at the site. By style, I mean those variables of artistic-creative variation on artifacts or the aesthetic arrangements of those artifacts rather than those variables of engineering morphology—mechanical and structural properties of artifacts that enable them to serve certain functions (e.g., the tensile strength of an anchor, which enables it to hold its vessel, vs. any decoration on the anchor).

Stylistic variation is considered in the human systems model to be a material cultural manifestation of the system's psychological component. Other factors, such as the use of enclosed space, can also reflect the psychological component. Stylistic variability at the site may be quite important in identifying the unknown human system that created the site in question.

Any printed or incised element of a writing system present on artifacts at the site (e.g., Chinese characters) would constitute a material indication of that human system's communicational component, and would indicate, of course, that the system present had been a literate, relatively advanced one.

In short, given the preservation and contextual integrity of the site, it would be feasible to test for factors of variability of several, if not all, components of the human system that generated the site.

Internal system variability would not be the only possibility in testing data from the site. Studies of cultural processes that were involved with the original site could also be conducted.

TESTING FOR CULTURAL PROCESSES
AT THE SITE

If the site proves to be a shipwreck, then the cultural processes that determined the operation of the vessel could be addressed. For instance, was the ship an exploratory vessel sent to discover, perhaps colonize, new lands? Or was it a trading vessel, such as an early one blown off course or a late nineteenth-century one conducting regular trade and transit along the California coast? If the vessel were not part of a local California human system, then it would involve, either intentionally

242

or inadvertently, the movement of persons, human behavior (see Mortin 1981), and material goods from one human system to another. This process has been termed "diffusion" in the anthropological literature. I prefer to term it "cultural flow" (see Koerper and Stickel 1980 for an extended discussion of the range of phenomena this process pertains to).

Several interesting hypotheses could be tested relative to this process. For instance, Renfrew (1975) recognized ten different types of trade and, depending on the home port of the vessel, different types of trade or exchange mechanisms could be tested for, such as Renfrew's, "down-the-line," "emissary," or "colonial enclave" types of trading, any one of which could have been involved in the origin of the site.

SUMMARY

It can be seen that underwater archaeology has gone through several developmental phases, each with different aims and goals. Now the field is in search of theory, research designs, and an attendant scientific approach to studying shipwrecks and other subaquatic sites. This was the goal of our seminar. And this is a healthy stage of development, for as the field becomes more scientific it will necessarily generate an expanded, and a more valid, knowledge of our cultural heritage in the hydrosphere. Underwater archaeology will now take its productive place alongside terrestrial archaeology, allowing us a better understanding of the past. I believe the best way to support the field is to implement a creative scientific testing methodology (Stickel 1979).

This paper attempted to provide a specific example of that methodology in terms of the proposed preliminary research design. This research design was developed for a site that has become a sensation in the current magazine and television media. The proposed research could debunk that "hype" over the site or, alternatively, support it. The basic thrust of the design is to gain information about the site in an objective, scientific manner. The experience and information to be gained by any such research will undoubtedly advance our knowledge.

Since most marine sites are located near the shore, they are rapidly being destroyed by a combination of natural sea and land processes, by modern cultural construction and waterway usage, and, most unfortunately, by nonprofessional vandalism and theft. The best way we can learn from these sites, before they are gone forever, is to explore them with highly organized, interdisciplinary research programs, for both underwater fieldwork and later analysis.

I hope this paper has indicated how interesting and useful such an interdisciplinary approach, based on theory, could be.

ACKNOWLEDGMENTS

The writer wishes to express his gratitude for the enthusiasm, help, and encouragement given to him by the discoverers of the Palos Verdes site, Wayne Baldwin and Robert Meistrel. The advice, input, research, and scholarly contributions of the following members and affiliates of the ERA Consortium (which is investigating the site) is deeply appreciated: Mr. Robert Arends, Dr. Rainer Berger, Dr. Alan Crawford, Ms. Cathy Crawford, Mr. Hiram Henry, Dr. Robert Jurmain, and Dr. Dwight Read. I would like to thank Thomas Levy for Figures 11.3 and 11.4 and Wayne Baldwin for Figures 11.1 and 11.5. I appreciate the review by Bruce Love (a previous investigator of the site from UCLA) of the original draft of this paper. Also I would like to express my grateful appreciation to Richard Gould and the other seminar participants for their constructive criticisms of the paper. And I would like to give my special thanks here to Dr. Douglas Schwartz, director of the School of American Research, Santa Fe, New Mexico for his special assistance during my stay at the school.

References

ALBRIGHT, ALAN B.
1977   "The Brown's Ferry Vessel," in *The Proceedings of the North American Society of Oceanic History* (Annapolis: U.S. Naval Academy).

ANDREWS, CHARLES M.
1938   *The Colonial Period of American History, vol. IV: England's Commercial and Colonial Policy* (New Haven: Yale University Press).

ARMYTAGE, FRANCES
1953   *The Free Port System in the British West Indies: A Study in Commercial Policy, 1766–1822* (New York: Longmans, Green).

ARNOLD, J. BARTO III
1974   "The Archaeological Applications of Computerized Contour and Perspective Plotting," *Newsletter of Computer Archaeology* 10:1–7.
1978a   "The *Flota* Disaster of 1554," in *Beneath the Waters of Time: Proceedings of the Ninth Conference on Underwater Archaeology*, ed. J. B. Arnold III, Texas Antiquities Committee Publication no. 6 (Austin).
1978b   "Underwater Site Testing: Results of the Texas Antiquities Committee's 1977 Field Season," in *Beneath the Waters of Time, Proceedings of the Ninth Conference on Underwater Archaeology*, ed. J. B. Arnold III, Texas Antiquities Committee Publication no. 6 (Austin).

ARNOLD, J. BARTO III, ED.
1978   *Beneath the Waters of Time: Proceedings of the Ninth Conference on Underwater Archaeology*, Texas Antiquities Committee Publication no. 6 (Austin).

ARNOLD, J. BARTO III, AND ROBERT S. WEDDLE
1978   *The Nautical Archaeology of Padre Island: The Spanish Shipwrecks of 1554* (New York: Academic Press).

ASCHER, ROBERT
1961a "Analogy in Archaeological Interpretation," *Southwestern Journal of Anthropology* 17: 317–25.
1961b "Experimental Archaeology," *American Anthropologist* 63: 793–816.
ATTON, HENRY, AND HENRY H. HOLLAND
1908 *The King's Customs* (London: John Murray).
BÄCKSTRÖM, MATTI, JUKKA LEINONEN, TURE MATTILA, AND JUSSI KOSONEN
1976 *Pienoismalli*, no. 2. Kustantaja, Oulu.
BAKER, MICHAEL
1981 "A Simulative Experiment in Simple Product Manufacture," in *Modern Material Culture: The Archaeology of Us*, ed. Richard A. Gould and Michael B. Schiffer (New York: Academic Press).
BANISTER, JOHN
1744– Newport Historical Society Archives, vol. 526, Waste Book, Vault
46 A.
1747– Newport Historical Society Archives, vol. 367, Ledger, Vault A.
52
1748– Newport Historical Society Archives, vol. 69, Receipt Book, Vault
68 A.
BARCK, OSCAR T., AND HUGH T. LEFLER
1958 *Colonial America* (New York: Macmillan).
BARRY, JAMES P.
1974 *Ships of the Great Lakes: 300 Years of Navigation* (Berkeley: Howell-North Books).
BARTH, F.
1966 "Models of Social Organisation," Occasional Papers of the Royal Anthropological Institute, no. 23.
BASCH, L.
1972 "Ancient Wrecks and the Archaeology of Ships," *International Journal of Nautical Archaeology* 1: 1–58.
BASCOM, WILLARD
1976 *Deep Water, Ancient Ships* (Garden City, N.Y.: Doubleday).
BASS, GEORGE F.
1961 "The Cape Gelidonya Wreck: Preliminary Report," *American Journal of Archaeology* 65: 267–76.
1966 *Archaeology Under Water* (New York: Frederick A. Praeger).
1967 *Cape Gelidonya: A Bronze Age Shipwreck*, Transactions of the American Philosophical Society, vol. 58, pt. 8 (Philadelphia).
1972 *A History of Seafaring Based on Underwater Archaeology* (London: Thames & Hudson; New York: Walker and Co.).
1975 *Archaeology Beneath the Sea* (New York: Frederick A. Praeger).
1979 "A Medieval Islamic Merchant Venture," *Archaeological News* 8: 84–94.
1980 "Marine Archaeology: A Misunderstood Science," in *Ocean Yearbook* 2, ed. Elizabeth Mann Borgese and Morton Ginsburg (Chicago and London: University of Chicago Press).

References

1981 Letter to the Editor, *Science*, July 16.

BASS, GEORGE F., AND PETER THROCKMORTON

1961 "Excavating a Bronze Age Shipwreck," *Archaeology* 14: 78–87.

1967 *The Discovery and the Excavation in Cape Gelidonya: A Bronze Age Shipwreck*, Transactions of the American Philosophical Society, 57: 14–39.

BASS, GEORGE F., AND FREDERICK H. VAN DOORNINCK, JR.

1982 *Yassi Ada I: A Seventh-Century Byzantine Shipwreck* (College Station: Texas A & M University Press).

BEKKER, CAJUS

1968 *The Luftwaffe War Diaries* (Garden City, N.Y.: Doubleday).

BENNETT, J. W.

1976 "Anticipation, Adaptation, and the Concept of Culture in Anthropology," *Science* 192: 847–52.

BERNDT, CATHERINE H.

1981 "Interpretations and 'Facts' in Aboriginal Australia," in *Woman the Gatherer*, ed. Frances Dahlberg (New Haven: Yale University Press).

BIGELOW, BRUCE M.

1930 "The Commerce of Rhode Island with the West Indies Before the American Revolution" (Ph.D. diss., Brown University).

BINFORD, LEWIS R.

1962 "Archaeology as Anthropology," *American Antiquity* 28: 217–25.

1968a "Archaeological Perspectives," in *New Perspectives in Archaeology*, ed. L. R. Binford and S. R. Binford (Chicago: Aldine).

1968b "Ethnographic Data and Understanding the Pleistocene," in *Man the Hunter*, ed. R. B. Lee and I. De Vore (Chicago: Aldine).

1968c "Some Comments on Historical versus Processual Archaeology," *Southwestern Journal of Anthropology* 24: 267–75.

1972 "Archaeological Perspectives," in *An Archaeological Perspective*, ed. L. R. Binford (New York: Seminar Press).

1977 "Introduction," in *Method and Theory in Historical Archaeology*, ed. Stanley South (New York: Academic Press).

BLACKMAN, D. J., ED.

1973 *Marine Archaeology* (London: Butterworth).

BRAUDEL, FERNAND

1981 *The Structures of Everyday Life, vol. 1: Civilization and Capitalism* (New York: Harper and Row).

BREW, JOHN O.

1971 "The Use and Abuse of Taxonomy," in *Man's Imprint from the Past*, ed. James Deetz (Boston: Little, Brown).

BRIDENBAUGH, CARL

1938 *Cities in the Wilderness* (New York: Ronald Press).

1955 *Cities in Revolt: Urban Life in America, 1743–1776* (New York: Alfred A. Knopf).

BROADWATER, JOHN D.
1981   "The York River Shipwreck Project: Results from the 1978 Survey,"
        in *In the Realms of Gold: The Proceedings of the Tenth Conference
        on Underwater Archaeology*, ed. W. A. Cockrell (San Marino, Calif.:
        Fathom Eight).
BRODBECK, MAY
1962   "Explanation, Prediction, and 'Imperfect' Knowledge," in *Scientific
        Explanation, Space and Time*, ed. Herbert Feigl and Grover Maxwell
        (Minneapolis: University of Minnesota Press).
BURLINGAME, R.
1959   "The Hardware of Culture," *Technology and Culture* 1: 11–19.
BUTZER, KARL
1975   "The 'Ecological' Approach to Prehistory: Are We Really Trying?"
        American Antiquity 40: 106–11.
1980   "Context in Archaeology: An Alternative Perspective," *Journal of
        Field Archaeology* 7: 417–22.
CALENDER OF STATE PAPERS, ELIZABETH
        Domestic Series.
        Foreign Series.
        Ireland (1586–1603).
CALENDAR OF THE CAREW MANUSCRIPTS
1589–1600
CABEZA DE VACA, ÁLVAR NÚÑEZ
1961   *Adventures in the Unknown Interior of America*, trans. Cyclone Covey
        (New York: Collier; rpt. 1983 Albuquerque: University of New Mex-
        ico Press).
CARR, LOIS GREEN
1974   "The Metropolis of Maryland: A Comment on Town Development
        Along the Tobacco Coast," *Maryland Historical Magazine* 69(2):
        124–45.
CARR-LAUGHTON, L. C.
1958   "English and Spanish Tonnage in 1588," *The Mariner's Mirror* 44:
        151–54.
CARSON, EDWARD
1972   *The Ancient and Rightful Custom: A History of the English Customs
        Service* (Hamden, Conn.: Archon).
CERAM, C. W., AND P. LYON
1958   "The Blue Museum," *Horizon* 1(2): 66–77.
CHAMPLIN, RICHARD
        Newport Historical Society Archives, Miscellaneous Papers, Vault
        A.
CHAPIN, HOWARD M.
1926   *Rhode Island Privateers in King George's War 1739–1748* (Providence:
        E. E. Johnson & Co.).
1928   *Privateering in King George's War, 1739–1748* (Providence: E. E.
        Johnson & Co.).

References

CHATTERTON, E. K.
1912 *King's Cutters and Smugglers 1700–1855* (Philadelphia: J. P. Lippencott Co.).
CHRISTENSEN, A. E., JR., AND I. MORRISON
1976 "Experimental Archaeology and Boats," *International Journal of Nautical and Underwater Exploration* 5: 275–84.
CHYET, STANLEY F.
1970 *Lopez of Newport: Colonial American Merchant Prince* (Detroit: Wayne State University Press).
CLAASSEN, CHERYL
1975 "Aleutian Island Homogeneity: A Near Island Perspective" (B.A. thesis, University of Arkansas).
1981 "Experimentation with Modern Materials," in *Modern Material Culture: The Archaeology of Us*, ed. Richard Gould and Michael B. Schiffer (New York: Academic Press).
CLARKE, DAVID L.
1968 *Analytical Archaeology* (London: Methuen).
1978 *Analytical Archaeology*, 2d ed., rev. Bob Chapman (New York: Columbia University Press).
CLAUSEN, CARL J.
1965 *A 1715 Spanish Treasure Ship*, Contributions of the Florida State Museum, Social Sciences, no. 12 (Tallahassee).
CLAUSEN, CARL J., AND J. BARTO ARNOLD III
1976 "The Magnetometer and Underwater Archaeology," *International Journal of Nautical Archaeology and Underwater Exploration* 5: 159–69.
CLAUSEN, CARL J., H. K. BROOKS, AND A. B. WESOLOWSKY
1975 "The Early Man Site at Warm Mineral Springs, Florida," *Journal of Field Archaeology* 2: 191–213.
COATES, JOHN
1977 "Hypothetical Reconstructions and the Naval Architect," in *Sources and Techniques in Boat Archaeology*, ed. S. McGrail, British Archaeological Report Supplementary Series 29: 215–26 (Oxford, England).
COCKRELL, WILBURN A.
1975a "Florida's Underwater Heritage," in *The Florida Handbook, 1975–1976*, 15th ed., comp. Allen Morris (Tallahassee: Florida Peninsular Publishing Co.).
1975b "Warm Mineral Springs 1975: A Multidisciplinary Approach to a 10,000 BP Archaeological Site," *Florida Scientist* 38.
1980 "The Trouble with Treasure: A Preservationist View of the Controversy," *American Antiquity* 45: 333–39.
1981 "Some Moral, Legal, and Ethical Considerations in Underwater Archaeology," in *In the Realms of Gold*, ed. W. A. Cockrell (San Marino, Calif.: Fathom Eight).

COCKRELL, WILBURN A., AND LARRY MURPHY
1978   "8 SL 17: Methodological Approach to a Dual Component Marine Site on the Florida Atlantic Coast," in *Beneath the Waters of Time: Proceedings of the Ninth Conference on Underwater Archaeology,* Texas Antiquities Committee Publication no. 6 (Austin).

COLES, JOHN
1966   "Experimental Archaeology," *Proceedings of the Society of Antiquities of Scotland* 99: 1–20.
1973   *Archaeology by Experiment* (London: Hutchinson).
1977   "Experimental Archaeology—Theory and Principles," in *Sources and Techniques in Boat Archaeology,* ed. S. McGrail, British Archaeological Report Supplementary Series 29: 233–43 (Oxford, England).
1979   *Experimental Archaeology* (New York: Academic Press).

COSANS, ELIZABETH J.
1974   "The Franklin Court Report," report for the National Park Service, Independence National Historic Park, Philadelphia.

CRUMLIN-PEDERSEN, OLE
1975   "Viking Seamanship Questioned," *The Mariner's Mirror* 61: 127–31.

CRUXENT, JOSE M., AND IRVING ROUSE
1969   "Early Man in the West Indies," in *New World Archaeology: Theoretical and Cultural Transformations,* ed. Ezra B. Zubrow, Margaret C. Fritz, and John M. Fritz (San Francisco: W. H. Freeman).

DANOWSKI, FRAN
1980   *Fishermen's Wives: Coping with an Extraordinary Occupation,* NOAA Sea Grant, Marine Bulletin no. 37 (Kingston: University of Rhode Island).

DAVIS, CHARLES G.
1929   *Ships of the Past* (New York: Bonanza Books).

DE BORHEGYI, STEPHAN F.
1963   "The Challenge, Nature, and Limitations of Underwater Archaeology," in *Diving into the Past: Proceedings of a Conference on Underwater Archaeology,* ed. June D. Holmquist and Ardis H. Wheeler (St. Paul: Minnesota Historical Society).

DEETZ, JAMES
1965   *The Dynamics of Stylistic Change in Arikara Ceramics,* Series in Anthropology, no. 4 (Urbana: University of Illinois).
1968   "The Archaeological Visibility of Food-gatherers," in *Man the Hunter,* ed. R. B. Lee and I. De Vore (Chicago: Aldine).
1977   *In Small Things Forgotten: The Archaeology of Early American Life* (Garden City, N.Y.: Doubleday).

DEETZ, JAMES, ED.
1971   *Man's Imprint from the Past: Readings in the Methods of Archaeology* (Boston: Little, Brown).

References

DE FRONDEVILLE, GUY
1966 "Some Notable Wreck Excavations—Mahdia," in *Marine Archaeology*, ed. Joan Du Plat Taylor (New York: Thomas Y. Crowell).
DEIGHTON, LEN
1977 *Fighter* (New York: Alfred A. Knopf).
1980 *Battle of Britain* (London: Coward, McCann and Geoghegan).
DE SALAZAR, EUGENIO
1968 "The Minor Horrors of the Sea," in *The European Reconnaissance: Selected Documents*, ed. J. H. Parry (New York: Walker and Co.).
DESAUTELS, R. J., ET AL.
1970 *Archaeological Report, Amchitka Island, 1969–70*, U.S. Atomic Energy Commission, TID-25481 (Washington, D.C.).
DEXTER, FRANKLIN B.
1901 *The Literary Diary of Ezra Stiles* (New York: Charles Scribner's Sons).
DIOLE, PHILIPPE
1953 *The Undersea Adventure* (New York: Julian Messner).
DOUGLAS, MARY
1966 *Purity and Danger* (London: Routledge and Kegan Paul).
DUGAN, JAMES
1953 *The Great Iron Ship* (New York: Harper & Bros).
DUMAS, FREDERICK
1962 *Deepwater Archaeology* (London: Routledge and Kegan Paul).
1966 "Underwater Work and Archaeological Problems," in *Marine Archaeology*, ed. Joan Du Plat Taylor (New York: Thomas Y. Crowell).
1972 *Thirty Centuries Under the Sea*, trans. P. Facey (New York: Crown).
DUNN, RICHARD S.
1972 *Sugar and Slaves: The Rise of the Plantation Class in the English West Indies, 1624–1713* (New York: Norton).
DUNNELL, ROBERT C.
1980 "Evolutionary Theory in Archaeology," *Advances in Archaeological Method and Theory* 3: 35–99.
DU PLAT TAYLOR, JOAN, ED.
1966 *Marine Archaeology: Developments During Sixty Years in the Mediterranean* (New York: Thomas Y. Crowell).
EGGAN, FRED
1954 "Social Anthropology and the Method of Controlled Comparison," *American Anthropologist* 56: 743–63.
EMERY, K. O., AND R. L. EDWARDS
1966 "Archaeological Potential of the Atlantic Continental Shelf," *American Antiquity* 33: 733–37.
ESSEX AVIATION GROUP
1978 *Guide to Exhibits and Information Book* (Chelmsford, Essex).
FALLON, NIALL
1978 *The Armada in Ireland* (Middletown, Conn.: Wesleyan University Press).

FARJEON, JEFFERSON
1938   *The Compleat Smuggler* (New York: Bobbs-Merrill).
FENWICK, VALERIE, ED.
1978   *The Graveney Boar: A Tenth-Century Find from Kent,* National Maritime Museum, Greenwich, Archaeological Series, no. 3; British Archaeological Reports, British Series 53 (Oxford, England).
FERGUSON, LELAND, ED.
1977   *Historical Archaeology and the Importance of Material Things* (Society for Historical Archaeology).
FINNEY, BEN
1979   *Hokule'a: The Way to Tahiti* (New York: Dodd, Mead).
FISCHER, GEORGE R.
1973   "Underwater Archaeology in the National Park Service: Problems in Resource Management," in *Cedam International Bulletin* (Texas: Cedam International).
1974   "The History and Nature of Underwater Archaeology in the National Park Service," in *Underwater Archaeology in the National Park Service: Model for the Management of Submerged Cultural Resources* (Santa Fe: U.S. Department of the Interior, National Park Service).
FLANNERY, KENT V.
1967   "Culture History v. Culture Progress: A Debate in American Archaeology," *Scientific American* 217: 119–22.
FLANNERY, KENT V., ED.
1976   *The Early Mesoamerican Village* (New York: Academic Press).
FLEMING, PETER
1957   *Operation Sea Lion* (New York: Simon and Schuster).
FRANZÉN, ANDERS
1961   *The Warship 'Wasa'* (Stockholm: Norstedts).
1963   "The Ghost Ship 'Vasa,' " in *Diving into the Past: Proceedings of a Conference on Underwater Archaeology,* ed. June D. Holmquist and Ardis H. Wheeler (St. Paul: Minnesota Historical Society).
FREEMAN, L. G., JR.
1968   "A Theoretical Framework for Interpreting Archaeological Materials," in *Man the Hunter,* ed. R. B. Lee and I. De Vore (Chicago: Aldine).
FROST, FRANK
1981   "The Palos Verdes Chinese Anchor Mystery" (unpublished paper).
FROST, H.
1973   "Anchors, the Potsherds of Marine Archaeology," in *Marine Archaeology,* ed. D. J. Blackman (London: Butterworth).
GIBBS, JIM
1977   *A Maritime History of Hawaii: Shipwrecks in Paradise* (Seattle: Superior Publishing Co.).
GLASGOW, TOM, JR.
1964   "The Shape of the Ships that Defeated the Spanish Armada," *The Mariner's Mirror* 50: 177–87.

References

GLASSIE, HENRY
1977 "Archaeology and Folklore: Common Anxieties, Common Hopes," in *Historical Archaeology and the Importance of Material Things*, ed. Leland Ferguson (Society for Historical Archaeology).

GLUCKMAN, STEPHEN J.
1976 "Underwater Archaeology: Theory and Method" (M.A. thesis, University of Florida).

GOGGIN, JOHN
1960 "Underwater Archaeology, Its Nature and Limitations," *American Antiquity* 25: 348–54.

GOODENOUGH, WARD H.
1965 "Yankee Kinship Terminology: A Problem in Componential Analysis," *American Anthropologist* 67: 259–87.

GOULD, R. A., ED.
1978 *Explorations in Ethnoarchaeology* (Albuquerque: University of New Mexico Press, School of American Research Advanced Seminar Series).

GRAHAM, WINSTON
1972 *The Spanish Armadas* (London: Collins).

GREENHILL, BASIL
1976 *Archaeology of the Boat* (Middletown, Conn.: Wesleyan University Press).

GRENIER, ROBERT
1979 "Underwater Survey on Two Mid-Sixteenth Century Basque Sites with Discovery of a Galleon on the Coast of Labrador," presentation at the Tenth Annual Conference on Underwater Archaeology, Nashville.

1981 "Excavation of a Sixteenth Century Basque Whaler in Red Bay, Labrador," paper presented at the Twelfth Annual Conference on Underwater Archaeology, New Orleans.

GUILMARTIN, JOHN FRANCIS, JR.
1974 *Gunpowder and Galleys* (London: Cambridge University Press).

GUINEY, D., AND G. VITELLI
n.d. Flume study videotape on file with J. E. Ericson, Department of Anthropology, Harvard University.

GUMERMAN, GEORGE, AND DAVID PHILLIPS, JR.
1978 "Archaeology Beyond Anthropology," *American Antiquity* 43: 184–91.

HAASUM, SIBYLLA
1974 *Vikingatidens Segling Och Navigation [Sailing and Navigation During the Viking Era]* (Stockholm: University of Stockholm Institute of Archaeology).

HAMSHERE, CYRIL
1972 *The British in the Caribbean* (Cambridge, Mass.: Harvard University Press).

HARDIE, R. P.
1912 *The Tobermory Argosy* (Edinburgh: Oliver and Boyd).

HEDGES, JAMES B.
1968   *The Browns of Providence Plantation: The Colonial Years* (Providence: Brown University Press).

HEIZER, R. F., ED.
1978   *California: Handbook of the North American Indians,* vol. 8 (Washington, D.C.: Smithsonian Institution).

HENDERSON, GRAEME
1980   "Indiamen Traders of the East," *Archaeology* 33: 18–25.

HEYERDAHL, THOR
1979   *Early Man and the Ocean: A Search for the Beginnings of Navigation and Seaborne Civilizations* (Garden City, N.Y.: Doubleday).

HILL, JAMES N.
1972   "The Methodological Debate in Contemporary Archaeology: A Model," in *Models in Archaeology,* ed. David L. Clarke (London: Methuen).

HISCOCK, K. B.
1979a   "Hutton's Heinkel-1," *Essex Aviation Group News,* September, pp. 8–11.

1979b   "Dig Diary," *Essex Aviation Group News,* November, pp. 3–4.

HISS, PHILIP H.
1943   *Netherlands America: The Dutch Territories in the West* (New York: Essential Books).

HOFFMAN, FRANK
1974   *The Mystery Ship from 19 Fathoms* (Au Train, Mich.: Avery Color Studios).

HOLE, F. D.
1961   "A Classification of Pedoturbations and Some Other Processes and Factors of Soil Formation in Relation to Isotropism and Anisotropism," *Soil Science* 91: 375–77.

HOLE, FRANK, AND ROBERT F. HEIZER
1965   *An Introduction to Prehistoric Archaeology* (New York: Holt, Rinehart and Winston).

HOLMQUIST, JUNE DRENNING, AND ARDIS HILLERMAN WHEELER, EDS.
1964   *Diving into the Past: Theories, Techniques, and Applications of Underwater Archaeology* (St. Paul: Minnesota Historical Society).

HOON, ELIZABETH E.
1938   *The Organization of the English Customs System 1696–1786* (New York: Appleton-Century).

HUDSON, KENNETH
1976   *The Archaeology of Industry* (New York: Charles Scribner's Sons).

HULSE, CHARLES A.
1981   "A Spatial Analysis of Lake Superior Shipwrecks: A Study in the Formative Process of the Archaeological Record" (Ph.D. diss., Michigan State University).

INVERARITY, ROBERT BRUCE
1963   "New York Report," in *Diving into the Past: Proceedings of a Conference on Underwater Archaeology,* ed. June D. Holmquist and Ardis

References

H. Wheeler (St. Paul: Minnesota Historical Society).

JAMESON, JOHN F., ED.
1923 *Privateering and Piracy in the Colonial Period: Illustrative Documents* (New York: Macmillan).

JENSEN, MERRILL
1968 *The Founding of a Nation* (New York: Oxford University Press).

JEWELL, DONALD P.
1961 "Freshwater Archaeology," *American Antiquity* 26: 414–16.

JOHNSTONE, PAUL
1974 *The Archaeology of Ships* (New York: Henry Z. Walck).

JONES, V. C., AND H. L. PETERSON
1971 *The Story of a Civil War Gun Boat, U.S.S. Cairo* (Washington, D.C.: U.S. Government Printing Office).

JUDGE, W. JAMES
1979 "Minimal Impact Archaeology: A Plea for a Formalized Ethic," in 1979 *Proceedings of the American Society for Conservation Archaeology* (1–9), assembled by Calvin R. Cummings.

KARO, GEORGE
1966 "Some Notable Wreck Excavations—Antikytheria," in *Marine Archaeology,* ed. Joan Du Plat Taylor (New York: Thomas Y. Crowell).

KATZEV, MICHAEL L.
1980 "A Replica of the Kyrenia Ship," *Institute of Nautical Archaeology Newsletter* 7.

KAY, H. F.
1977 "Review of Haasum," *International Journal of Nautical Archaeology and Underwater Exploration* 6: 79–80.

KEITH, DONALD
1980 "A Fourteenth-Century Shipwreck at Sinan-gun," *Archaeology* 33: 33–43.

KENYON, WALTER A.
1963 "Ontario Report," in *Diving into the Past: Proceedings of a Conference on Underwater Archaeology,* ed. June D. Holmquist and Ardis H. Wheeler (St. Paul: Minnesota Historical Society).

KESKINEN, KALEVI, KARI STENMAN, AND KLAUS NISKA
1977 "Venalaiset Havittajat," *Suomen Ilmavoimien Historia,* 7 (Espoo, Finland).

KING, THOMAS F., PATRICIA PARKER HICKMAN, AND GARY BERG
1977 *Anthropology in Historical Preservation* (New York: Academic Press).

KIRCH, PATRICK, AND TOM DYE
1979 "Ethno-Archaeology and the Development of Polynesian Fishing Strategies," *Journal of the Polynesian Society* 88: 53–76.

KLUCKHOHN, CLYDE
1940 "The Conceptual Structure in Middle America Studies," reprinted in *Contemporary Archaeology: A Guide to Theory and Condition,* ed. Mark P. Leone (Carbondale: Southern Illinois University Press).

KNOLLENBERG, BERNHARD
1960   *Origins of the American Revolution, 1759–1766* (New York: Macmillan).
KOERPER, HENRY C., AND E. G. STICKEL
1980   "Cultural Drift: A Primary Process of Culture Change," *Journal of Anthropological Research* 36(4): 463–69.
LARABEE, LEONARD WOOD, ED.
1935   *Royal Instructions to British Colonial Governors 1670–1776* (New York: Appleton-Century).
LAUGHTON, JOHN KNOX, ED.
1895   *State Papers Relating to the Defeat of the Spanish Armada*, 2 vols. (London: Navy Records Society).
LENIHAN, DANIEL J.
1974a   "Shipwrecks as Archaeological Phenomena," in *Underwater Archaeology in the National Park Service*, ed. Daniel J. Lenihan (Santa Fe: National Park Service).
1974b   "Underwater Archaeology in the National Park Service: A Model for the Management of Submerged Cultural Resources," in *Underwater Archaeology in the National Park Service*, ed. Daniel J. Lenihan (Santa Fe: National Park Service).
1979   "Impounding the Past," *Water Spectrum*, Spring, pp. 44–50.
LENIHAN, DANIEL J., ET AL.
1977   *The Preliminary Report of the National Reservoir Inundation Study* (Washington, D.C.: Cultural Resource Management Division, U.S. Department of the Interior, National Park Service).
LENIHAN, DANIEL J., AND LARRY MURPHY
1981   "Considerations for Research Designs in Shipwreck Archaeology," paper presented at the Twelfth Annual Conference on Underwater Archaeology, New Orleans.
LEONARD, JOHN
1982   Review of *The Structures of Everyday Life* by Fernand Braudel, *New York Times* 20 May, p. C21.
LEONARD, MARIE RYAN
1973   "Braziers in the Bodrum Museum," *American Journal of Archaeology* 77: 19–25.
LEONE, MARK P., ED.
1972   *Contemporary Archaeology* (Carbondale and Edwardsville: Southern Illinois University Press).
LÉVI-STRAUSS, CLAUDE
1962   *The Savage Mind* (Chicago: University of Chicago Press).
LEWIS, MICHAEL
1960   *Armada Guns* (London: Allen and Unwin).
1961   *The Spanish Armada* (New York: Thomas Y. Crowell).
LIGGETT, BARBARA
1978   *Archaeology at New Market*, exhibit catalog (Philadelphia: Atheneum).

256

References

LIPE, WILLIAM D.
1974   "A Conservation Model for American Archaeology," *The Kiva* 39: 213–44.

LUUKKANEN, EINO
1963   *Fighter over Finland* (London: Macdonald).

LYON, D. J.
1974   "Documentary Services for the Archaeological Diver: Ship Plans at the National Maritime Museum," *International Journal of Nautical Archaeology and Underwater Exploration* 3: 3–19.

LYON, EUGENE
1981   *The Treasure of 1622* (Key West, Fla.: Treasure Salvors, Inc.).
1982   "Treasures from the Ghost Galleon," *National Geographic* 161: 228–43.

MCCLELLAN, WILLIAM S.
1912   *Smuggling in the American Colonies at the Outbreak of the Revolution* (New York: Moffat, Ward and Co.).

MCGIMSEY, CHARLES R. III, AND HESTER A. DAVIS, EDS.
1977   *The Management of Archaeological Resources: The Airlie House Report*, Special Publication of the Society for American Archaeology.

MCGRAIL, SEAN
1975   "Models, Replicas and Experiments in Nautical Archaeology," *The Mariner's Mirror* 61: 3–8.
1977   "Aspects of Experimental Boat Archaeology," in *Sources and Techniques in Boat Archaeology*, ed. S. McGrail, British Archaeological Reports 29 (Oxford, England).

MCKAY, JOYCE
1976   "The Coalescence of History and Archaeology," *Historical Archaeology* 10: 93–98.

MCKEE, ALEXANDER
1963   *From Merciless Invaders* (London: Souvenir Press).
1964   "Ships that Fought the Armada," *The Mariner's Mirror* 50: 331–32.
1968   *History Under the Sea* (London: Hutchinson).
1972   "The Influence of British Naval Strategy on Ship Design: 1400–1850," in *A History of Seafaring Based on Underwater Archaeology*, ed. George Bass (New York: Walker and Co.).
1973   *King Henry VIII's 'Mary Rose'* (London: Souvenir Press).

MARKINSON, DAVID H.
1964   *Barbados: A Study of North American–West Indian Relations 1739–1789* (The Hague: Mouton & Co.).

MARSDEN, PETER
1972   "The Wreck of the *Amsterdam* near Hastings 1749," *International Journal of Nautical Archaeology and Underwater Exploration* 1: 73–96.
1974   *The Wreck of the Amsterdam* (Briarcliff Manor, N.Y.: Stein and Day; London: Hutchinson).

MARSDEN, PHILIP R. V.
1967   A *Ship of the Roman Period, from Blackfriars, in the City of London* (London: Guildhall Museum).
MARSHALL, DON B.
1978   *California Shipwrecks: Footsteps in the Sea* (Seattle: Superior Publishing Co.).
MARSHALL CAVENDISH PUBLICATIONS LTD.
1975   *The History of the Sailing Ship* (New York: Arco Publishing Co.).
MARSTRANDER, S.
1976   "Building a Hide Boat: An Archaeological Experiment," *International Journal of Nautical Archaeology and Underwater Exploration* 5: 13–22.
MARTIN, COLIN J. M.
1972   "*El Gran Grifón*: An Armada Wreck on Fair Isle," *International Journal of Nautical Archaeology and Underwater Exploration* 1: 59–71.
1973   "The Spanish Armada Expedition, 1968–70," in *Marine Archaeology*, ed. D. H. Blackman (London: Butterworth).
1975   *Full Fathom Five* (New York: Viking).
1978   "The *Dartmouth*, A British Frigate Wrecked Off Mull 1690: The Ship," *International Journal of Nautical Archaeology and Underwater Exploration* 7: 29–58.
1979a   "*La Trinidad Valencera*: An Armada Invasion Transport Lost Off Donegal," *International Journal of Nautical Archaeology and Underwater Exploration* 8: 13–38.
1979b   "Spanish Armada Pottery," *International Journal of Nautical Archaeology and Underwater Exploration* 8: 279–302.
MARTIN, KILCHER
1979   "Ferdinand Keller und die Entdeckung der Pfahlbauten," *Archaeologie der Schweiz* 2(1): 3–11.
MARX, ROBERT F.
1965   *The Battle of the Spanish Armada, 1588* (London: Weidenfeld and Nicholson).
1971   "The Early History of Diving," *Oceans* 4: 66–74.
1978   "History of the Council of Underwater Archaeology," in *Beneath the Waters of Time: Proceedings of the Ninth Conference on Underwater Archaeology*, ed. J. B. Arnold III, Texas Antiquities Publication no. 6 (Austin).
MATHEWSON, R. DUNCAN
1977   "Method and Theory in New World Historic Wreck Archaeology: Hypothesis Testing on the Site of *Nuestra Señora de Atocha*, Marquesas Keys, Florida" (M.S. thesis, Florida Atlantic University).
MATHEWSON, R. DUNCAN, LARRY MURPHY, AND BILL SPENCER
1974   "New Concepts in Marine Archaeology: Shallow Water Historical Archaeology in the Lower Florida Keys," paper presented at the Fifth Annual Conference on Underwater Archaeology, Berkeley.

258

References

MATTINGLY, GARRETT
1959   *The Armada* (Boston: Houghton Mifflin).
MEGGERS, BETTY J., AND CLIFFORD EVANS
1966   "A Trans Pacific Contact in 3,000 B.C.," in *New World Archaeology*, ed. Ezra B. W. Zubrow, Margaret C. Fritz, and John M. Fritz (San Francisco: Freeman).
MELTZER, DAVID
1979   "Paradigms and the Nature of Change in American Archaeology," *American Antiquity* 44: 644–55.
MORAN, GEOFFREY P., EDWARD F. ZIMMER, AND ANNE E. YENTSCH
1977   "Archaeological Investigations at the Narbonne House, Salem Maritime National Historic Site, Salem Massachusetts," Report for the U.S. National Park Service, Public Archaeology Laboratory (Providence, R.I.: Brown University).
MORISON, SAMUEL ELIOT
1971   *The European Discovery of America: The Northern Voyages* A.D. *1500– 1600* (New York: Oxford University Press).
MORRISON, J. S., O. CRUMLIN-PEDERSEN, AND G. VAN DER HEIDE
1970   *Aspects of the History of Wooden Shipbuilding*, Maritime Monographs and Reports, no. 1 (Greenwich: National Maritime Museum).
MORTIN, HARRY
1981   *The Wind Commands: Sailors and Sailing Ships in the Pacific* (New York: Columbia University Press).
MOSTERT, NOËL
1974   *Supership* (New York: Alfred A. Knopf).
MROZOWSKI, STEPHEN A.
1981   "Archaeological Investigations in Queen Anne Square, Newport, Rhode Island: A Study in Urban Archaeology" (M.A. thesis, Brown University).
MROZOWSKI, STEPHEN A., SUSAN GIBSON, AND PETER THORBAHN
1979   "The Archaeological Investigations of Queen Anne Square, Newport, Rhode Island," Report of the Newport Redevelopment Agency, Public Archaeology Laboratory (Providence: Brown University).
MUCKELROY, KEITH W.
1975   "A Systematic Approach to the Investigations of Scattered Wreck Sites," *International Journal of Nautical Archaeology and Underwater Exploration* 4: 173–90.
1977   "Historic Wreck Sites in Britain and their Environs," *International Journal of Nautical Archaeology and Underwater Exploration* 6: 47–57.
1978   *Maritime Archaeology* (Cambridge, England: Cambridge University Press).
MUCKELROY, KEITH W., ED.
1980   *Archaeology Under Water: An Atlas of the World's Submerged Sites* (New York and London: McGraw-Hill).

MUELLER, JAMES, ED.
1975   *Regional Sampling in Archaeology* (Tucson: University of Arizona Press).
MULVANEY, D. J.
1975   *The Prehistory of Australia* (Ringwood, Victoria: Penguin).
MURDOCK, G. P.
1967   *Ethnographic Atlas* (Pittsburgh: University of Pittsburgh Press).
MURPHY, LARRY
1981   "Isle Royale Shipwreck Management Program: Phase I (Preliminary Assessment," paper presented at the Twelfth Annual Conference on Underwater Archaeology, New Orleans.
MURPHY, LARRY, AND ALLEN SALTUS
1981   *Phase II Identification and Evaluation of Submerged Cultural Resources in the Tombigbee River Multi-Resource District, Alabama and Mississippi.* Report of Investigations, no. 17 (Tuscaloosa: University of Alabama).
NEEDHAM, JOSEPH
1954   *Science and Civilization in China* (Cambridge, England: Cambridge University Press).
1969   *The Grand Titration* (Toronto: University of Toronto Press).
NEWPORT HISTORICAL SOCIETY ARCHIVES
        NHS 1: Vault A, Lopez Letter Books, Misc.
        NHS 2: Vault A, Lopez Day Books, vol. 475, April–December 1756.
        NHS 3: Vault A, Lopez Day Books, vol. 475, November 23, 1756.
        NHS 4: Vault A, Lopez Store Blotter, vol. 475, 1759.
        NHS 5: Vault A, Lopez Day Book, vol. 726, 1762.
        NHS 6: Vault A, Lopez Store Blotter, vol. 726, June–July 1762.
        NHS 7: Vault A, Lopez Copy Book, 1764–65.
        NHS 8: Vault A, Champlin Miscellaneous Papers.
        NHS 9: Vault A, Lopez Miscellaneous Papers, Letters, Box 168.
        NHS 10: Vault A, Customs House Letter Book, vol. 90, 1768.
        NHS 11: Vault A, Customs House Letter Book, vol. 90, 1768.
        NHS 12: Vault A, Customs House Letter Book, vol. 90, October 21, 1768.
        NHS 13: Vault A, Lopez Miscellaneous Papers and Letters.
        NHS 14: Vault A, Vernon Copy Book, vol. 77.
        NHS 15: Vault A, Lopez Letter Book, vol. 624.
        NHS 16: Vault A, Miscellaneous Receipts in Lopez Letter Book, vols. 632–36.
        NHS 17: Vault A, Lopez Letter Book, vol. 624.
        NHS 18: Vault A, Lopez Letter Book, vol. 632.
        NHS 19: Vault A, Lopez Letter Book, vol. 632.
        NHS 20: Vault A, Lopez Letter Book, vol. 632.
        NHS 21: Vault A, Lopez Letter Book, vol. 632.
        NHS 22: Vault A, Lopez Miscellaneous Papers, Box 166.

References

NOËL-HUME, IVOR
1969   *Historical Archaeology* (New York: Alfred A. Knopf).
1974   *A Guide to Artifacts of Colonial America* (New York: Alfred A. Knopf).
ODYSSEY
1980   "Shipwreck: *La Trinidad Valencera*," Public Broadcasting Associates (Boston).
OLSEN, STEPHEN, DONALD D. ROBADUE, JR., AND VIRGINIA LEE
1980   *An Interpretive Atlas of Narragansett Bay*, Coastal Resources Center, Marine Bulletin 40 (Kingston: University of Rhode Island).
ORME, BRYONY
1981   *Anthropology for Archaeologists: An Introduction* (Ithaca: Cornell University Press).
ORWELL, GEORGE
1952   *Homage to Catalonia* (Boston: Beacon Press).
PARRY, J. H., ED.
1968   *The European Reconnaissance: Selected Documents* (New York: Walker & Co.).
PARRY, J. H., AND P. M. SHERLOCK
1956   *A Short History of the West Indies* (London: Macmillan).
PERLEY, SIDNEY
1891   *Historic Storms of New England* (Salem, Mass.: Salem Publishing and Printing Co.).
PETSCHE, JEROME
1974   *The Steamboat Bertrand: History, Excavation, and Architecture* (Washington, D.C.: U.S. Government Printing Office).
PIERSON, L. J., AND J. R. MORIARTY
1980   "Stone Anchors: Asiatic Shipwrecks Off the California Coast," *Anthropological Journal of Canada* 18(3): 17–23.
PINSON, ANN
1980   "The New England Rum Era: Drinking Styles and Social Change in Newport, R.I., 1720–1770," Working Papers on Alcohol and Human Behavior, no. 8 (Providence: Brown University).
PLOG, STEPHEN, FRED PLOG, AND WALTER WAIT
1978   "Decision Making in Modern Surveys," in *Advances in Archaeological Method and Theory*, vol. 1, ed. Michael B. Schiffer (New York: Academic Press).
POGGIE, JOHN, AND CARL GERSUNY
1974   *Fisherman of Galilee: The Human Ecology of a New England Coastal Community*, Sea Grant, Marine Bulletin Series 17 (Kingston: University of Rhode Island).
POLLOCK, MARVIN
1980   "The Defeat of the Spanish Armada," *Odyssey*, Public Broadcasting Associates (Boston).
PRATTIS, J. I.
1973   "A Model of Shipboard Interaction on a Hebridean Fishing Vessel," *Journal of Anthropological Research* 29: 210–19.

261

PRICE, R., AND KEITH W. MUCKELROY
1977   "The *Kennemerland* Site: The Third and Fourth Seasons, 1974 and 1976: An Interim Report," *International Journal of Nautical Archaeology and Underwater Exploration* 6: 187–218.

QUIMBY, IAN M. G.
1973   *Ceramics in America* (Charlottesville: University of Virginia Press, Winterthur Museum).

RACKL, HANS-WOLF
1968   *Diving into the Past: Archaeology Underwater* (New York: Charles Scribner's Sons).

RAMSEY, WINSTON G., ED.
1980   *The Battle of Britain Then and Now* (London: After the Battle Magazine).

RATHJE, WILLIAM L.
1979   "Modern Material Culture Studies," in *Advances in Archaeological Method and Theory*, vol. 2, ed. Michael B. Schiffer (New York: Academic Press).

REBIKOFF, DIMITRI
1972   "History of Underwater Photography," in *Underwater Archaeology: A Nascent Discipline* (Paris: UNESCO).

RENFREW, COLIN
1975   *The Emergence of Civilization* (London: Methuen).

RICHMOND, JOHN
1979   "Dig Diary," *Essex Aviation Group News*, September, pp. 4–5.

ROBERTS, ADOLPHE WALTER
1942   *The French in the West Indies* (Indianapolis and New York: Bobbs-Merrill).

ROBERTSON, BRUCE
1977   *Aviation Archaeology* (Cambridge, England: Patrick Stephens).

RUOFF, ULRICH
1972   "Palafittes and Underwater Archaeology," in *Underwater Archaeology: A Nascent Discipline* (Paris: UNESCO).

1981   "Der Kleine Hafner in Zurich," *Archaologie der Schweiz* 4(1): 2–14.

SACHS, WILLIAM S., AND ARI HOOGENBOOM
1965   *The Enterprising Colonials: Society on the Eve of the Revolution* (Chicago: Argonaut).

SCANDURRA, ENRICO
1972   "The Maritime Republics: Medieval and Renaissance Ships in Italy," in *A History of Seafaring Based on Underwater Archaeology*, ed. George Bass (New York: Walker and Co.).

SCHIFFER, MICHAEL B.
1972   "Archaeological Context and Systemic Context," *American Antiquity* 37: 156–65.

1976   *Behavioral Archaeology* (New York: Academic Press).

SCHIFFER, MICHAEL B., AND WILLIAM C. RATHJE
1973   "Efficient Exploration of the Archaeological Record: Penetrating

References

Problems," in *Research and Theory in Current Archaeology*, ed. Charles L. Redman (New York: John Wiley and Sons).

SCHLESINGER, ARTHUR M.
1939   *The Colonial Merchants and the American Revolution 1763–1776* (New York: Facsimile Library).

SCHUYLER, ROBERT L.
1978   "Historical and Historic Sites Archaeology as Anthropology: Basic Definitions and Relationships in Historical Archaeology," in *Historical Archaeology: A Guide to Substantive and Theoretical Contributions*, ed. Robert L. Schuyler (Farmingdale, N.Y.: Baywood Publishing Co.).

SEVERIN, T.
1977   "Preliminary Report on the Brendan Project," in *Sources and Techniques in Boat Archaeology*, ed. S. McGrail, British Archaeological Reports 29 (Oxford, England).

SHERIDAN, RICHARD B.
1974   *Sugar and Slaves* (Baltimore: Johns Hopkins University Press).

SHINER, JOEL L.
1978   "Underwater Archaeology, European vs. American," in *Beneath the Waters of Time: Proceedings of the Ninth Conference on Underwater Archaeology*, ed. J. B. Arnold III, Texas Antiquities Committee Publication no. 6 (Austin).

SHOMETTE, DONALD G.
1979   "The Patuxent River Submerged Cultural Resource Survey: Historic Overview," report prepared for the Maryland Historical Trust, Annapolis.

SHOMETTE, DONALD G., AND RALPH E. ESHELMAN
1981   *The Patuxent River Submerged Cultural Resource Survey, Drum Point to Queen Anne's Bridge, Maryland: Reconnaissance, Phase I and Phase II*, 2 vols., Maryland Historical Trust Manuscript Series, no. 13.

SIMMONS, JOE J.
1981   "Nautical Hygiene," paper presented at the Twelfth Annual Conference on Underwater Archaeology, New Orleans.

SNOW, EDWARD R.
1943   *Great Storms and Famous Shipwrecks of the New England Coast* (Boston: Yankee Publishing Co.).

SOUTH, STANLEY
1977   *Method and Theory in Historical Archaeology* (New York: Academic Press).

SPAULDING, ALBERT C.
1968   "Explanation in Archaeology," in *New Perspectives in Archaeology*, ed. Sally R. Binford and Lewis R. Binford (Chicago: Aldine).

SPEISER, E. A., TRANS.
1955   "The Epic of Gilgamesh," in *Religions of the Ancient Near East*, ed. Isaac Mendelsohn (New York: Liberal Arts Press).

263

SPOTSWOOD GREEN, WILLIAM
1906   "The Wrecks of the Spanish Armada on the Coast of Ireland," *Geographical Journal* 27: 429–51.
STEFFY, J. RICHARD
1976   "The Institute's Model Ship," *American Institute of Nautical Archaeology Newsletter* 3: 1–4.
1978a   "Maximum Results from Minimum Remains," in *Beneath the Waters of Time: Proceedings of the Ninth Conference on Underwater Archaeology*, ed. J. B. Arnold III, Texas Antiquities Committee Publication no. 6 (Austin).
1978b   "Construction Details of the Brown's Ferry Ship," in *Beneath the Waters of Time: Proceedings of the Ninth Conference on Underwater Archaeology*, ed. J. B. Arnold III, Texas Antiquities Committee Publication no. 6 (Austin).
STEIN, CHARLES FRANCIS
1960   *A History of Calvert County, Maryland* (Baltimore: privately printed).
STEIN, JULIE K.
1981   "The Earthworm: An Unsuspected Nemesis for Archaeologists," manuscript on file, Department of Anthropology, University of Washington, Seattle.
STÉNUIT, ROBERT
1971   *Treasures of the Armada* (New York: Dutton).
1973   *Treasures of the Armada* (Newton Abbot, England: David and Charles).
STICKEL, E. GARY
1974   *A Spatial and Temporal Analysis of Underwater Neolithic Settlements in the Alpine Foreland of Switzerland* (Ann Arbor, Mich.: University Microfilms).
1979   "More on Theory Building in Archaeology," *Current Anthropology* 10: 621–22.
1982   "A General Human Systems Model for Archaeological Analysis," in *New Uses of Systems Theory in Archaeology*, ed. E. G. Stickel (Los Altos, Calif.: Ballena Press).
STICKEL, E. GARY, AND JOSEPH C. CHARTKOFF
1973   "The Nature of Scientific Laws and Their Relationship to Law-building in Archaeology," in *The Explanation of Culture Change: Models in Prehistory*, ed. Colin Renfrew (London: Duckworth).
SWITZER, DAVID G.
1978   "Provision Storage and Galley Facilities Onboard the Revolutionary War Privateer, Defence," in *Beneath the Waters of Time: Proceedings of the Ninth Conference on Underwater Archaeology*, ed. J. B. Arnold III, Texas Antiquities Committee Publication no. 6 (Austin).
TAYLOR, WALTER W.
1948   *A Study of Archaeology*, Memoir Series of the American Anthropological Association, no. 69 (Carbondale: Southern Illinois University Press).

References

TAYLOR, WALTER W., ED.
1967   A Study of Archaeology, (Carbondale: Southern Illinois University Press).
THOMAS, DAVID HURST, AND ROBERT L. BETTINGER
1976   Prehistoric Piñon Ecotone Settlements of the Upper Reese River Valley, Central Nevada, Anthropological Papers of the American Museum of Natural History 53, pt. 3 (New York).
THOMPSON, I. A. A.
1969   "The Appointment of the Duke of Medina Sidonia to the Command of the Spanish Armada," Historical Journal 12: 197–216.
THROCKMORTON, PETER
1969   Shipwrecks and Archaeology: The Unharvested Sea (Boston: Atlantic-Little, Brown).
TRIGGER, BRUCE
1980   "Archaeology and the Image of the American Indian," American Antiquity 45: 662–76.
TRINGHAM, RUTH E.
1978   "Experimentation, Ethnoarchaeology, and the Leapfrogs in Archaeological Methodology," in Explorations in Ethnoarchaeology, ed. Richard A. Gould (Albuquerque: University of New Mexico Press, School of American Research Advanced Seminar Series).
UNESCO
1972   Underwater Archaeology: A Nascent Discipline (Paris).
VALENTINE, J. MANSON
1976   "Underwater Archaeology in the Bahamas," Explorers Journal 54: 176–83.
WADBURY, GEORGE
1951   The Great Days of Piracy in the West Indies (New York: Norton).
WADE, NICHOLAS
1981   "Galleon Yields Gold, Silver, and Archaeology," Science 212: 1486–87.
WARFEL, STEPHEN G.
1980   "A Critical Analysis and Test of Stanley South's Artifact Patterns" (M.A. thesis, Brown University).
WATKINS, MALCOLM C.
1973   "Ceramics Used in America: Comparisons," in Ceramics in America, ed. Ian M. G. Quimby (Charlottesville: University of Virginia Press, Winterthur Museum).
WATSON, PATTY JO
1973a   "The Future of Archaeology in Anthropology: Culture History and Social Science," in Research and Theory in Current Archaeology, ed. Charles L. Redman (New York: John Wiley and Sons).
1973b   "Explanation and Models: The Prehistorian as Philosopher of Science and the Prehistorian as Excavator of the Past," in The Explanation of Culture Change, ed. Colin Renfrew (London: Duckworth).

265

WATSON, PATTY JO, STEVEN A. LEBLANC, AND CHARLES L. REDMAN
1971   *Explanation in Archaeology: An Explicitly Scientific Approach* (New York and London: Columbia University Press).
WATTS, GORDON P.
1975   "The Location and Identification of the Ironclad U.S.S. *Monitor*," *International Journal of Nautical Archaeology and Underwater Exploration* 4: 301–31.
WHEATLEY, RONALD
1958   *Operation Sea Lion* (London: Oxford University Press).
WHEELER, R. C., ET AL.
1975   *Voices from the Rapids*, Minnesota Historical Archaeology Series, no. 39 (St. Paul: Minnesota Historical Society).
WHITING, J. W. M., AND B. AYRES
1968   "Influences from the Shape of Dwellings," in *Settlement Archaeology*, ed. K. C. Chang (Palo Alto, Calif.: National Press).
WIGNALL, SYDNEY
1973   "The Armada Shot Controversy," in *Marine Archaeology*, ed. D. J. Blackman (London: Butterworth).
WILLEY, GORDON R., AND P. PHILLIPS
1958   *Method and Theory in American Archaeology* (Chicago: University of Chicago Press).
WILLEY, GORDON R., AND JEREMY A. SABLOFF
1974   *A History of American Archaeology* (London: Thames & Hudson).
WILLIAMS, NEVILLE
1961   *Contraband Cargoes: Seven Centuries of Smuggling* (Hamden, Conn.: Shoe String Press).
WISEMAN, JAMES
1980   "Archaeology in the Future: An Evolving Discipline," *American Journal of Archaeology* 84: 279–85.
WIT, JOEL S.
1981   "Advances in Antisubmarine Warfare," *Scientific American* 244: 31–41.
WOOD, DEREK, AND DEREK DEMPSTER
1961   *The Narrow Margin* (London: Hutchinson).
WOOD, RAYMOND W., AND DONALD LEE JOHNSON
1978   "A Survey of Disturbance Processes in Archaeological Site Formation," in *Advances in Archaeological Method and Theory*, vol. 1, ed. Michael B. Schiffer (New York: Academic Press).
WOOLWORTH, ALAN R.
1963   "Minnesota Report," in *Diving into the Past: Proceedings of a Conference on Underwater Archaeology*, ed. June D. Holmquist and Ardis H. Wheeler (St. Paul: Minnesota Historical Society).
ZHONGPU, FANG
1980   "Did Chinese Buddhists Reach America 1,000 Years Before Columbus?," *China Reconstructs*, pp. 65–66.

Index

Index

documents, 4, 54, 68, 72, 74, 118, 145,
147, 177, 180, 187; on smuggling, 155,
157, 162, 164, 170; primary, 149–50;
ships' manifests, 30, 58
Douglas, Mary, 61
Douhet doctrine, 110
Drake, Francis, Sir, 15, 107, 119, 125
Drenning, June, 220
Dugan, James, 56
Dumas, Frederick, 24, 77
Dunnell, Robert C., 33
Du Plat Taylor, Joan, 220
Dutch colonies, 154–68 passim
Dye, Tom, 196–97

ecofacts, 241
ecological degradation, 179–80
economics, 174, 179–80; world, 30, 84
Edwards, R. L., 46
Eggan, Fred, 194, 195
Egyptian tomb paintings, 17
Elizabeth I (queen of England), 107, 108,
125, 136
Elizabethan State Papers, 128, 137, 138
Emery, K. O., 46
Engelhardt, Conrad, 40, 197
England, 8, 43, 55, 85, 110, 117, 124, 129,
133, 136; British at Chesapeake Bay, 178,
184; smugglers and, 151–63 passim;
shipwreck archaeology of (British), 25, 38,
43
English Channel, 110, 124
environment: influences of, 68, 76, 80–82;
influence of wrecks on, 81; river
evolution, 174, 180
Eshelman, Ralph E., 174
Essex Aviation Group, 111, 114, 116, 117,
133
ethnoarchaeology, 15–16, 18, 21, 34, 87,
196–97, 204. *See also* cultural context
Ethnographic Atlas, 74
ethnography, 15, 34, 234, 235
ethnology, 63, 204
Europe, 8, 21, 25, 72, 74, 107, 110, 125,
180, 190, 214
Evans, Clifford, 71
excavation, 3, 21, 29, 31–32, 36, 42, 48,
64, 81, 117, 146, 147, 204, 222, 239;
partial/total, 11; research for, 13; strategies
of, 9; stratigraphy for, 45, 78, 81; value
of, 8, 41

Fallon, Niall, 112, 113, 117, 128
Fenton, Edward, 130
Fenwick, Valerie, 27
Ferguson, Leland, 63

Finney, Ben, 198
Fischer, George R., 47, 48, 209
fishermen, 194
flags of convenience, 10
Flags of Truce, 152
Flannery, Kent V., 31, 94, 96
fleets, 73, 86, 214. *See also* armadas
Fleming, Peter, 109
Florida, 19, 20, 26, 31, 58, 77, 79, 80, 86
Florida Division of Archives, 47
Florida Keys, 73, 213, 214
forecastle, 60
Fort Jefferson National Monument, 85
France, 8, 101, 108, 136, 217; and
smugglers, 151, 152; French
Structuralism, 6
Freeman, L. G., Jr., 16
Frost, Frank, 233, 236, 237

Gagnan, Emile, 8
Gersuny, Carl, 194, 205
Getty Museum, 220
Gibbs, Jim, 75
Gibson, Susan, 148
Glasgow, Tom, Jr., 124, 125
Glassie, Henry, 63
global communication dynamics, 30
Gluckman, Stephen J., 47, 221
Goering, Hermann, 133
Goggin, John, 38, 45, 105, 221
Gould, Richard, 15, 16, 87, 223
Graham, Winston, 110, 117
Gravelines, 129–30
Great Lakes, 3, 10, 11, 12, 15, 32, 54, 55,
59, 75, 85
Greenhill, Basil, 71
Grenier, Robert, 48, 215
Guilmartin, John Francis, Jr., 110, 128
Guiney, D., 200
Gumerman, George, 33

Haasum, Sibylla, 196
Hardie, R. P., 112
Hasslöf, O., 15
Hedges, James B., 158, 160
Heizer, R. F., 236
Henry, Hiram, 244
Heyerdahl, Thor, 71, 198
Hickman, Patricia Parker, 94
Hill, James N., 70
Hiscock, K. B., 115
Hispaniola, 71, 164
Historical Archaeology, 46
history, 42, 149, 150; historians, 8, 15, 50,
52, 56, 58, 62, 68, 149; historical
identity, 170; historiography, 27, 144–47;

269

Index

shipping on the, 73, 99, 112, 124–28, 214
Meggers, Betty J., 71
Meighan, Clement, 236
Meistrel, Robert, 233–35, 244
Meltzer, David, 33
metallurgy, 28–29, 92; bronze, 13; Bronze Age, 101–2, 193; copper, 17; iron, 14, 55, 127, 130–32; mercury, 57
methodology: a definition, 221
Moran, Geoffrey P., 148, 149
Moriarty, James, 222, 223, 231–37 passim
Morison, Samuel Eliot, 61
Morrison, I., 190
Mortin, Harry, 243
Mostert, Noël, 10, 127
Mrozowski, Stephen A., 12, 30, 148
Muckelroy, Keith W., 5, 7, 13, 15, 25, 27, 30, 45, 49, 73, 76, 77, 86, 92, 94, 105, 112, 140, 192, 197, 200–204, 210, 211, 224, 227, 230, 236, 237, 239
Mueller, James, 239
Mulvaney, D. J., 16
Murdock, G. P., 74
Murphy, Larry, 9, 12, 15, 16, 19, 25, 27, 44, 48, 58, 78, 81, 85, 214
museologists, 42–43

Narragansett Bay, 12. *See also* Newport, Rhode Island
National Oceanographic and Atmospheric Administration, 64
National Park Service, 3, 32, 47, 56, 64, 201
National Science Foundation, 94, 101
nautical archaeology, 43, 189; experiments in, 191–97, 204; methods of, 193, 197–98; processes of, 200–201. *See also* underwater archaeology
Navigation Acts, 148, 150; Hovering Act, 155; Molasses Act, 151, 152, 154, 156; Plantation Duties Act, 150; Staple Act, 150; Sugar Act, 154
Needham, Joseph, 231
Neolithic Revolution, 22
Newport, Rhode Island, 148–69 passim
New World: archaeology of, 25–26, 31, 45, 69, 95, 97–98, 100, 103, 143, 222, 234; shipping of, 71, 187; Spain and the, 29, 57–58, 84, 212
Noël-Hume, Ivor, 4, 67, 148
N-transforms, 76

Oceania, 196
"Odyssey," 114

Old World: archaeology of, 27, 95, 98, 100, 234; shipping of, 71; Spain and the, 231
Orme, Bryony, 92
Orwell, George, 214

Pacific Ocean, 71, 222
Padre Island, Texas, 47, 48, 54, 209, 215, 217
Palos Verdes, California, 222, 223, 224, 230, 231; experimental archaeology at, 232, 235, 239, 240, 242; hypotheses on, 231–40
Parma, Duke of, 107–9, 119, 122
Parry, J. H., 217
Patuxent River, 173, 174, 175, 177; economy along, 178–80, 182–87; hypotheses on, 174, 180, 183, 186
pedoturbation, 82
Peterson, H. L., 47
Petsche, Jerome, 47
Philip II, 109, 118–25 passim
Phillips, David, Jr., 33
Phillips, P., 63
Phuket Island, Thailand, 197, 202
Pierson, L. J., 222, 223, 231–37 passim
Pinson, Ann, 149
Plog, Fred, 82
Plog, Stephen, 82
Poggie, John, 194, 205
Pollock, Marvin, 114
port visitation, 81
Prattis, J. I., 62
preservation, 10, 40, 54, 59, 77, 94, 209
Price, R., 73
proxemics, 51, 53
Purdy, Barbara, 19

Rackl, Hans-Wolf, 41, 50
radar, 108, 133, 220
Ramsey, Winston G., 115, 117, 139
Rathje, William L., 76, 87
Rayner, G., 115
Read, Dwight, 239, 244
Rebikoff, Dimitri, 221
Redman, Charles L., 94
remote sensing, 175, 220
Renfrew, Colin, 234, 243
replication, 189, 203; Brendan project, 190, 195, 198; *Falls of Clyde*, 75; Gokstad faering, 190, 196; Graveney, 190, 196; *Hokule'a*, 190, 198; Kalnes skin boat, 189, 190, 192; Kyrenia models, 100, 196, 200
research designs, 10, 13, 21, 28, 32, 36, 44, 64, 81, 84, 88, 100, 221, 224, 243; idiographic, 27; nomothetic, 28–31;

Made in the USA
San Bernardino, CA
21 August 2014